Fighting Words

FIGHTING WORDS

The Politics of Hateful Speech

Laurence R. Marcus

Westport, Connecticut
London

Library of Congress Cataloging-in-Publication Data

Marcus, Laurence R.
    Fighting words / the politics of hateful speech / Laurence R.
Marcus.
      p.   cm.
    Includes bibliographical references and index.
    ISBN 0-275-95438-2 (alk. paper)
    1. Discrimination in higher education—United States. 2. Hate
speech—United States. 3. Education, Higher—Political aspects—
United States. 4. Freedom of speech—United States. 5. College
students—Civil rights—United States. 6. Kean College of New
Jersey. I. Title.
LC212.42.M37 1996
378.1'012—dc20   95-26516

British Library Cataloguing in Publication Data is available.

Library of Congress Catalog Card Number: 95-26516
ISBN: 0-275-95438-2

First published in 1996

Praeger Publishers, 88 Post Road West, Westport, CT 06881
An imprint of Greenwood Publishing Group, Inc.

Printed in the United States of America

The paper used in this book complies with the
Permanent Paper Standard issued by the National
Information Standards Organization (Z39.48–1984).

10 9 8 7 6 5 4 3 2 1

Copyright Acknowledgment

The author and publisher gratefully acknowledge permission to quote from the
following material:

"Diversity and Its Discontents" by Laurence R. Marcus. Originally published in
The Review of Higher Education v. 9 n. 3 (Spring 1994). Reprinted by permission
of *The Review of Higher Education*, 2002 School of Education, The University of
Michigan, Ann Arbor, Michigan 48109–1258.

Contents

Preface

I undertook this book project to try to make sense of the issues raised by a series of hateful-speech events at Kean College, near Newark, New Jersey. I was an assistant chancellor in the New Jersey Department of Higher Education and a member of the college's Board of Trustees throughout the period of turmoil until June 1994. But this is not simply, or primarily, about Kean and the idiosyncratic factors that may have contributed to its explosion. Indeed, in addition to his vituperative speech at Kean, Khalid Abdul Muhammad spoke at more than fifty institutions of higher learning in the year or so before he was shot in the leg during a California appearance in the spring of 1994. Twice that semester he spoke at Howard University, the first appearance ending up on the CBS News program *Eye to Eye*, which showed the audience joining a student in anti-Semitic chanting. Other speakers carried similar messages at other colleges. For example, Abdul Alim Musa presented a "vituperatively anti-Semitic speech" at the University of Washington. Also, even though in the few years leading up to the incidents at Kean, the predominant number of outside hate speakers invited to college campuses who made news were African Americans carrying extreme messages, they did not have a monopoly on the market. For example, Stockton State College (NJ) fought hard, but lost, a court battle to keep the Ku Klux Klan from speaking on its campus.

Kean College is used as a point from which to initiate the discussion, as well as a touchstone to explore specific issues. For instance, there were differences and similarities in how each of the above-mentioned situations played out. The aftermath of the Howard incident differed from Kean's in that the chair of Howard's Afro-American Studies Department, Russell Adams, along with a number of African American students, publicly spoke out in condemnation of Muhammad's message and those who cheered him (Shea, 1994), while counterparts at Kean were either silent or spoke in support of portions of Muhammad's speech. Similar to what occurred at Kean, there was too much silence from too many proponents of diversity at the University of Washington, and a high-ranking official appeared to trivialize the matter by indicating that "only a few Jews were upset" (Alexander, 1994: 63).

Since hateful speech is not an isolated matter, this book looks at the broad context to determine the extent to which most colleges and universities share the same vulnerability. Moreover, I came quickly to understand that my first impression of hateful speech was too narrow, that it includes much more than formal speeches made by inflammatory orators or statements published or broadcast by extremists; that it includes the more common occurrence of words and symbolic speech acts that are mean, malicious, and defamatory (coming in the college setting from students) and that are intended to subordinate one group to another. Although I recognize that hateful speech is also used to subordinate people based on other characteristics such as national origin, gender, sexuality, religion, and so on, my focus here is primarily on the crisis in black and white, a problem that has dominated our nation since its earliest days.

As a reminder of the need to look to the circumstances that foster hateful speech, Henry Louis Gates (1993: 48) admonishes that the "pendulum has swung from the absurd position that words don't matter to the equally absurd position that only words matter." If we do not like the message, we must address the situation from which it arises. To gain insight, I looked at the status of race and intergroup relations in our rapidly changing nation. It was useful to focus on some of the controversial race- or ethnicity-based issues of our time, including immigration, affirmative action, multiculturalism, and identity politics, in order to understand the context in which our colleges and universities exist. I moved then to a consideration of the intergroup climate on our campuses, and of efforts undertaken by many institutions to constrain the number of hateful acts, which, according to a 1990 report from the National Institute Against Prejudice and Violence (1990), affected some 65–70 percent of the nation's minority students. My position brought me in contact with students, faculty, and staff throughout New Jersey's public and independent system of higher education; in certain parts of this book, I have recounted some of what I heard from people at Kean and other institutions on issues of intergroup relations. Finally, I sought to draw some conclusions that might help higher education come to grips with hateful speech.

An expression of thanks is due to Dr. Herman James, President of Rowan College of New Jersey, who made it possible for me to undertake this effort, as well as to the Dean of the School of Education, David Kapel, and my colleagues in the Department of Educational Administration—Ted White, Jack Collins, Chris Johnston, Ted Johnson, Dick Smith, and Mario Tomei—who not only supported my endeavor but also eased my transition back to the academic life. Finally, a special acknowledgement is owed to my wife, Maureen Flanagan Marcus, for her love, her support, and her having put up with me through this process.

REFERENCES

Alexander, Edward. "Multiculturalists and Anti-Semitism." *Society* v. 31 n. 6 (September/October 1994), pp. 58–64.

Gates, Henry Louis, Jr. "Let Them Talk, Why Civil Liberties Pose No Threat to Civil Rights." *The New Republic* v. 209 n. 12/13 (September 20/27, 1993), pp. 37–49.

National Institute Against Prejudice and Violence. *Campus Ethnoviolence and the Policy Options, Institute Report No. 4*. Baltimore, MD: NIAPV, 1990.

Shea, Christopher. "Howard U Condemns Bigotry and Attacks on Its Reputation." *The Chronicle of Higher Education*. April 27, 1994, p. A32.

Introduction

HATEFUL SPEECH AT KEAN COLLEGE

In the 1993–1994 academic year, the lid blew off of the Kean College pressure-cooker. Not yet fully recovered from the open intergroup conflict that had resulted from a speech nearly two years earlier by the controversial Afrocentrist Leonard Jeffries, the college was battered first by a November 29, 1993, speech that brought Khalid Abdul Muhammad to national prominence, and then in the spring by a follow-up appearance of Louis Farrakhan. The internal strife and the harm to the college's external reputation took significant tolls, resulting in a tumble in enrollments and in fundraising; the college's foundation arm reported a virtual halt to the Library Capital Campaign and a 24 percent increase in the number of alumni declining to make contributions during the annual alumni phone-athon (Trustee Subcommittee, 1994). The weight of the controversy was also felt heavily by the college's president, who during the summer of 1994 announced her resignation, effective June 30, 1995.

To many, it was unbelievable that a public college—or any college where "Truth" is the ultimate goal—would permit hate speakers to come on campus to spew their venom. To others, it was a shock that a college could be so rocked by an outside speaker, since the exploration of controversial views is an accepted and everyday occurrence on most campuses. To those who knew Kean as a college that sought to provide a multicultural education to a diverse population, there was consternation about its apparent inability to deliver its message in an effective manner—or, perhaps, the turmoil was the inevitable outcome of multicultural education. The issues raised by the Kean hate speech saga deserve attention, given their implications for our democracy and higher education's centrality to a more desirable American future.

SETTING THE STAGE

Originally a teachers college located in the city of Newark, the college moved along with many of America's urban dwellers to the suburbs in the late 1950s, changing its name (pronounced like "Kane") and expanding its educational program. However, while many new suburbanites shed their liberal values, Kean College maintained its commitment, which ran deep within its institutional culture, to the democratic goal of providing educational opportunity to low and moderate-income students. In 1985, it was honored as one of the first two New Jersey state colleges to win a Governor's Challenge Grant of $3.9 million to further its mission of providing an excellent education to the increasingly diverse undergraduate population that, by choice, it was serving.

The college's demographics reflect its commitment. At the time of the Muhammad speech, the nine publicly appointed members of the board of trustees included two African Americans, one of whom was chair, and two Latinos, one of whom was vice chair; both elected student representatives on the board were African American. The president was Hispanic. The acting vice president for academic affairs was African American, as were two of the academic deans and the associate vice president for student affairs; another of the academic deans was Hispanic. African Americans and Latinos accounted for about 14 percent of the faculty. In the fall of 1993, the college's enrollment was about two-thirds white; African Americans and Hispanics each accounted for 14 percent and Asians for approximately 4 percent. Diversity among the student body appeared to be accepted, as a high proportion of African Americans were among the elected student leaders, including the most prestigious positions, such as the presidency of the Student Organization (the undergraduate student government), class presidencies, and the elected representatives to the board of trustees.

However, while many courses took a multicultural approach, and the student activities program celebrated the diverse backgrounds of its undergraduate population, the spirit of multiculturalism appears to have been little more than a veneer. A public split developed at the end of February 1992, around Leonard Jeffries's speech at a blacks-only dinner, the culminating event in the observance of Black History Month. Jeffries had been at the center of a storm within his own institution, City College of the City University of New York, for his teaching that Europeans and those of European descent are "ice people" imbued with overwhelmingly negative characteristics; his comments, such as allegations of a Jewish conspiracy behind the trade in African slaves, had also been labelled as blatantly anti-Semitic and anti-white. Although Jeffries had been on the Kean campus without incident on numerous prior occasions as a result of his membership on a panel that advised the college's Africana Studies Department, this was his first visit since he had gained national attention by attacking Jews and Italians for purportedly orchestrating portrayals of negative racial stereotypes in the film industry in order to continue the suppression of African Americans.[1]

When a group of Jewish students, staff, and faculty (including some of the college's most ardent supporters of multiculturalism) sought entrance to the speech, they learned that it was "private dinner," restricted to the members of an African American student organization and their guests. As a result, they picketed the function, much to the chagrin of the sponsoring group. While a compromise admitted several Jewish students as observers, Jeffries further inflamed the situation by telling his audience that he could not deliver his full message with the Jewish students in the room, and that those who wished to hear all that he had to say should come to a subsequent appearance scheduled at a nearby black church.

The campus erupted. The African American students and faculty who participated in the dinner were furious that their cultural event and one of their "revered elders" had been treated with disrespect. Jewish students, faculty, and staff were upset that the college would permit a person who had publicly advanced anti-Semitic notions on previous occasions to speak without having to confront those whom he defamed. While appreciating that intellectual, social, and cultural functions may not always attract audiences fully reflective of the college's demographics, many members of the college community (including people of all races and ethnicities) were disturbed that a student group had been permitted to utilize college facilities for an event at which admission was restricted on the basis of race or ethnicity. Many were also concerned about the razor-thin edge between free speech and hate speech, and about whether the institution should somehow seek to establish a dividing line. Some viewed the matter more in terms of an ethnic battle between blacks and whites or between blacks and Jews.

Intemperate statements and accusations abounded from many quarters. In the event's aftermath, some African American students alleged that Jewish faculty were retaliating for the Jeffries appearance by intimidating them in class. Faculty, too, alleged intimidation when a group of African American students marched into a faculty senate meeting (set to discuss the issues regarding the closed dinner speech), ringed the perimeter of the room, and glared at the assembled body as it deliberated. Delegations representing the various groups protested at the trustee meetings and at a meeting of the State Board of Higher Education. For the rest of that semester and well into the next year, the student newspaper seemed to focus on little else, particularly on its op-ed pages, which seemed to be devoid of any moderate views. Through it all, much of the college's Hispanic community was concerned that the battling whites and blacks had another agenda; that is, to rid the college of its Hispanic president.

At first the president sought to minimize the matter by indicating that only a few Jewish faculty were troubled by the episode. However, when the tumult proved that it had staying power, she sought to quell the situation with a multicultural speakers series and an all-college retreat that opened the fall 1992 semester. However, it was the mediation activity undertaken by the U.S. Justice Department's Community Relations Service that showed the most promise, since it brought together several of the primary players, the leadership of the Concerned Black Personnel and the Jewish Faculty and Staff Association. But however useful the discussion between those involved in the mediation, the charge to the Justice Department unit was too narrow, since it defined the root problem simply as between blacks and Jews. Thus, with the two parties on the verge of signing an agreement of understanding during the summer of 1993, the president made a set of personnel appointments that both groups saw as being ethnically divisive, and everything fell apart. An African American woman who was an associate vice president was made acting vice president for academic affairs to serve for a year and then to retire from the administration; a Jewish woman who was an assistant vice president was elevated to associate vice president (no "acting") and, under the direct supervision of the president, was assigned several key functions formerly undertaken directly by the previous vice president. Those involved in the mediation between the two groups saw this action as throwing gasoline on the fire which had been was almost extinguished; in protest, they backed away from the agreement of understanding.

Kean College was an uneasy place in the fall of 1993. When classes resumed in September, it was learned that Jeffries was to return as a speaker at a conference being held at the college by a regional scholarly association. Just prior to that appearance, the president released a draft of a new campus speakers policy, nearly a year and a half in the making, and said that it would be an interim measure. Among the provisions were prohibitions on racially or ethnically restricted events, a requirement that outside speakers be taped, and a stipulation of advance notice for external speakers. Given its timing, the African American students viewed this as a "Jeffries Policy," and several black student leaders came to a trustee meeting seeking the president's resignation. Jeffries's speech itself occurred without incident, but it resulted in the final dissolution of the Justice Department's mediation initiative, which had stalled during the summer, and probably led to the invitation to Muhammad (Trustee Subcommittee, 1994).

KHALID ABDUL MUHAMMAD SPEAKS

An African American student leader, who was treasurer of the student government, sought funding from several student groups to establish an alternative multicultural speakers series, since he thought that the president's series was too one-sided. The first speaker would be Khalid Abdul Muhammad, national spokesman from the Nation of Islam; other speakers would be determined later.

Several broad-based organizations (the student government, two groups that planned student activities, the sophomore and junior classes, and a student lobbying group) agreed to contribute to the event, many believing that the money generated from ticket sales would return their investment and provide the source of funds for the second speaker in the student-sponsored series. Few, however, were prepared for what Muhammad would say.[2]

As people began to arrive for the speech, Muhammad made it known that he would not go on stage unless everyone entering the auditorium were searched by his security team, known as the Fruit of Islam. College officials, fearing the repercussions of a last-minute cancellation, sought counsel from the Attorney General's Office, which advised that patrons could be asked if they would permit a search; those objecting could not be forced to submit to a search but could be barred from admission if given a refund. Thus everyone who wanted to hear the speech, "The Secret Relationship between Blacks and Jews," was frisked by Muhammad's body-guards, as members of the college police force stood nearby. Several hundred people, the majority of whom were not members of the Kean community (and many of whom were given free tickets, since ticket sales were slack), entered the auditorium. As a result of the audio-taping requirement, there was no uncertainty regarding what Muhammad said either during his remarks or in the question-and-answer period. During the three-hour session, Muhammad established himself in the nation's eyes as a major purveyor of hatred.

Muhammad began with a warning, "before we even get started. It's going to be a rough ride, buddy." He said, "I didn't come here to take no prisoners." He let loose on the Jews, noting that they had criticized his leader, Louis Farrakhan. He proclaimed that "I'm one of his flame throwers, and I came here to burn your behind up." Complete with scatological references and a put-on Yiddish accent, he evoked all the anti-Semitic stereotypes, accusing the Jews of being behind the slave trade and calling them "murderer[s] . . . from the beginning," "the father of the lie." Stating that Jews controlled the Federal Reserve, he said that they were "no good bastard[s]" who "were always looking for gold." He said that they deserved the Holocaust and called Hitler "wickedly great." An example of his anti-Semitism:

The so-called Jews . . . crawled out of the caves and heels of Europe just a little over 4,000 years ago. . . . You left your dead right in the caves with you and you slept with your dead for 2,000 years, smelling the stench coming up from the decomposing body. . . . You did your number one and number two, your pee-pee and your doo-doo, which should be a don't don't, right in the caves . . . You slept in your urination and your defecation, generation after generation for 2,000 years. . . . You knocked your animals in the head with clubs . . . and suck[ed] the blood from the raw meat, and you still eat your meat raw to this very day.

His vitriol was not limited to Jews; he called the pope a "no good . . . cracker," suggesting that someone should "raise that dress up and see what's really under there." He said that the King James Version of the Bible was named after a "screaming sissy" and went on to postulate that "God does not name holy books after homosexuals."

He gave no quarter to blacks whose views were less extreme than his, mentioning (among many others) "Uncle Tom" Bradley, "stinkin'" David Dinkins, and "Spook" Lee. Referring to Henry Louis Gates, who had spoken at one of Kean College's multicultural forums, he said, "when white folks can't defeat you, they'll always find some Negro, some boot-lickin', butt-lickin', butt-dancin', bamboozled, half-baked, half-fried, sissified, punkified, pasteurized, homogenized nigger that they can trot out in front of you." He saved some of his best for Nelson Mandela's non-retribution policy and for South Africa's white population:

We don't owe the white man nothing in South Africa. . . . If we want to be merciful at all, when we gain enough power from God Almighty to take our freedom and independence from him, we give him 24 hours to get out of town, by sundown. That's all. If he won't get out of town by sundown, we kill everything white that ain't right in South Africa. We kill the women. We kill the children. We kill the babies. We kill the blind. We kill the crippled. We kill the faggot. We kill the Lesbian. We kill them all. . . . Kill the old ones, too. Goddammit, if they [are] in a wheelchair, push 'em off a cliff. . . . Kill the crazy. Goddammit, and when you get through killing 'em all, go to the God damn graveyard and dig up the grave and kill 'em, God damn, again, cause they didn't die hard enough.

Muhammad spewed three hours' worth of hatred, but what was more appalling than his remarks was the appreciation that he was receiving from much of his audience, including Kean College

students, staff, and faculty, who laughed in response to his characterizations and cheered him on with supportive comments and
applause, even at his most outrageous, and even when he belittled
an African American student who was brave enough to ask a
challenging question. One of the few whites in the audience, a
faculty member who had been urged by some of his African
American students to attend the speech to hear an Afrocentric
perspective, wrote to the trustees that he was shocked to see "the
leading Kean College faculty and student exponents of Afrocen-
trism [sitting] in the front row cheering" (Nordheimer, 1993: B6).

A CAMPUS BATTERED

There was no physical violence as a result of the speech, but,
needless to say, there were many who were fighting mad. The
aftermath proved as raucous as the event, but significantly more
enduring. Tensions rose on the campus. It was not until December
9, ten days after the event, that the college president issued a short
statement condemning Muhammad's speech (without mentioning
his name), calling his remarks "intolerable, especially in an academic community like Kean College, whose members are committed to living together harmoniously" (Gomez, 1994a: 4).

However, by then the college had fragmented like never before,
with few maintaining neutral positions. A group of senior faculty,
many of whom had not been party to earlier criticism of the
president, subsequently visited the state's higher education chancellor to voice their displeasure about the state of affairs at the
college. On the other hand, one prominent member of the faculty
circulated a letter to the college community, later published as a
letter to the editor in several newspapers, criticizing the press
coverage and defending the college and its president. Other support
for the president came from members of the Hispanic community,
but there was no unanimity from that quarter. The leader of the
faculty union lamented to the *Newark Star Ledger*, the state's most
important newspaper, that while many at the college were issuing
statements akin to war communiqués, no one was talking to each
other (Spoto, 1993). The division on campus would only get worse
as the academic year proceeded.

The response from off campus was swift and strong. Articles
appeared in most of the state's newspapers as well as those in New

York City and Philadelphia, followed by op-ed columns and editorials, all denouncing Muhammad and his message of hatred; many faulted the college's president for lack of leadership and the college itself for having miseducated students who cheered Muhammad. Letters to the editor abounded. For weeks, television and radio call-in programs focused on the incident. Just prior to the president's initial statement, the state's chancellor called for an independent investigation into the event, particularly regarding the frisking of audience members by Muhammad's bodyguards. New Jersey's outgoing governor, many state legislators, and members of the state's congressional and senatorial delegation spoke out. The town council of the municipality in which the college is located passed a resolution blasting the college president and condemning racially motivated, disparaging remarks.[3]

When a full-page ad with excerpts from the speech was placed in *The New York Times* by the Anti-Defamation League (ADL) of B'nai B'rith, the matter entered the broader awareness, and national columnists and political figures entered the fray. Vice President Albert Gore spoke out. Prominent African Americans including Jesse Jackson, Benjamin Chavis, William Gray, and Congressman Charles Rangel denounced Muhammad's message. Kweisi Mfume, Representative from Maryland and chair of the Congressional Black Caucus, wrote to Louis Farrakhan asking whether the speech, whose excerpts he characterized as "extremely agonizing for me to even read," represented the views of the Nation of Islam (Holmes, 1994: A1). Farrakhan, who had been seeking to establish a less extreme image for himself replied that the Jews are "plotting against us even as we speak" (Goodman, 1994: E1). On February 2nd the United States Senate weighed in with a 97 to 0 vote condemning the November 29th speech, and the Congressional Black Caucus indicated that it was considering distancing itself from Farrakhan and the Nation of Islam. Three weeks later, the House of Representatives followed the Senate's lead with a vote of 361 to 34 denouncing Muhammad's speech, despite the warning by California's Don Edwards that the Congress was "making a national and international hero of this scoundrel"[4] (Hook, 1994: 458).

The day after the Senate vote, and under mounting pressure, Farrakhan suspended Muhammad as his national spokesperson; "While I stand by the truths that he spoke, I must condemn in the

strongest terms the manner in which those truths were represented." He said that the speech had been "vile, repugnant, malicious and spoken in mockery of individuals and people, which is
against the spirit of Islam." Farrakhan went on to assert that the
real issue, however, was not Muhammad's remarks but the ADL's
aim "to destroy the reputation and character of Louis Farrakhan . . . and to ultimately destroy the Nation of Islam" (Cohen,
1994: 1). The college's president and the chair of the board of
trustees promptly released statements praising Farrakhan's action
but ignoring his related statements, which many at Kean saw not
as rhetorical but as strongly anti-Semitic in tone and intent.

This apparent insensitivity on the part of Kean's two top leaders
threatened the fragile willingness of the college community to
participate in a trustee review, brokered by the chancellor just
before Christmas, of campus climate, college policies, and the
events of November 29th. The president had opposed the review,
accusing the chancellor, who was Jewish, of "respond[ing] emotion-
ally" to the speech instead of defending the college as a place where
the right of free speech is absolute (Gomez, 1993). (It should be
noted that the State Assembly was to pass in 1994 a resolution
commending the chancellor for his "prompt and forceful response"
to the hate speech incident, and that the incoming governor cited
his actions in her announcement that she would retain him in her
new cabinet.) However, with tensions high on campus, the faculty
senate and other campus groups speaking out against the manner
in which the event had been handled and supporting the chancellor's call for an investigation, and with the college community
shaken by the solid chorus of rebuke from the outside, the chair of
the board of trustees broke with the president. With the consent
of the board he established a subcommittee of trustees to undertake
a review.

Chaired by an African American woman, the committee also
included a male trustee (a Puerto Rican Jew), a student trustee (an
African American male), and the faculty representative to the board
(a white male). Serving as the group's facilitator was the vice
president of the Washington-based American Arbitration Association. The state Attorney General's Office, the county prosecutor,
and the US Justice Department's Community Relations office
agreed to provide assistance as necessary. Faculty leadership,
initially favoring a study by a group totally external to the college

in order to assure objectivity, agreed to participate. The study, delayed by unusually severe winter weather, had yet to begin when the president and board chair issued their statements praising Farrakhan's suspension of Muhammad. The flurry that resulted, however, proved brief, and the study commenced.

In mid-February 1994, Rabbi Avi Weiss, national president of the Coalition for Jewish Concerns, was invited to campus to provide "A Response to Bigotry and Hatred." His well attended and well received speech was marred by the rudeness of several African American students, prompting the college president to send him a written apology. This did not sit well with some within the college's black community, who felt that their freedom of expression was being trampled upon. The Pan African Student Union upped the ante by inviting Louis Farrakhan to speak.

Farrakhan accepted, but because the students had not met the letter of the speakers policy requiring notice to the administration in advance of the proposed date, the appearance was delayed. In the meantime, the president sought the advice of the Attorney General's Office regarding whether Farrakhan could be barred from speaking. In a March 16, 1994, advisory letter, the Attorney General indicated that "any content-based restriction imposed by a state college on student-sponsored speakers invited by campus groups or organizations is subject to a strict scrutiny analysis and is likely to be held unconstitutional" (Poritz and Brown, 1994).

In announcing Farrakhan's March 28th appearance, the president called upon the college community to "stand firm in denouncing bigotry and racism" and indicated her belief that the "presence of yet another controversial speaker on the campus has the potential of distracting this community from the healing process now begun" (Gomez, 1994b). Few on campus agreed that any healing was in process, and few were listening to the president by that point. Many of both races rallied to the call to condemn bigotry and racism. A protest vigil was organized to occur simultaneously with the speech.

Minister Farrakhan delivered a relatively mild address to a packed theater. *The New York Times* characterized his speech as "a performance that swelled with defiance at perceived enemies in the news media . . . and at a mass culture he accused of robbing black Americans of the chance to succeed" (Nordheimer, 1994: B4). While saying that he was not anti-Semitic, he indicated that the image-makers in Hollywood responsible for limiting the life chances of blacks were dominated by Jews. He also expressed solidarity with the protest against hateful speech that was occurring outside in the rain. An estimated seven hundred people, including United States Senator Frank Lautenberg, Congressman Robert Franks, numerous state legislators, the higher education chancellor, and many from the college, participated in the "United Against Hatred" vigil.

The harshest winter and spring in recent memory—both in terms of weather and intergroup relations—drew to a close at Kean College, and everyone concentrated on the end of classes and final exams. The board of trustees subcommittee released its report in early June. A few weeks later, the president announced her intention to step down.

As is probably the case in many high-profile conflicts, whether on a college campus or off, the turmoil actually involves smaller numbers of people than one might assume from press accounts. Thus, a student leader (who was Hispanic) told the *Philadelphia Inquirer* that she did not believe that the wrangling "affected the relationship of the majority of students" (John-Hall, 1995: B6), and the trustee subcommittee (in 1994) heard from students that the conflict did not reach the classroom.

Nevertheless, when classes resumed in September 1994, enrollments were lower than they had been a year earlier, and, while the 1994–95 academic year proved to be much less eventful than the previous year, intergroup relations were still strained, with tensions bubbling to the surface from time to time. For example, African American students bridled under rules that they believe were aimed at them, such as the requirement of six-weeks' notice for guest speakers and the administration's policy of increasing security for events that it deemed controversial (John-Hall, 1995). The bitterness between the college's African American and Jewish communities persisted. Such incidents as the carving of swastikas into study carrels near the college's Holocaust Center and the appearance of other anti-Semitic graffiti on campus, while it was not attributed to African American students, served as a reminder of the unresolved feelings between the two groups (*The Chronicle of Higher Education*, 1995a).

ISSUES IN SEARCH OF ANSWERS

In the aftermath of the Jeffries speech, I was concerned about what I perceived to be a general lack of leadership throughout the institution, as some players became increasingly strident, others sought to gain advantage through political jockeying and behind-the-scenes, manipulation, and some simply ran for the hills. While I thought that the Justice Department mediation effort held promise for pulling the campus back together, I was concerned that it envisioned a two-party dispute involving only African Americans and Jews,and that even then, students were not part of the dialogue. I was distraught that the parties to the mediation chose to show their unity by protests against the president rather than by filling the leadership void, staking out common ground on which to re-anchor the college. I was also distressed that the board of trustees was not acting more definitively to pull the college out of its crisis.

After the Muhammad speech, I was angry that frisking had been permitted (in the name of free speech) and that the president and the chair of the board did not come out immediately after the speech to condemn it in no uncertain terms, to act quickly to defuse what had to be considered a ticking bomb. I must even admit that for a few fleeting moments (and not out loud), I questioned whether Muhammad should have been permitted to speak. More lasting, however, was my concern that our effort at multiculturalism had appeared to produce the opposite of what we had intended, and my bafflement that students would invite such a speaker, that students and faculty would cheer his viciousness, that so many on all sides wanted to get back at the other side—even if it meant serious disruption of a college in which they had invested so dearly.

The subsequent chapters seek to achieve an understanding of why the events at Kean played out as they did, and of the extent to which the Kean experience is within higher education's mainstream. We begin with an examination of the prevailing racial climate in America.

NOTES

1. Shortly after his speech at Kean, the City University of New York sought to remove Jeffries from his role as chair of the Black Studies Department, returning him exclusively to faculty responsibilities, because of his prior attacks on Jews and Italians. Some saw this action as

an infringement of his free-speech rights, while others concluded that the university had a legitimate right to limit its administration to people who acted in accordance with institutional goals (Kaus, 1993). Jeffries's attempt to retain his administrative post see-sawed through the courts. A month after his removal, a federal district court ordered him reinstated. This decision was upheld at the appellate level, but in November 1994 the Supreme Court ordered the appeals court to review its decision in accordance with *Waters v. Churchill*, a recent case in which the Court ruled that a government employer could fire an employee for speech that was likely to be disruptive. Upon rehearing, the appellate court ruled in favor of the university, in April 1995. Jeffries announced his determination to appeal that ruling to the Supreme Court, but he stepped down from his administrative position at the expiration of his term on June 30, 1995 (*The Chronicle of Higher Education*, 1995b).

2. While Muhammad was not widely known prior to his Kean speech, he was familiar to Jewish groups that track anti-Semitic speakers. A member of one such group called a member of the board of trustees to warn him of Muhammad's extremism. The information was passed on to the president's office in the hope that the college might prepare for the visit.

3. The college sought to minimize damage through a series of letters from the president to the college community, to friends of the college, and to political leaders. Further, it published a special issue of its widely circulated biweekly newsletter, *Kean Today*. That issue included excerpts from statements made in condemnation of Muhammad's remarks by members of the board of trustees at their December 13, 1993, meeting; a statement from the president; and a declaration by the thirty members of the President's Council (an administrative group) joining the president in her disavowal of hateful expressions and pledging to continue their efforts to create a supportive climate on campus. The newsletter also took a slap at the chancellor, and it asserted that "Jewish newspapers, present the night of the speech, began the denunciation on the College and its administration for its lack of response immediately following the event." Further, it "reminded the community that the issue [of hate speech] is confronting Kean College but also the state, nation, and world" (Kean College, 1994: 1, 4). While the statements about the Jewish newspapers and the pervasiveness of hate speech were factual, they were viewed by some critics in the college as an effort to reduce the Kean problem to a "Jewish problem," making it seem less severe than they thought it to be.

4. The African Americans in the House voted on the prevailing side 20 to 11, with four voting "present" and three not voting.

REFERENCES

Cohen, Robert. "Farrakhan Suspends Lecturer." *Newark Star Ledger.* February 4, 1994, pp. 1, 18.

Editors of *The Chronicle of Higher Education.* "'In' Box." *The Chronicle of Higher Education.* January 13, 1995a, p. A15.

————. "'In' Box," *The Chronicle of Higher Education.* July 7, 1995b, p. A13.

Gomez, Elsa. "Letter to Chancellor Edward D. Goldberg." December 20, 1993.

————. " December 9 Statement from Dr. Gomez," reprinted in *Kean Today.* January 13, 1994, p. 4.

————. "Administrative Report, Special Edition." March 4, 1994.

Goodman, Howard. "Blacks, Jews Strive Amid New Wounds," *Philadelphia Inquirer.* January 30, 1994, pp. E1–E2.

Holmes, Steven A. "Farrakhan Is Warned over Aide's Invective." *The New York Times.* January 25, 1994, p. A1.

Hook, Janet. "House Denounces Remarks as 'Racist' Speech." *Congressional Quarterly* v. 52 n. 8 (February 26, 1994), p. 458.

John-Hall, Annette. "N.J. College Still Feels Speech's Stigma." *Philadelphia Inquirer.* January 8, 1995, pp. B1, B6.

Kaus, Mickey. "TRB in Washington, Speech Defect." *The New Republic* v. 208 n. 24 (June 14, 1993), pp. 6, 49.

Kean College. "Controversy Follows Muhammad Speech." *Kean Today.* January 13, 1994, pp. 1, 4.

New Jersey State Assembly. "An Assembly Resolution Concerning Free Speech, Tolerance, and Responsibility, and Commending Dr. Edward Goldberg, Chancellor of Higher Education." January 10, 1994.

Nordheimer, Jon. "Divided by Diatribe, College Speech Ignites Furor over Race." *The New York Times.* December 29, 1993, pp. B1, B6.

————. "Farrakhan Softens Tone but Sticks to Message." *The New York Times.* March 30, 1994, p. B4.

Poritz, Deborah T. and William C. Brown. "Letter to Elsa Gomez Re: Constitutionality of Conduct-Based Restrictions on Speakers at State Colleges." D.O.L. No. 94–80057. March 16, 1994.

Spoto, Mary Ann. "Kean President Blasts Farrakhan Aide's Talk." *Newark Star Ledger.* December 11, 1993, p. A10.

Trustee Subcommittee (Patricia Weston Rivera, Chair). *Report of the Subcommittee.* Union, NJ: Kean College Board of Trustees, June 1994.

Chapter 1

A Changing America

Race pervades the American existence. Fred Bruning (1992: 11), writing in the Canadian weekly *MacLean's* after the Los Angeles riots prompted by the Rodney King affair, offered that, "race is the fundamental issue of this country. It touches every aspect of our communal being." The closer, it seems, that race is to the heart of any matter, the more thorny, emotional, and difficult that matter is to resolve. Bruning contends that "we are going to feel the dyspeptic burn of suspicion and hate around our hearts and nothing is going to offer quick antacid relief. And, what's worse, we are not going to be pleased with ourselves. Not at all." This journalistic alarm must be considered not simply in the context of a white suburban jury acquitting a group of white police who had beaten a black man, as abhorrent as that act was. It is also consistent with the findings of a national commission, whose honorary chairs were former presidents Gerald R. Ford and Jimmy Carter, that "America is moving backward—not forward—in its efforts to achieve the full participation of minority citizens in the life and prosperity of the nation" (Commission on Minority Participation, 1988: 1).

Students arrive at college holding attitudes reflective of their families and communities. If we hope that they will graduate as enlightened souls committed to the improvement of intergroup relations, it is useful to understand the thoughts and feelings that they bring with them, which are significantly affected by the dramatic changes that have been occurring in our dynamic society.

America is a nation with a constitutional (and cultural) tension between individual rights and group protection. For the first three-quarters of a century of our republic, most blacks were counted as three-fifths of a person, treated as property, and accorded no civil rights. It took another century to establish that the constitutional rights recognized in aftermath of the Civil War were, indeed, the same as those enjoyed by whites since the Revolutionary War. Sadly, the American Dream of a society in which, all things being equal, everyone can achieve in accordance with ability and persistence, and enjoy the fruits of our democracy, has yet to be realized for millions. For millions of others, that dream appears to be precipitously close to slipping away.

In the past half-century, we have been deeply influenced by important accomplishments: putting legal segregation into history's scrap heap, walking on the moon, triumph in the Cold War, and extension of opportunity to receive a higher education to nearly all adults. However, our economy has taken a roller coaster ride that is different from normal cycles of boom and recession, as the end of the industrial age and the globalization of the marketplace knock us from our position of international economic supremacy. Our confidence has also been shaken by such experiences as the assassination and attempted assassinations of presidents, presidential candidates, and civil rights leaders; the deep divisions that accompanied our tragic losses in the war in Vietnam; the explosion of the space shuttle *Challenger* as millions of school children watched on television; recurrent urban unrest that has led to devastating riots periodically since the early 1960s; and a growing sense that many of our most important institutions are failing to meet current needs. Yet at the same time that we are questioning our own direction, events and trends in other parts of the world are sustaining America's attractiveness to their tired, poor, and huddled masses, "yearning to breathe free." Several of these factors—our changing social conditions, our changing demography, our changing attitudes, and our changing politics—bear closer scrutiny.

CHANGING SOCIAL CONDITIONS

In the three decades following World War II, America followed a slow but steady course toward ending *de jure* segregation and legal discrimination, a cause that had moral dimensions that permitted the development of a broad coalition of Americans. Even so, it was a struggle; the giant steps of the *Brown* decision, the Civil Rights Act of 1964, and the Voting Rights Act of 1965 required strong government enforcement to give them meaning. While the intensity of the federal effort may have varied through the five presidencies from Kennedy to Carter (three Democrats and two Republicans), federal policies were in the direction of promoting the equality and civil rights of minorities as a group, in order to overcome their prior discrimination as a group.

Those civil rights successes happened before today's college students (those matriculating at the usual age, at least) were born. They have no memory of life under Jim Crow laws, nor of the battles that tore down that way of life. For them segregation is a matter of history, just as slavery was for their grandparents. Their "real time" experience with official separation of the races comes from the South African context, not the American. Thus, they do not share the passion for that cause that earlier generations of students did. In some important ways, that shows the tremendous growth that has occurred in our national thinking; in other ways, it increases the challenges of bringing about a better America.

When the *Brown* decision was rendered, approximately 55 percent of Americans approved. By 1961 that proportion had increased to 63 percent. At the time of the *Brown*'s fortieth anniversary, the Gallup Poll found that 86 percent of whites and 94 percent of African Americans agreed with the Supreme Court's basic finding. Nearly two-thirds of those polled credited the decision with having increased the quality of education for African Americans as well as with having improved race relations between blacks and whites (McAneny and Saad, 1994).

However, while the American public still agrees with the fundamental concept that legal segregation is wrong, the electoral majority that had put teeth into the effort to bring about a more equal society began to erode, as school busing and housing integration litigation moved north (where segregation had been *de facto* rather than *de jure*) and as affirmative action programs began to be implemented. While many saw these policies as logical and necessary next steps in the Civil Rights Movement, others disagreed. Julius Lester (1991: 7) believes that the battle against *de facto* segregation represented in reality a "shift from fighting for civil rights to fighting against racism," one that moved the American people away from attempts to find common ground, with disastrous results: "to fight against racism divides humanity into an 'us against them' situation." Similarly, Richard Kahlenberg (1995: 24) argues that since liberals continued to focus on issues of race rather than shift to issues of class, they created today's "angry white males."

Economic Uncertainty

Further, the policies that began to break apart the civil rights coalition came to the national forefront in a time of domestic economic downturn that proved to be the vanguard of a global economic restructuring. Competition increased for pieces of an economic pie that was not growing as fast as the population. For example, hourly wages adjusted for inflation were lower in 1988 than they had been in any year since 1966. In 80 percent of two-parent families with children, adults worked more hours in 1989 than in 1979. However, since the increases in real wages for wives did not compensate for declines in the real earnings of husbands, the families were not wealthier for working more. Equally as discouraging, in 1992 there were 36.9 million Americans living in poverty, the highest number in three decades (Piliawsky, 1994). Further, the home ownership proportion—an indication of the strength of the economy and the ability to realize the American dream—was lower in 1990 than it had been four decades earlier (Abernathy, 1993). During this time, much of white America assumed that federal mandates and programs were improving the lot of most African Americans, often at the expense of whites. While we will explore that issue in greater depth in the next chapter, it is important to understand that, as a study by the National Urban League revealed, the increase in economic status of 8 percent of the African American population moving into the upper and middle classes was outweighed by the decrease in status of the 16 percent who moved from the working class to the underclass (Kilson and Cottingham, 1991).

The recession of the late 1980s and early 1990s added more stress. The economic restructuring continued; corporate America began to down-size its middle management and shift to a leaner, more customer-oriented approach. International competition and the need to reduce expenses caused reliable companies like IBM, which had been known for protecting their workforce even in the worst of times, to undertake massive personnel cuts. The end of the Cold War reduced employment in defense-related industries, and the advance of technology (particularly in the area of telecommunications) resulted in greater job loss than gain. A review of reports filed with the Equal Employment Opportunity Commission reveals that during the recession female workers fared better than male workers, increasing their share in higher-paying occupations, and that Asians and Hispanics increased their employment shares generally. White males suffered as a result of their concentration in industries and occupations that were especially hard hit. African Americans, particularly in blue-collar occupations, lost ground as well. (At the recession's end, the overall share of white male employment in the diminished job force increased somewhat [Badgett, 1994].)

Sadly, our thinking has taken an "un-American" turn, as many have come to view their own prospects and our collective future in pessimistic terms. Many Americans have begun to fear that their children may well experience a lower standard of living. We have also seemingly begun to accept the notion that America is bound to have an underclass with little opportunity for escape. Further, losses of economic position of some white males and of African Americans set the stage for increased racial polarization.

CHANGING DEMOGRAPHICS

The proportion of whites and African Americans feeling increased challenge to their position and prospects is on the rise as a result of changing demography. The 1990 census revealed that our population is being transformed in fundamental ways: we are becoming a nation of minorities. In that year, eight of ten Americans were white (down from the peak of 90 percent in 1960); if white Hispanics are subtracted, whites drop to 75 percent of the nation's population. African Americans account for 12 percent, Hispanics (some of whom are also black) represent 9 percent, Asians and Pacific Islanders three percent, and Native Americans 1 percent (Riche, 1991). (The figure for the Hispanic population may be too low, given its members' ability to list themselves in several categories, including "Other" [McDaniel, 1995].)

The current proportion of the population that is white (non-Hispanic) is roughly what it was in 1810, after which European immigration and high fertility rates brought the white population to more than 88 percent by 1930 (McDaniel, 1995). However, after the post–World War II "baby boom," white fertility rates—as well as those of all native-born Americans—began to drop off precipitously. By the late 1970s, the American fertility rate was 1.7 births per woman, well below replacement. With population growth linked closely with the economy, fertility bottomed-out in the recession of 1980–1981, with white fertility at 1.4 and black fertility at 2.09 births per woman, both below replacement. With the economic expansion of the 1980s fertility grew again, the white rate increasing to 1.7 and the black rate to 2.4 by 1990 (Abernathy, 1993).

Fertility rates among native-born Hispanic women are comparable to the national average. However, foreign-born Hispanics—as well as other immigrants—tend to mirror the fertility rates of their counties of origin. Thus, for example, the fertility rate of mainland-born Puerto Rican women is 1.9, while it is 2.5 for those born on the island. Thus, because of the combined effect of high levels of immigration from Latin America (particularly Mexico) and the Caribbean, the Hispanic population began to accelerate in the 1980s (Abernathy, 1993).

Similarly, the Asian population not only began to grow substantially but also began to shift in terms of ethnicity. As late as the 1970 census, Japanese Americans were the largest Asian American group. By the 1980 census, they had been surpassed by Chinese Americans. In 1990, Filipino Americans came close to matching the Chinese American population, and Americans whose descent was from the Indian sub-continent, and also Korean Americans, approached the Japanese American population in size (Riche, 1991).

The shift in place of origin of immigrants can be seen in the drop-off of the proportion of Americans of European descent who were immigrants from 5 percent in 1960 to 3 percent in 1990; immigrants accounted for 1 percent of the Native American population in both years. Over the same period, the proportion of foreign-born blacks increased from 1 to 4 percent, among Hispanics from 32 percent to 41 percent, and among Asians from 32 to 63 percent (McDaniel, 1995).[1]

A Nation of Minorities

As may be readily surmised, the demographic trend lines indicate that non-Hispanic whites will continue to decline as a proportion of the American population. When today's baby-boomers were babies, nine of every ten Americans were white; today, it is three of every four. When the baby-boomers reach old age, their share of the American population will have slid to three out of every five (Edmondson, 1994). The number of whites is projected to grow by only six-tenths of a percent per year in the 1990s and by three-tenths of a percent per year for the first decade of the next century. The fastest growing cohorts among whites will be in the older age groups, while there will be an absolute decline in their numbers aged 25–44. The growth rate throughout the 1990s of 1.3 percent per annum among white children will lag behind that of Hispanics (5 percent) and African Americans (3 percent). Immigration will account for 57 percent of the growth among the Asian American population through 2010, and for 36, 20, and 5 percent respectively for Hispanics, African Americans, and whites (Exter, 1993).

While at present approximately one-third of Americans under the age of thirty-five are minority, in thirty years the majority under age thirty-five will be minority (Edmondson, 1994). Hispanics will surpass African Americans as the second-largest group in the nation. By 2050, whites will be 55 percent of the population, Hispanics will be 22 percent, African Americans will be 14 percent, Asian Americans 8, and Native Americans 1 (McDaniel, 1995). If demographic projections hold up, by sometime between 2060 and 2080 there will be no racial or ethnic majority in the United States (Riche, 1991; Exter, 1993).

The demographic changes are showing in the schools. For example, in fall 1984 America's elementary and secondary schools were 73.3 percent white, 15 percent African American, 8.2 percent Hispanic, and 3.5 percent from other groups. Ten years later, the proportions were 68.1 percent, 15.9 percent, 11.7 percent, and 4.3 percent respectively (National Center for Educational Statistics, 1994a). By 2000 one-third of all school-aged children will be from minorties (Commission on Minority Participation, 1988), and for many, English will not be the native or best language. In Dade County, Florida, the nation's fourth-largest school district, the students' parents come from 123 countries. Similarly, in Fairfax

County, Virginia, there are more than a hundred languages spoken (Browder, 1994). In New York City one out of four children in the public schools has non-English-speaking immigrant parents. The US Department of Education reports increases of 40 percent or more in the numbers of school children who have difficulty speaking English in eighteen states (including all three West Coast states and most of the Southeast), 21–39 percent in eight states (including Pennsylvania, Ohio, and Indiana), and 1–20 percent in eleven states (including New York, New Jersey, Michigan, and Illinois). Decreases occurred in only thirteen states (including Florida and Texas) and the District of Columbia (National Center for Educational Statistics, 1994b).

One significance of this trend toward an increased proportion of minorities among young people lies in the fact that they will constitute accordingly a growing share of the workforce, accounting for one-third of the net addition to the labor force between 1985 and 2000 (Commission on Minority Participation, 1988). The pace will accelerate between 1990 and 2005, when more than half of new workers will be from minorities (Exter, 1993).

More than ever, success in the labor market is a function of educational attainment (a topic to be discussed in more detail in the next chapter). Many minority children, particularly African Americans and Hispanics, have not fared well in our schools. True, in recent years gaps in learning proficiency appear to have been declining (some very dramatically). For example, among seventeen-year-olds in 1978, 96 percent of whites, 71 percent of blacks, and 78 percent of Hispanics performed at or above proficiency levels in basic mathematics; by 1992 the proportions stood at 98 percent, 90 percent, and 94 percent, respectively. For algebra, the equivalent figures were 8 percent of whites, a negligible percentage of blacks, and 1 percent of Hispanics; by 1992 the proportions were 9, 7, and 1 percent, respectively (National Center for Educational Statistics, 1994a). Further, in reading, 60 percent of the proficiency gap between blacks and whites has been eliminated since 1971 (Smith, 1993). Scores on the Scholastic Aptitude Test (SAT) have also narrowed; African American students increased their math scores by twenty points and their verbal scores by twenty-one between 1977 and 1987, while scores of white students on the verbal test increased one point and remained constant in math (Commission on Minority Participation, 1988). However, problems remain. The

Armed Forces Qualifying Test still reveals a significant difference in the skill levels of African Americans who have left school, relative to similarly situated whites (Maxwell, 1994).

As long as any gaps in proficiency remain, America's ability to compete economically will be seriously constrained. While the publication of *A Nation at Risk* (1983), which spurred the educational reform movement of the 1980s, brought home the message that the quality of schools was poor enough to threaten our economic well-being and national security, we seem to have lost that sense of urgency. One indication is that school bond issues and budgets are not faring particularly well with voters. In part, this has to do with a frustration that, despite substantial efforts at reform, the schools have yet to enjoy broad respect again, but also with a belief of many that to overcome the problems of educating minority children would bankrupt us, if it were even accomplishable. Indeed, the publication of Murray and Hernstein's *The Bell Curve* (1994), which has renewed the debate regarding the racial and ethnic, i.e., genetic, basis of intelligence, is likely to add fuel to these concerns—and reduce willingness to support a public education system that is becoming more a province of minorities. Thus, as we approach the twenty-first century the discussion is not so much about strengthening the public schools as it is about providing publicly subsidized alternatives to them.

Anti-Immigrant Sentiment

The increased challenges of demographics and immigration felt by many whites and African Americans came to the fore in California in 1994, when voters passed Proposition 187, a measure that, on its face, meant to curb public services to illegal immigrants but actually had much to do with growing anti-immigrant (and to a certain extent anti-minority) sentiment. California is often a national bell-weather. In many respects, the demographic trends discussed earlier have already reached the Golden State: two-thirds of the 800,000 people who move to California each year are foreign born, and legal immigration increases the state's population by 28 percent each year. As a result, in California's 46th congressional district, for example, there are more than fifty languages spoken, and in a recent election there were candidates from six different cultural groups (Browder, 1994).

Immigration increased total fertility in California from 1.95 births per woman in 1982 to 2.5 in 1990; Hispanic fertility rose over 23 percent from 3.16 to 3.9 in that period. The combined effect of immigration and fertility increases caused the non-Hispanic white majority in Los Angeles County to become a minority in the 1980s. If high immigration continues, by 2020 non-Hispanic whites will be approximately one-third of the state's population, and African Americans will be less than 7 percent (Abernathy, 1993).

According to the Center for Immigration Studies, California's illegal immigrants used in 1990 an estimated $5.4 billion worth of services from thirteen major federal and state programs, including Medicaid, uncompensated health care, Aid to Families with Dependent Children, public education, and food stamps. The magnitude of these expenditures is demonstrated by the fact that the welfare case-load attributable to illegal immigrants in California represented 25 percent of the state's total (or 6 to 7 percent of the national total) (Abernathy, 1993). During the referendum campaign it was estimated that of the 2.9 million illegal immigrants in the United States, 86.4 percent were concentrated in seven states (Arizona, California, Florida, Illinois, New Jersey, New York, and Texas); as many as 2.1 million were living in California. The seven states were reported to spend $471 million per year on correctional facilities, $209 million on emergency medical care and child birth, and $3.1 billion for education from kindergarten through grade twelve. These expenditures were not fully offset by the $1.9 billion that these individuals paid in various state taxes. California's expenses included $1.4 billion per year for education, non-emergency health, and welfare, approximately 10 percent of the state budget, but illegal immigrants paid only about half of that amount (approximately $732 million) in state taxes (Anderson and Farragher, 1994; *The Economist*, 1994).

Proponents of Proposition 187 hoped that without access to services the illegal immigrants would go somewhere else, relieving the drain on California's budget, and that once they left, the jobs that they had held would become available to legal residents. Throughout the campaign, the issues regarding the effect of illegal immigration on wages and employment were muddled with general concerns regarding legal immigration and trends in the job market. It is pretty clear that in fact most illegal immigrants work in low-skilled, oppressive settings and that many earn substandard wages; they occupy jobs that are not attractive to citizens and other documented workers.

The effect of *legal* immigration on American workers, however, is not so clear. Some flatly assert that immigration suppresses weekly wages of unskilled labor by as much as 10 percent and that African Americans, who constitute much of the unskilled labor pool, bear a disproportionate share of the job competition from immigrants (Abernathy, 1993). Conservative scholar Edward Luttwak believes that underclass jobs are being eroded from both sides, the better ones being taken by more educated workers, the least attractive by immigrants (Browder, 1994). Others argue that black wage rates and employment levels have either benefited or are unaffected as a result of immigration. More recent studies that focus on localized impacts of immigrants on low-skilled urban labor appear to bridge the gap. For example, between 1985 and 1990 economic conditions led nearly 12 percent of the poor whites and nearly 5 percent of the poor blacks to leave Los Angeles; even greater emigrations occurred from Chicago, New York, and other metropolitan areas. Those who remained in the city—the ones who appear in the studies of the effects of immigration—were not negatively affected: while those who had been were not studied, since they had sought more opportunity elsewhere (Skerry, 1995).

Whether immigration does or does not affect employment, the perception is that it does. The president of New York's National Association for the Advancement of Colored People, Hazel Dukes, has asked, "Why let foreigners or newcomers have . . . jobs while blacks, who have been here for hundreds of years, can't support themselves or their families?" (Browder, 1994: 39). She is joined by others who are not in direct competition with immigrants for jobs but do not like the new immigrants. Such sentiment was voiced during a New York City mayoral campaign, when a liberal candidate speaking of the success of immigrants to that city was interrupted by another elected official: "It was true of the immigrants who came from Europe, and also the Orientals. But these others. The quality is not good." There was hearty applause from the audience (Klein, 1991: 37–8).

The debate leaves one wondering whether immigrants are welfare-collecting, social service–consuming ne'er-do-wells or hardworking people who take jobs away from others. Cash-strapped, recession-ridden, and tax-rebellious Californians were tantalized with the prospect of saving huge amounts of money by keeping illegal immigrants and their children out of the public schools, hospitals, welfare lines, etc., as well as of having someone to blame for the condition of their economy and their waning confidence that it might soon return to the glorious conditions that had made their state so special. They responded by overwhelmingly passing the measure, even garnering 47 percent of the black vote (despite the opposition of most African American leaders who saw its racist, xenophobic overtones) (Skerry, 1995).[2]

CHANGING ATTITUDES

In matters beyond immigration and demographics, polls appear to reveal general agreement on goals but significant divergence on the nature of the problems to be overcome and the strategies to be used. For example, a recent *Wall Street Journal*/NBC poll showed that 70 percent of African Americans and 65 percent of whites feel that not enough progress had been made in recent years toward the goal of improved race relations (*Society*, 1995). An ABC News/*Washington Post* poll of a few years earlier indicated that blacks are more likely than whites to perceive race relations as problematic, seeing white hostility toward blacks and black hostility toward whites as more widespread.[3] Whites, on the other hand, are more likely to see race relations as fairly congenial (Sigelman and Welch, 1993). Thus, while neither group is satisfied with the quality of race relations, whites appear to believe that the distance to the goal is shorter than African Americans do.

The ABC News/*Washington Post* poll revealed that although race relations are not necessarily improved in settings where interracial social contact is commonplace, interracial friendships do reduce among blacks the perception of the level of white hostility, and vice versa (Sigelman and Welch, 1993). Interracial friendships are most likely to develop where friendships in general tend to develop—at work, at school, in the neighborhood, etc., and even then it may be difficult for people of different races to move beyond casual contact to close friendships, given stereotyping and status differentials (Ellison and Powers, 1994). Consider that two-thirds of whites still live in neighborhoods that are at least 90 percent white, with three-quarters in mostly white areas, and that, similarly, two-thirds of African Americans live in overwhelmingly black neighborhoods (Edmondson, 1994; McAneny and Saad, 1994). Further, irrespective of level of income, African Americans show a greater tendency than Hispanics or Asian Americans to be residentially isolated, thus linking residential segregation more to racial stratification than to class inequality (McDaniel, 1995).

Although the *Wall Street Journal*/NBC poll indicated that most in both groups think that integration had slipped in importance as a national goal (*Society*, 1995), the extent to which both groups want more integration differs greatly. The Gallup Poll found that 40 percent of African Americans and only 17 percent of whites want to see more integration in housing. Further, while 56 percent of whites and 84 percent of blacks believe that more should be done to improve integration in the schools, 88 percent of the former and 64 percent of the latter prefer that children attend local schools, even if it means that most of the students would be of the same race (McAneny and Saad, 1994). A 1992 survey of fifteen- to twenty-four-year-olds conducted by People for the American Way found that while most think that integration is an important goal, the proportions of African Americans and Hispanics who think so is significantly higher (Collison, 1992).

According to the *Wall Street Journal*/NBC poll, 92 percent of whites and 97 percent of African Americans see crime as being a serious problem, and 70 percent and 74 percent, respectively, think that welfare dependency is also. However, the poll reported very different views on the fundamental nature of the problems and how they should be approached. African Americans, the poll found, feel to a much greater extent than whites that government should play a substantial role in resolving the economic woes that they saw as being at the heart of these matters. Whites, on the other hand, are more likely to see the same problems as a matter of moral decline, where government cannot be particularly helpful (*Society*, 1995). This is consonant with other studies that show 72 percent of African Americans, compared to 36 percent of whites, attributing the white-black socioeconomic gap mainly to discrimination and 54 and 24 percent, respectively, seeing "a lot" of discrimination on the job (Bobo and Kluegel, 1993). The differences among the respondents in a national poll taken by NBC's Project RACE are also consistent: 39 percent of African Americans agree that there should be preferential treatment for blacks in the workplace, compared to only 9 percent of whites; 67 percent of the former supported racial quotas, as against 25 percent of the latter (Singer, 1990).

The People for the American Way survey of youth found differences regarding issues of discrimination and how they should be approached. When asked whether a white or a minority would be more likely to be denied a scholarship or a job due to discrimination, 49 percent of the whites thought that the white would lose out while 68 percent of the African Americans thought that it would be the minority. Fifty-one percent of the whites indicated opposition to "special consideration" to minorities in college admissions, and 65 percent were opposed to giving minorities special consideration in employment; when the questions substituted "preference" for "special consideration," the proportions opposed jumped to 64 and 78 percent, respectively. On the other hand, 74 percent of African Americans approved of "special consideration" in college admissions, while 52 percent supported "preference"; special consideration in employment was favored by 60 percent, while 40 percent approved of the according preference. Hispanics responding to the same questions fell in between African Americans and whites (Collison, 1992).

The Self-Interest Factor

Bobo and Kluegel (1993), using data from the 1990 General Social Survey (GSS) along with their own data, also found that though whites are not supportive of "preferential" policies in job hiring or college admissions, they do favor "compensatory" policies, such as racially targeted job training or special education programs. They also learned that white support for compensatory programs increases when the programs are income-linked. The researchers concluded that self-interest plays a greater role in these inclinations than does racism, since the lower the income and education levels of the white respondents the more likely they are to oppose race-targeted programs and to support income-targeted programs.

This notion of perceived self-interest appears to be related not just to income but to population size as well. Taylor (1994), also using data from the 1990 GSS, found that white support for race-targeted intervention varies inversely with the proportion of African Americans in the local population. Where the black population is large and the white-black economic gap is narrow, whites tend to believe that African Americans possess too much societal influence; that preferential treatment in hiring and promotion is prevalent; that blacks are lazier than whites and more likely to prefer living off of welfare; and that racial inequality is due to black inferiority. Her research supports the "racial competition" model used to explain white racial views.

CHANGING POLITICS

Giles and Hertz (1994) demonstrate that such thinking carries into the voting booth. Analyzing elections in Louisiana between 1975 and 1990, they found that the higher the black concentration in a parish, the lower the percentage among the white registered voters who are Democrats and the greater the percentage who are Republicans. They also found an income link: the higher the median income of white voters, the smaller the growth of both Republican and independent registration, so much so that Republican registration in the parishes with the highest white median income is unrelated to the level of black concentration. Voting followed the same patterns in the 1990 U.S. Senate election and the 1991 gubernatorial elections: the greater the percentage of African American registered voters in a parish, the greater the proportion of white registered voters who cast their ballots for avowed racist David Duke.

According to Richard Cohen (1991), the proportion of the population in an area that is black also affects the way that African Americans vote; the larger the black proportion, the greater the tendency of black voters to be racially polarized. This phenomenon is in keeping with the "perceived threat pattern," since the African American voters in such situations believe that the white voters will be voting their own perceived race-based interests as well.[4]

A change in perceived interest has affected the national balance of power. As policies such as busing and fair housing began to descend on their neighborhoods, and as they began to see themselves in economic competition with African Americans (who seemed to have the weight of the government on their side), much of the white working class that had been so important to the Democratic coalition first put together by Franklin Roosevelt followed poor whites into the conservative bloc. Beginning with Richard Nixon in the 1968 presidential election, Republicans have cultivated the disenchanted white voters through racial issues hidden behind such code words as "busing," "law and order," "welfare queen," and "quotas" (Piliawsky, 1994). By 1980, formerly liberal working and middle-class white voters, who began to feel that they were being left behind formed a new coalition with traditional conservatives to sweep Ronald Reagan into the presidency. In 1988, then Vice President George Bush played directly to white fears with his campaign advertisement exploiting the continued criminal activity of Willie Horton in Massachusetts, who had been parolled in accordance with the rules in effect under Governor Michael Dukakis, Bush's opponent for the presidency.[5]

During the Reagan-Bush years, the White House worked very deliberately to put the old Roosevelt/Democratic coalition permanently out to pasture. On a policy level, it sought to redirect the national civil rights policy away from a paradigm of race consciousness, in order to remedy group injustice, to one based on color blindness and individual action, to deal with individual injustice. The government's shift was evident in a number of high-profile civil rights cases that ended up before the Supreme Court (Marcus, 1988). Additionally, the Reagan and Bush administrations generally stepped up the pace of deregulation, a notion that had begun to gain momentum during the mid-1970s. In some agencies of government, including the Department of Education and the Department of Labor's affirmative-action enforcement effort, deregulation was accomplished by reducing the size of the staff, by changing regulations where congressional approval could be garnered, and by shifting the agency thrust from enforcing regulations to providing technical assistance. Further, a choice was made by President Reagan, in keeping with the national mood, to focus on bringing inflation under control, in part by reducing federal spending. Social programs took the brunt of the cuts. For example, between 1981 and 1987 federal housing programs were reduced by 79 percent, training and employment programs by 70 percent, the Work Incentive Program by 71 percent, and block grants for community development and nongovernment-operated community services by more than one-third (Marcus and Stickney, 1990). Also, at the same time that its purview was being expanded beyond matters of race and gender, the budget of the Equal Employment Opportunity Commission fell in constant dollars, and its staff was slashed by almost a thousand positions (Smith, 1993). Further, and specifically affecting the education sector, the staff and budget of the Office for Civil Rights (OCR) in the Department of Education were reduced by a quarter, and the Office's budget was intentionally underspent. To diminish the possibility that the consequences of these policy changes would be documented, the OCR (under Reagan) reduced its collection of statistical data and ordered its staff not to provide such information even when requested under the Freedom of Information Act (Wilson, 1989).

Continuing on the tack of racial divisiveness that had proved so effective in election campaigns, Reagan and Bush consciously, in the eyes of some observers, directed the attention of whites away from such issues as the massive loss in manufacturing jobs, drops in real wages of the middle and working classes, and the increasing inability of average Americans to buy homes, by focusing it on how African Americans might benefit from proposals coming from liberals and the Democrat-controlled Congress (Kilson and Cottingham, 1991). While the positions taken by these two presidents were in keeping with the views of the political majorities that put them in power, they had the effect of substantially turning the clock back on civil rights. Seizing upon the growing national sentiment that Washington's reach was too long and its approach out of touch with the ordinary American, they argued strongly that the best solutions came from the crucible of the states. They conceded the position advocated in earlier times by such people as Lester Maddox, George Wallace, and Strom Thurmond that states' rights should prevail over federal prerogatives in the area of equity policy and civil rights.

Their efforts were buoyed by a conservative-dominated Supreme Court that chipped away at many of the civil rights protections that had been sanctioned by the Warren and Burger courts. The Democratically controlled Congress responded by passing the Civil Rights Act of 1991, which had such effects as restoring the use of statistics to prove the existence of disparities in order to establish a *prima facie* case of discrimination (which the Court had ruled invalid in the *Wards Cove* case in 1989).

While the majority did not change its view, a sour and stagnant economy caused voters to turn away from George Bush in 1992, making Bill Clinton only the second Democratic presidential candidate since 1948 to garner more white votes than the Republican opponent (Piliawsky, 1994). Clinton's rise to the presidency brought with it hopes for a return to the civil rights paradigm that had dominated during the administrations of Presidents Kennedy through Carter. However, the coalition that put him into the White House (not even a majority of those voting in 1992, due to the candidacy of Ross Perot) proved to be extremely fragile, making it difficult for him to govern. During his first several months in office, he was forced to confront the reality of a massive federal debt, tied in large measure to the military buildup of the Reagan years and the Bush administration's bail-out of investors in failed savings and loan associations. There was not even enough revenue to pay for current operations. Even worse were the trend lines indicating that by 2012, payments on the national debt and existing entitlement programs would leave precious little for anything else (Hager, 1994). As a result, Clinton was unable to develop any momentum to shift federal spending in the direction of social programs. A major setback occurred when his response to one of the most pressing concerns of Americans at the time of the 1992 election, universal health care, was deemed too costly and failed to receive congressional endorsement in 1994.

Indeed, Clinton's inability in the eyes of the voting public to develop a compelling and affordable agenda resulted in an unprecedented Republican sweep the 1994 mid-term elections. It gave the GOP control both of the Senate (for the first time in a decade) and of the House (for the first time in four decades). The new House majority sought to place much of its conservative "Contract with America" into statute within its first three months in power as it promised the voters it would do.

Its ideological efforts were supported by the Supreme Court, which continued to overturn or restrict important race-related measures. For example, in order to combat the gerrymandering of congressional districts that kept whites in office although the Voting Rights Act of 1965 had added African Americans to the voting registers in large numbers, district lines were being redrawn, often at the insistence of federal courts, to enhance the likelihood of the election of blacks. Since some of those new districts were themselves to some extent gerrymandered, the Court set the practice aside, jeopardizing numerous congressional seats recently won by minorities. It also acted to permit the revocation of school desegregation orders when a school district could demonstrate that it had done what it could to minimize majority-black schools even if there were schools that remained majority-black. It also extended to the federal government the strict standard that it had earlier imposed on the efforts of state and local governments to promote minority and women-owned business through preferential contract awards, thus calling all affirmative action programs into question. Further, in a First Amendment case, it required the state of Ohio to permit the Ku Klux Klan to erect a cross on public property during the holiday season (along with the Christmas trees and menorahs of other groups), despite the Klan's well known use of that otherwise religious symbol as a symbol of hatred. Even though President Clinton had the opportunity within his first two years to appoint two justices (the first by a Democrat since Thurgood Marshall's appointment in 1967), the Court's conservative, strict-constructionist orientation is likely to be felt for some time to come, given the relative youth of the Reagan and Bush appointees.

INCREASING HOSTILITY

Racism and prejudice run deep in America, and these feelings bubble up to the surface when times are tough, particularly since those who are economically or socially threatened often find it necessary to project their anxieties onto those they feel are the source of the threat, whatever the accuracy of that analysis. *Washington Post* columnist Juan Williams (1991: 35) believes that it was President Reagan who "free[d] the monster of alienation" that set Americans sniping at each other, by saying to the nation, "Well, you know, we've done enough on this civil rights stuff. We don't need to do anymore." The incidence of hate-based activity has been on the upswing: in 1992 the Southern Poverty Law Center reported a rise in hate crimes for the fourth consecutive year and cited the existence of 346 white supremacy groups, a 27 percent increase over the previous year (Billings, 1992). The ADL (1995) reported 2,066 anti-Semitic incidents in 1994, the highest number in the sixteen-year history of its annual survey and the fourth increase in a row; in the ten years leading up to 1994, acts of harassment and personal assault increased by 291 percent. New Jersey, the home of Kean College, ranked fourth on that 1994 ADL list, with eighty-eight reported anti-Semitic incidents. The Anti-Defamation League also saw a general rise in bias crimes, with consecutive annual increases from 593 in 1988 (the first year that such statistics were maintained by state police) to 1,303 in 1992, the bulk of the growth in bias crimes against people rather than property. African Americans were the most frequently targeted racial group, Hispanics the most frequently victimized ethnic group, and Jews the most frequent religious group (Commission on Racism, Racial Violence and Religious Violence, 1993).

Traditional hate groups like the Ku Klux Klan and the American Nazi Party were joined in the 1980s by such new neo-nazi groups as the Aryan Nation and by anti-government militias (that we came to learn so much about in the aftermath of the 1995 bombing of the federal building in Oklahoma City). Further, the level of hate-based activity by teenagers and young adults increased, particularly as "skinhead" groups emerged. These skinheads have proven to be violent, undisciplined bands of marauders who think nothing of brutalizing any African American or Jew whose path they cross. In New Jersey, there has been an increase in the number of juveniles arrested for bias crimes, as well as in the number who were targets. While there may be some relationship between this increase and the approximately four hundred skinheads in the state, no statistics have been kept relative to skinhead incidents, because those groups do not meet the FBI's criteria of an organized hate group (Commission on Racism, Racial Violence and Religious Violence, 1993). Obviously, not all bias-related crime is committed by skinheads, nor just by whites. Groups of black youth bent on race-based violence have also come to public attention, for example the Jersey City teenagers whose "dot busting" (assaults on people of Indian subcontinental ancestry) made the national press, and the bands of teenagers on "wilding" expeditions in New York's Central Park.

As frightening as these developments are, it would be short-sighted and inaccurate to believe that all hate-based activity comes from extremist groups. The director of the New York Civil Rights Coalition, Michael Meyers, said three years ago of the status of intergroup relations that it's "becoming fashionable to hate. It's become pedestrian, commonplace, and acceptable" (Billings, 1992: 37). That view was underscored by the report of the Los Angeles County school district of the incidence of more than 2,200 hate crimes during a single school year in its region (O'Neil, 1993). One such example can be seen in the five white male high school seniors in affluent Greenwich (Connecticut) High School, who reportedly included letters in the printed captions under their senior yearbook pictures that all together, spelled out "'kill' 'ALL' 'ni' 'gg' 'ERS'" (Steinberg, 1995).[6] Indeed, Kilson and Cottingham (1991: 522) argue that the situation has deteriorated to the point that "it is open season on black folks, even among decent people."

A NEED FOR LEADERSHIP

While many would contend that it is the responsibility of political and moral leaders to combat this creeping divisiveness and hostility, as well as to keep us focused on the broad goal of improving racial and intergroup harmony, their eyes and voices have been turned elsewhere. Some believe that political leaders are so worried about alienating voters that they engage in "a conspiracy of silence—a fear of speaking candidly about the causes and possible solution to [race-related] problems" (Klein, 1991: 39). Other political leaders, however, appear to have been swept up in the tide of intolerance. For example, the intemperate speech given by presidential candidate and journalist Patrick Buchanan at the 1992 Republican Convention was clearly intended to stake out a claim among the most disenchanted, racially, and homophobically polarized white voters. Two more recent episodes add to the evidence. In early 1995, House Majority Leader Dick Armey referred during an interview with several reporters to Representative Barney Frank, one of the few openly gay members of Congress, as "Barney Fag" (Gray, 1995: A1). A few months later, on a nationally syndicated radio program, Senator Alfonse D'Amato used a mock Japanese accent in accusing Judge Lance Ito of poorly handling the O. J. Simpson murder case (Henneberger 1995). While both politicians apologized for their remarks, the pain that they caused is not easily erased.

Into the void left by the silence of most political leaders on the issues of racial and intergroup relations has come a group of leaders, white and black, who appear to be doing all that they can to erect barriers between people. People with such views are making themselves felt politically at the grass roots and national levels. Among them are leaders on the religious right, members of the clergy like Jerry Falwell and Pat Robertson, who have a reach well beyond their own religious communities. The political activity of religious fundamentalists first resulted in textbook censorship and a boiling-down of values education and multicultural curricula in many school districts. The executive director of the Christian Coalition (which reports a membership of 1.4 million people) predicted that this local success would "sweep from one side of the country to the other like a tsunami" (Otto, 1994: A2). The organization's founder, evangelical leader and former presidential candidate Pat Robertson, speaking before an assembled 3,000 delegates to the coalition's September 1994 convention (which attracted most of the major contenders for the 1996 Republican presidential nomination), proclaimed that "we are seeing the Christian Coalition rise to where God intends it to be in this nation, as one of the most powerful political forces that have ever been in the history of the United States" (Edsall, 1994: A4). This is not a boast (or threat) to be taken lightly, since white, evangelical Protestants constitute about a quarter of the nation's voting-age population; between 40 and 60 percent of them are conservative, the equivalent of 10 to 15 percent of the electorate. This strength has permitted the half-dozen politically active groups on the religious right to raise an estimated $20–25 million per year to devote to their causes (Green, 1994). Their singular emphasis on fundamentalist Christian (and politically conservative) values, including the desire to tear down the walls between church and state by codifying many of those values into law, appeals to many disenchanted, economically threatened whites and can only add to the level of societal hostility.

Feeling disenchanted is not an emotion limited to whites. As a result, the African American community, too, has its share of divisive leaders, including clergymen such as Minister Louis Farrakhan and the Reverend Al Sharpton, who preach an aggressively ethnocentric, pro-black, anti-white position. Just as David Duke and Pat Robertson represent minority factions among whites, Farrakhan and Sharpton are also leaders of minority factions within the African American community. All of these divisive spokesmen, while not responsible on each side for the animus of the other, reinforce the cleavage between the races and offer each other a confirmation of their views.

This, then, is a society whose political leadership at the highest levels has moved from an active effort to reduce the walls that surround race, to the "benign neglect" of the early 1970s, to the regressive policies of the eighties and early nineties; a society whose attention has been focused on matters other than intergroup harmony; whose moral leaders did not speak out when intergroup tensions began to surface, or even exacerbated the divisions; a society becoming increasingly diverse yet with interracial friendships more the exception than the rule. In this context, it is little wonder that students bring to campus a whole set of prejudices, some that they are not even aware of. Further, eighteen-year-olds of all ethnic groups, not having first-hand knowledge of legally mandated segregation, see civil rights in historical terms rather than as a current national priority (Stern, 1990). College faculty and administrators, it would appear, have their work cut out for them.

We will turn next to affirmative action, a policy that embodies many of the points advanced in this chapter. To some it represents an important tool for solidifing the gains of the civil rights movement. To others it is responsible for the loss of common ground shared by the coalition which brought about the successes of that earlier day.

NOTES

1. The change in the ethnic mix of immigrants also brings a change in the national religious make-up. For example, in Chicago there are now more Muslims than Methodists, and more Hindus than Presbyterians (Oldaker, 1994).

2. Given previous Supreme Court decisions according certain rights to illegal immigrants—including the right to receive a public education—this matter is likely to wind up before the high court.

3. The Gallup Poll revealed that the difference in how the races view race relations also extends to how they view the media in its coverage of race relations and of issues where race may be a factor. African Americans believe, by better than two to one, that newspaper and television reporting worsens, rather than improves, race relations. The opposite sentiment is shared by Hispanics, Asian Americans, and whites, by almost the same margins (McAnney, 1994).

4. Juan Williams (1991: 35) argues that black political leaders reinforce the behavior. There are times, he says, when they call on the African American community for solidarity in support of black politicians who "should absolutely be hooted out of office," simply to assure that they have their piece of the political pie.

5. Street crime is an issue that has been on the American political scene since Richard Nixon focused on it in 1968. By the time that George

Bush brought Willie Horton's name into the picture, much of white America was fearful of crime and in particular of crime committed by black men. However, most crime committed by blacks is against other blacks—and to the detriment of black neighborhoods, not only in terms of those assaulted, murdered, and robbed or whose property is destroyed but also in terms of lost business and employment opportunities. When the War on Poverty died, a war on crime took its place; but that war has been fought on the "arrest, convict, and incarcerate" front only. Instead of alleviating the conditions that have bred crime, it built more jails and filled then with black men. In the early 1990s, 42 percent of prison inmates were black (Kilson and Cottingham, 1991). Sadly, when the Omnibus Crime Act of 1994 was being debated, conservatives fought to keep out of the bill job training programs and funding for such proven crime-reducing programs as "midnight basketball," characterizing them as "useless pork" that the country could ill afford; instead, they sought to put more police on the streets. President Clinton strongly advocated the inclusion of crime-reducing programs, but only watered-down provisions survived.

6. Unfortunately, a 1990 Harris poll found that more high school students said that they would join in or silently support a racial confrontation than said that they would either openly condemn or try to stop one (O'Neill, 1993).

REFERENCES

Abernathy, Virginia. *Population Politics, The Choices That Shape Our Future.* New York: Plenum Press, 1993.

Anderson, P. and T. Farragher. "States Spend Billions to Provide Services to Illegal Immigrants." *Philadelphia Inquirer.* September 15, 1994, p. A4.

Anti-Defamation League. "ADL Special Summary Report: 1994 Audit of Anti-Semitic Incidents, Overview." New York: Anti-Defamation League, 1995.

Badgett, M. V. Lee. "Where the Jobs Went in the 1990–91 Downturn: Varying (Mis)Fortunes of Homogenous Distress?" Paper presented at the National Conference on Race Relations and Civil Rights in the Post Reagan-Bush Era. Minneapolis, MN, October, 1994.

Billings, Jessica C. "Racism in the '90s: Is It Hip to Hate?" *Education Digest* v. 58 n. 2 (December 1992), pp. 35–39.

Bobo, Lawrence and James R. Kluegel. "Opposition to Race-Targeting: Self-Interest, Stratification Ideology, or Racial Attitudes." *American Sociological Review* v. 58 n. 4 (December 1993), pp. 443–464.

Browder, Lesley H., Jr. "'Can We All Get Along?' The Politics of Diversity." *Leadership and Diversity in Education,* ed. Joel L. Burdin. Lancaster, PA: Technomic Publishing, 1994, pp. 36–54.

Bruning, Fred. "Black and White in America." *MacLean's* v. 105 n. 22 (June 1, 1992), p. 11.

Cohen, Richard. "Nixon's the One." *Second Thoughts about Race in America.* ed. Peter Collier and David Horowitz. Lanham, MD: Madison Books, 1991, pp. 19–24.

Collison, Michelle N.-K. "Young People Found Pessimistic About Relations Between the Races." *The Chronicle of Higher Education.* March 25, 1992, pp. A1, A32.

Commission on Minority Participation in Education and American Life. *One-Third of a Nation.* Washington, DC: American Council on Education and Education Commission of the States, 1988.

Commission on Racism, Racial Violence and Religious Violence. *Report of the Commission on Racism, Racial Violence and Religious Violence.* Trenton, NJ: NJ Department of Law and Public Safety, 1993.

Editors of *Society.* "Social Science and the Citizen." *Society* v. 32 n. 2 (January/February 1995), pp. 2–4.

Editors of *The Economist.* "Illegal Immigrants, to the Rescue." *The Economist* v. 332 n. 7879 (September 3, 1994), p. 35.

Edmondson, Brad. "The Trend You Can't Ignore." *American Demographics* v. 16 n. 7 (July 1994), p. 2.

Edsall, T. "Christian Coalition Sounds Charge for '96." *Washington Post.* September 17, 1994, p. A4.

Ellison, Christopher G. and Daniel A. Powers. "The Contact Hypothesis and Racial Attitudes among Black Americans." *Social Science Quarterly* v. 75 n. 2 (June 1994), pp. 385–400.

Exter, Thomas. "The Declining Majority." *American Demographics* v. 15 n. 1 (January 1993), p. 59.

Giles, Michael W. and Kaenan Hertz. "Racial Threat and Partisan Identification." *American Political Science Review* v. 88 n. 2 (June 1994), pp. 317–326.

Gray, Jerry. "House Leader Refers to Colleague with Anti-Gay Slur." *The New York Times.* January 28, 1995, p. A1.

Green, John C. "The Grassroots Clout of the Religious Right." *The Chronicle of Higher Education.* October 26, 1994, pp. B1–B2.

Hager, George. "Commission Moves Carefully on Entitlement Cuts." *Congressional Quarterly* v. 52 n. 32 (August 13, 1994), p. 2318.

Henneberger, Melinda. "D'Amato Gives a New Apology on Ito Remarks." *The New York Times.* April 7, 1995, p. A1.

Kahlenberg, Richard. "Class, Not Race, an Affirmative Action That Works." *The New Republic* v. 212 n. 14 (April 3, 1995), pp. 21–27.

Kilson, Martin and Clement Cottingham. "Thinking about Race Relations, How Far Are We Still from Integration?" *Dissent* v. 38 n. 4 (Fall 1991), pp. 520–530.

Klein, Joe. "Race: The Issues." *Second Thoughts about Race in America*. ed. Peter Collier and David Horowitz. Lanham, MD: Madison Books, 1991, pp. 37–50.

Lester, Julius. "Whatever Happened to the Civil Rights Movement?" *Second Thoughts about Race in America*, ed. Peter Collier and David Horowitz. Lanham, MD: Madison Books, 1991, pp. 3–9.

Marcus, Laurence R. "Federal Civil Rights Enforcement in Higher Education: Shadow or Substance." *Educational Policy* v. 2 n. 2 (1988), pp. 189–208.

Marcus, Laurence R. and Benjamin D. Stickney. "A Concluding Note: The Challenge Ahead." *Politics and Policy in the Age of Education*, ed. Laurence R. Marcus and Benjamin D. Stickney. Springfield, IL: Charles C Thomas Publishers, 1990.

Maxwell, Nan L. "The Effect on Black-White Wage Differences of Differences in the Quantity and Quality of Education." *Industrial and Labor Relations Review* v. 47 n. 2 (January 1994), pp. 249–264.

McAneny, Leslie. "Ethnic Minorities View the Media's View of Them." *The Gallup Poll Monthly* n. 347 (August 1994), pp. 31–41.

McAneny, Leslie and Lydia Saad. "America's Public Schools: Still Separate? Still Unequal?" *The Gallup Poll Monthly* n. 344 (May 1994), pp. 23–29.

McDaniel, Antonio. "The Dynamic Racial Composition of the United States." *Daedalus* v. 124 n. 1 (Winter 1995), pp. 179–198.

Murray, Charles A. and Richard Hernstein. *The Bell Curve: Intelligence and Class Structure in American Life*. New York: The Free Press, 1994.

National Center for Educational Statistics. *Mini-Digest of Educational Statistics 1994*. Washington, DC: US Government Printing Office, 1994a.

National Center for Educational Statistics. *The Pocket Condition of Education 1994*. Washington, DC: US Government Printing Office, 1994b.

National Commission on Excellence in Education. *A Nation at Risk: The Imperative for Educational Reform*. Washington, DC: US Government Printing Office, 1983.

Oldaker, Lawrence L. "Coping with 'Hate Speech' in Educational Settings." *Leadership and Diversity in Education*, ed. Joel L. Burdin.

Lancaster, PA: Technomic Publishing Company, 1994, pp. 76–85.

O'Neil, John. "A New Generation Confronts Racism." *Educational Leadership* v. 50 n. 8 (May 1993), pp. 60–63.

Otto, M. "Christian Coalition Looks to November." *Philadelphia Inquirer*. September 17, 1994, p. A2.

Piliawsky, Monte. "The Clinton Administration and African-Americans." *Black Scholar* v. 24 n. 2 (Spring 1994), pp. 2–10.

Riche, Martha Farnsworth. "We're All Minorities Now." *American Demographics* v. 13 n. 10 (October 1991), pp. 4–8.

Sigelman, Lee and Susan Welch. "The Contact Hypothesis Revisited: Black-White Interaction and Positive Racial Attitudes." *Social Forces* v. 71 n. 3 (March 1993), pp. 781–795.

Singer, Eleanor. "The Polls—A Review, NBC's 'R.A.C.E.' " *Public Opinion Quarterly* v. 54 n. 4 (Winter 1990), pp. 605–608.

Skerry, Peter. "The Black Alienation, Why African Americans Are Increasingly Nativist." *The New Republic* v. 212 n. 5 (January 30, 1995), pp. 15–23.

Smith, James P. "Affirmative Action and the Racial Wage Gap." *The American Economic Review* v. 83 n. 2 (May 1993), pp. 79–84.

Steinberg, Jacques. "Code Hate in Yearbook Evokes Anger." *The New York Times*. June 16, 1995, p. B1.

Stern, Kenneth S. *Bigotry on Campus: A Planned Response*. New York: American Jewish Committee, 1990.

Taylor, Marylee. "Local Racial Inequality and White Racial Attitudes." Paper presented at the National Conference on Race Relations and Civil Rights in the Post Reagan-Bush Era. Minneapolis, MN, October 1994.

Williams, Juan. "The Movement Continues." *Second Thoughts about Race in America*, ed. Peter Collier and David Horowitz. Lanham, MD: Madison Books, 1991, pp. 33–36.

Chapter 2

The Affirmative Action Debate

Fundamental to the thinking behind the conservative wave is the belief that the goal of the civil rights movement—a society with no group identity–related legal barriers to the achievement of the American Dream (i.e., "equality of opportunity")—has been achieved, and further that public policy has gone too far in the direction of seeking "equality of results." The policy at the heart of this concern is "affirmative action," a strategy rooted in the World War II goal of demonstrating the superiority of democracy over totalitarianism. Originally it sought to limit war-related federal contracts to non-discriminatory employers. In 1964, as part of his program to "level the playing field" for persons who had historically been the objects of discrimination, President Lyndon Johnson issued Executive Order 11246, which required employers wishing to remain eligible for federal contracts to seek out qualified women and minorities for positions in which they were underrepresented. Colleges and universities with federal contracts (including student financial aid) were also required to comply in their employment and admissions practices. Thirty years later, there were 160 race and gender preferences administered by the federal government, according to the Congressional Research Service (Rosen, 1995). Most states and many municipalities today also have similar policies for organizations wishing to remain eligible for their contracts.

THE PHILOSOPHICAL DEBATE
AND ECONOMIC THREAT

Affirmative action has proven to be a controversial policy for philosophical reasons. On the one hand are those who believe that the historical experience of African Americans has been so different from that of other ethnic groups that it justifies favored treatment. As Columbia's Charles V. Hamilton (1992: 13) argues, most ethnic groups came to America voluntarily as a means of improving their status; even if they were the targets of discrimination upon arrival (and many were), they were not dehumanized. More often, in many respects they were welcomed as a source of cheap labor to contribute to the nation's economic development. They and their off-spring "were politicized to believe that if they worked hard, they could achieve and contribute to the overall vitality and growth of society as productive human beings." As a result, they felt a sense of gratitude for the opportunity accorded to them. By and large, however, African Americans came involuntarily, as property. They had to struggle politically to be viewed as humans and to become citizens. While whites were willing to join blacks in their successful quest to overturn *de jure* segregation, many felt that the *de facto* discrimination that continued to plague African Americans was something that imperfect societies must live with. Thus it became necessary for African Americans to rely on the same political approach of pushing for their right to fair and equal treatment as they sought to usher *de facto* discrimination out of the workplace.

Affirmative action proponents argue that even after three decades, opportunities for African Americans remain limited by *de facto* discrimination, even for those who are of the middle class, who must contend with a "glass ceiling" in much of the corporate world. Further, "the black *prominenti* remain, as always, largely confined to entertainment such as sports, the arts, and media, and to religion and education"; also, the few African American intellectuals who have been able to gain broad attention "have weight only as information about the other America" (Rose, Ross, et al., 1995: 38).

On the other side are those who might concede a certain portion of the argument to affirmative action proponents but contend that the time for preferential treatment has passed. This argument has its roots in an 1883 Supreme Court decision that struck down the Civil Rights Act of 1875: "When a man has emerged from slavery, and by the aid of beneficent legislation has shaken off the insepa- rable concomitants of the state, there must be some stage in the progress of his elevation when he takes the rank of mere citizen, and ceases to be the special favorite of the law" (Wilson, 1989: 2). Still others would argue against the policy by citing the constitu- tional protection for equal treatment irrespective of race, ethnicity, religion, creed, etc., and our cultural norm of reward based on individual initiative. In this vein, Glenn Loury (1992) holds that affirmative action results in minority employees investing less in their work because the policy makes it easier for them to achieve higher-level positions. Finally there are those who contend that the "goals and timetables" required in affirmative action plans are, in effect, quotas, which have a reverse discriminatory result for whites, particularly white males.

Not withstanding the rhetoric about affirmative action's dis- criminatory effect on whites, it should be noted that the US Labor Department has revealed that reverse discrimination was alleged in less than 3 percent of all discrimination cases brought between 1990 and 1994 and that the plaintiffs won in 30 percent of the twenty-one instances (Rosen, 1995). Louis Gordon (in Rose, Ross, et al., 1995: 43), an African American professor at Purdue, points to his own experience to discount the notion of reverse discrimi- nation. At the time he was hired by the university, "there were sixteen black faculty members out of two thousand white ones. I was the only black hired that year in my division. There were forty hires. . . . Throughout the year, the school paper published a constant stream of dribble about the displacement of workers by blacks and the lowering of 'standards' at the institution. . . . Apparently [whites] are only displaced when blacks are hired."

The level of noise regarding affirmative action has risen and fallen inversely with the economy. As a nation, we have experi- enced a domestic economic transformation that has accompanied our rapid technological development and the globalization of the marketplace. The bipolar capitalist/communist world has been replaced by a new order: our international friends are now our economic competitors; newly developed nations are successfully competing for increasing shares of the market; and rising multina- tional corporations are willing to export jobs to places where labor costs and regulations are low. Feeling a threat to their long-term economic well-being and that of their children, much of the middle class has soured on affirmative action, and the noise has reached a crescendo, particularly among young white males who feel that the door of opportunity has slammed shut on them. Some political leaders have sought to capitalize on this anger by very consciously and obviously playing the "race card." For example, in his 1990 reelection campaign Senator Jesse Helms ran a television ad that depicted a white worker being denied a job because the prospective employer used a quota system to hire blacks over whites (Taylor and Liss, 1992). Prior to the 1994 election, a state senator in Kentucky wrote to eleven white students telling them that they had been passed over by eleven minorities with lower scores in awarding a state scholarship for college students who agreed to teach certain subjects or in certain areas of the state having teacher shortages (Zapler, 1994).[1]

POLITICAL AND JUDICIAL ACTIVITY

With white males voting for the Republicans in landslide proportions (57 percent) in the 1994 congressional elections, politicians perceived that they were being sent a message of anger regarding preferential treatment for women and minorities. In California, an initiative that would end state affirmative action is being prepared for the 1996 election. It has the support of Governor Pete Wilson (a 1996 GOP presidential hopeful), who vetoed a 1991 measure passed by the legislature that would have required the state's universities to produce "step-by-step plans" to achieve ethnic parity in college graduation rates (Schrag, 1995). (More on California follows.) National leaders are not to be left out of the action. In early February 1995, Senate Majority Leader Bob Dole, himself a 1996 presidential contender, announced that the Senate would undertake a review of affirmative action programs (*The New York Times*, 1995). By month's end President Clinton had called for a "national dialogue" on affirmative action and announced his administration's "top to bottom" review of the policy, hoping to determine "whether there is some other way we can reach our objective without giving a preference by race or gender" (Holmes, 1995: 9; Kahlenberg, 1995: 21).

Several recent court decisions may make the matter legally moot. For example, in August 1994 a federal district court judge invalidated the affirmative action program at the University of Texas Law School. As an institution that had previously discriminated in its admissions policies, the university had pledged to admit African Americans and Mexican Americans in accordance with their proportion among students graduating with bachelor's degrees from Texas colleges and universities (5 percent and 10 percent, respectively). If the law school had used color-blind admissions to select its class of five hundred in 1992, only nine blacks and eighteen Mexican Americans would have been selected, all of whom were being courted by extremely prestigious law schools. Thus, the law school had set its rejection mark for African Americans and Mexican Americans three index points lower than for others. The judge, however, found this practice to be unconstitutional (Rosen, 1994).

Toward the end of its 1994–1995 term, the Supreme Court refused to hear an appeal of a lower court ruling that overturned a University of Maryland scholarship program for high-achieving African American students. The program had been challenged by a Hispanic student who claimed that his high school grades and test scores would have qualified him for a Benjamin Banneker Scholarship if he had been black. The Fourth Circuit Court of Appeals had earlier rejected the university's argument for the race-based scholarship, i.e., that it had openly discriminated against blacks during segregation; the court felt that past discrimination against blacks did not justify current discrimination against others. It also rejected the university's contention that it needed the scholarships because the proportion of African Americans in the total enrollment at its College Park campus was less than half of their proportion among the state's population; the court pointed to the factor of student choice as the basis for the disparity. When the university followed the Fourth Circuit's ruling and merged the Banneker program into a non-race-based merit scholarship program, African Americans received nineteen scholarships, compared to the thirty to forty under the banned program. (Jaschik, 1995b).[2]

Several weeks after the Supreme Court's refusal to hear the Maryland case, it struck another blow to affirmative action when it reversed itself on the matter of set-asides for minority contractors in public projects. Six years earlier, in *City of Richmond v. Croson,* 488 U.S. 469 (1989), the Court had barred the practice by states and localities of requiring that a certain proportion of contracts be issued to women and minority-owned businesses unless the set-asides were to make up for demonstrated past discrimination. The following year, in *Metro Broadcasting v. FCC,* 110 S.Ct. 2297 (1990), it indicated that programs mandated by Congress did not need to meet that strict standard set forth in *Croson.* However, in a June 1995 decision in *Adrand Constructors, Inc. v. Pena,* the Court ruled 5–4 that the "strict scrutiny" standard by which it would be necessary to demonstrate "a compelling government interest" within a "narrowly tailored" program was indeed applicable to federal programs that accorded racial preference. At issue was a Department of Transportation incentive program for general contractors who use minority subcontractors. A white subcontractor sued, claiming that his company should have received work but that its low bid was passed over in favor of a higher bid from a minority firm so that the general contractor could receive the financial incentive. Justice Sandra Day O'Connor's majority opinion concluded that "any person, of whatever race, has the right to demand that any governmental actor subject to the Constitution justifies any racial classification subjecting that person to unequal treatment under the strictest judicial scrutiny." Seeking to preserve a place for affirmative action, she went on to note the majority of the Court "wish[ed] to dispel the notion that strict scrutiny is 'strict in theory, but fatal in fact.' . . . The unhappy persistence of both the practice and the lingering effects of racial discrimination against minority groups in this country is an unfortunate reality, and government is not disqualified from acting in response to it." However, when racial preferences are utilized "it is especially important that the reasons for any such classification be clearly identified and unquestionably legitimate" (Jaschik, 1995a: A21–2).

In the aftermath of the Court ruling, the Justice Department distributed a report to all federal agencies to help them assess the impact of the decision on the affirmative action programs under their purview. The report questioned whether colleges and universities could still use the principles of the *Bakke* decision in their admissions practices; that 1978 case had precluded racial and ethnic quotas in determining whom to admit but permitted race and ethnicity to be included as a factor in an admissions decision.

The Justice Department report theorized that the Court would demand evidence that the use of race and ethnicity as a factor in admissions and faculty hiring actually produces the benefit of diversifying the viewpoints on campus (Jaschik, 1995c).

Several weeks later, President Clinton, a Southerner whose formative years were at the end of the era of segregation, came out strongly in support of affirmative action. Acknowledging the policy's divisiveness, the president spoke of a two-fold challenge confronting the nation: "first to restore the American dream of opportunity and the American value of responsibility; and second, to bring our country together amid all our diversity into a stronger community so that we can find common ground and move forward as one." He said that "affirmative action is an effort to develop a systematic approach to open the doors of education, employment, and business development opportunities to qualified individuals who happen to be members of groups that have experienced long-standing and persistent discrimination." He spoke to America's "angry white males" by conceding that "some people are honestly concerned about the times affirmative action doesn't work, when it's done the wrong way." He said that the study that he had initiated in February led him to conclude that "affirmative action has not always been perfect, and affirmative action should not go on forever." Seeking to appeal both to disenchanted moderates and to liberals, as well as to shore up his support within the African American community, he said that rather than abandoning the policy, "it should be changed now to take care of things that are wrong, and it should be retired when its job is done." He indicated, however, that since discrimination against women and minorities still exists, "the job . . . is not over" (Clinton, 1995: B10).

The immediate reaction was not unexpected. As reported by *The New York Times*, the NAACP chair, Myrlie Evers-Williams, said that the public would appreciate the president's policy; she called it "a brave speech." Jesse Jackson, who was said to have been considering a challenge to Clinton in the 1996 election if the president retreated from affirmative action, lamented that the lengthy White House review had permitted the opposition to score points but said that Clinton had "set a good moral tone for the country" by speaking "to America's hopes and not its fears." On the other side of the ledger, Republican presidential hopefuls were critical. For example, Senate Majority Leader Bob Dole said that it was time "to get the

Federal Government out of the group-preference business" (Purdum, 1995: B10). California Governor Wilson asserted sharply that the president was "trying to keep in place a system that will contain a virus that threatens to tribalize America" (Locke, 1995: A1).

The day after Clinton spoke, the Board of Regents of the University of California—whose membership is dominated by appointees of Governor Wilson—culminated an eleven-hour debate with a 15–10 vote to end affirmative action in the nine-campus University System. Wilson, as president of the Board, opened the debate by asking whether the Regents were "going to continue to divide Californians by race." Numerous legislators also appeared, taking opposing positions. The state's most powerful black politician, Assemblyman Willie L. Brown, spoke of how he had been helped by affirmative action when he moved to California in 1951 and was able to fulfill his dream of getting a college education because he was given a "break" by admissions officers despite his "inadequate" high school education. Some at the meeting suggested that since there was a great likelihood that there would be a referendum on affirmative action in the 1996 California ballot, the Regents should take no action and let the voters decide. Jesse Jackson also appeared at the session, speaking for forty-five minutes. He called the proposal "politics at its lowest," saying that "the consequence of going backwards is the loss of hope, the furthering of despair, the hardening of cynicism we can ill afford." The projected effect on the admissions process—which would permit socioeconomic status, but not race or ethnicity, to be a factor—would be to increase the number of Asian students and decrease the numbers of African American and Hispanic students; the effect on the proportion of white students is understood to be negligible (Locke, 1995: A1, A14; Ayres, 1995: A1, A14).[3]

SOCIOECONOMIC INDICATORS BY RACE AND ETHNICITY

An examination of socioeconomic indicators reveals that social policies such as affirmative action meant to eliminate disparities between racial and ethnic groups have resulted in uneven progress.

Education

A positive effect of such initiatives has been a narrowing of several education-related gaps. For example, high school graduation rates for African Americans increased from 65 percent in 1975 (compared to 83 percent for whites) to 76 percent by 1985 (compared to 84 percent for whites); at the same time the Hispanic graduation rate increased from 56 percent to 63 percent. The proportions of African Americans going directly on to college from high school during that period rose and fell, reaching a high of 48 percent; Hispanic proportions stagnated through the period and then dropped to 47 percent; white proportions increased to 55 percent (Commission on Minority Participation, 1988).[4]

Mirroring demographic changes (discussed in the previous chapter) as much as changes in aspirations, college enrollments by race and ethnicity shifted somewhat between 1976 and 1992. For African Americans they increased from 9.6 to 9.9 percent, having fallen to 9 percent in 1984. Hispanics increased from 3.6 to 6.8 percent, Asians increased from 1.8 to 5 percent, Native Americans remained a relatively constant proportion of college enrollments (0.7 percent in 1976 and 0.8 percent in 1992), and whites decreased from 84.3 to 77.5 percent (National Center for Educational Statistics, 1994b). The trend continued in 1993 as Asian American enrollments increased by 3.9 percent, Hispanic by 3.6 percent, Native American by 2 percent, and African American by 1.3 percent. However, this overall minority enrollment increase of 2.6 percent (compared to a decrease in white enrollments by 2.5 percent), was the lowest in several years, the figure having risen by 7 percent in 1992 and 9 percent in 1991 (Gose, 1995).

As one might expect, there were significant variations in minority enrollment by state, ranging from a high of 69.9 percent in Hawaii to a low of less than 5 percent in Maine, New Hampshire, and Vermont. In Florida, Georgia, Illinois, Louisiana, Maryland, Mississippi, New Jersey, New York, and Texas, minorities accounted for between one-quarter and one-third of collegiate enrollments. In California and New Mexico they exceeded two of every five students (Gose, 1995).

According to the National Longitudinal Study of Youth, the mean number of years of schooling in 1970 stood at twelve years for white males and ten years for African American males; by 1988, it was slightly more than 12.5 years for whites and slightly less than 12.5 years for African Americans (Maxwell, 1994), and the typical black male worker had only 0.8 years of schooling, less than the typical white male worker (Smith, 1993). The proportion of white males completing high school increased from 55 percent in 1970 to 79 percent in 1988, while the proportion among African American males increased from 30 to 62 percent. The proportion of white males going on to college increased from 22.5 percent in 1970 to 38 percent in 1988, while the increase among African American males was from 10 to 26 percent (Maxwell, 1994). By 1993, 42 percent of white high school graduates aged eighteen to twenty-four were attending colleges, compared to 33 percent of African Americans and 36 percent of Asian Americans (Gose, 1995).

Blacks with abilities comparable to whites are less likely than whites to go on to college, and the gap appears to be growing; also, those who do attend are more academically able compared to other blacks than is the case with white college attendees relative to other whites (Maxwell, 1994). However, they are less likely to go to the most prestigious institutions. For example, in the early 1990s African Americans, Hispanics, and Native Americans accounted for less than 9 percent of the enrollments (out of more than 100,000 students) in ten of the nation's most highly rated colleges and universities (Hacker, 1992).

Degree attainment by minorities at the doctoral level has also followed a roller coaster effect. Increases occurred in the sixties and seventies but then tailed off. Between 1982 and 1992 the numbers of doctorates in all fields awarded to African Americans declined by 9 percent; among African American males the drop was more precipitous, 20 percent (Darity, 1995). However, in 1992 a turnaround occurred, with the number of doctoral degrees awarded to African Americans increasing by 15 percent over 1991. Gains were also achieved by Hispanics (up 7.2 percent), Asian Americans (up 6.5 percent), and whites (up 1.4 percent); a decrease of 20 percent among Native Americans occurred, but the sample was too small to be statistically significant. While their largest gains in 1992 occurred in engineering and the life sciences, African Americans still are underrepresented in those fields (Gose, 1995). In 1990, blacks held only 1.5 percent of the 75,000 doctorates among living engineers and scientists. Hispanics and Native Americans were also underrepresented, accounting for 1.7 and 0.1

percent, respectively; whites and Asians were 88 and 9 percent, respectively, of living engineers and scientists with doctorates (Darity, 1995).

Employment and Earnings

The increase in educational attainment, both in terms of years of schooling and of acquiring skills, proficiencies, and knowledge, provided a basis for the advancement of many African Americans into the economic and social mainstream. Affirmative action was intended as a mechanism to overcome the lingering vestiges of prejudicial behavior acting to keep them subordinate. Together, education and affirmative action have resulted in a growth of the African American middle class from about one-tenth of the black population in 1960 to about one-third in 1990 (*The Economist*, 1991). However, we are far from a parity situation across the board.

Between 1970 and 1990, African Americans filled 3.8 percent of the new positions for physicians (bringing them to 3.0 percent of all physicians), 4.3 percent of the new positions for lawyers (for 3.2 percent of all lawyers), 12.7 percent of new electrician jobs (to a total of 6.2 percent), 16.3 percent of new bank teller positions (to a new level of 9.9 percent), 33.8 percent of bus driver positions (to a new level of 24.4 percent), and 41.1 percent of new police officer hires (to a total of 13.5 percent) (Hacker, 1992). In federal civil service employment, African Americans rose from 11.1 percent of the workforce in 1970 to 16.5 percent in 1990; their proportions increased in the two highest classifications from 3.8 to 11.1 percent. Total minority workforce in the federal civil service rose from 14.7 percent to 26.4 percent, in the two highest classifications from 6.1 percent to 20.4 percent (Kellough, 1992).

In higher education, African Americans won 6.3 percent of new college faculty positions between 1970 and 1990 (for a new level of 4.5 percent) (Hacker, 1992). They did not, however, do as well as Asians in this area; between 1975 and 1985, the number of full-time Asian faculty increased by 9,300, while the number of African Americans increased by five hundred. As a result of this hiring pattern, by 1990 the number of Asian faculty had surpassed African American faculty, 24,250 compared to 23,225 (Orlans, 1992).[5] A similar pattern was evident at many of the most prestigious universities, including Harvard, where between 1982 and 1990 minorities increased as a proportion of tenured faculty (from 5.3 percent to 6.8 percent) and among tenure track faculty (from 8.1 to 8.4 percent); Asians accounted for the increase, while the proportion of African Americans among both tenured and tenure-track faculty actually decreased (Williams, 1992).

Aggregate wage studies using a variety of databases reveal that the gap between African Americans and whites decreased in the 1970s but that since then the picture has been mixed; some sources show a deterioration of the black position. The Current Population Survey (which uses a constant age structure) shows a 4 percent increase in the wage disparity between 1979 and 1985. However, data from the Panel Study of Income Dynamics (whose sample ages over time and is slightly older and better educated than the general workforce) indicate a slight narrowing during that same period (Card and Lemieux, 1994). Discouragingly, while the median income of black families rose from 54 percent of that of whites in the 1950s to 61.5 percent in 1975, it fell to 57.5 percent in 1985 (Commission on Minority Participation, 1988). A recent report from the US Census Bureau indicates that the income of black families, adjusted for inflation, did not change between 1969 and 1993 (Schulte, 1995).

Disaggregation of the data provides helpful insights. In the decade following the enactment of the Civil Rights Act of 1964, there was a dramatic increase in the earnings of black men relative to white men (O'Neill and O'Neill, 1992). In 1968 black males earned 45 percent less than white males; by 1980 the gap was 28 percent; in 1989 it was 27 percent (Smith 1993), and according to the Census Bureau it remained constant through 1993 (Schulte, 1995). Controlling for both experience and education, African American males earned within 8 percent of white males with similar qualifications in 1975 (Ferguson, 1995). Since then, the disparity among those older than forty-five years of age has remained essentially the same, but it has grown among younger workers. New black male college graduates in 1967–1968 earned 83 percent of the salaries of their white counterparts; four years later blacks earned 2 percent more than whites. At that point, however, blacks began to lose ground (Smith 1993); by 1989 the gap was at 16 percent, essentially where it began. Indeed, according to the Commission on Minority Participation (1988), between 1973 and 1986 the average real annual earnings for black males aged

twenty to twenty-four, fell by 50 percent. Since there is an association between wages and type of job, the decline might mean that
young black college graduates in the 1970s were as likely as white
males to be in managerial and professional occupations but that by
the late 1980s they were 13 percent less likely than whites to be in
those occupations. Similarly, for recent high school graduates, the
10 percent gap of 1975 grew to 16 percent in 1989. Among young
workers, black male high school graduates had more than their
share of jobs as operatives in the 1970s but less than their share in
craft positions. By the late 1980s, they had lost further ground as
craft workers and were at a point of parity as operatives. The wage
gap for high school dropouts remained a constant 16 percent, but
this only tells part of a bleak story, for during the 1980s no more
than half of the black high school dropouts with fewer than ten
years of experience were employed (Ferguson, 1995).

Among workers aged twenty to fifty-nine in 1989, white males
were the best compensated. Controlling for years of schooling,
blacks earned between 78 and 82 percent of what equally educated
whites did, while Hispanics earned between 81 and 86 percent and
Asians earned between 89 and 94 percent. Interestingly, in no
instance were the gaps the lowest between the respective minority
male group and the white male group for the groups with sixteen
or more years of education, which equates to at least a college
degree (O'Neill and O'Neill, 1992). This finding was confirmed by
a later study by the Economic Policy Institute that indicated that
the wage gap grew faster for African American males with more
education (McClain, 1995).

A cohort analysis of the African American males who had
entered the job market earning 2 percent more than whites revealed
that in 1989, eighteen years into their careers, they were earning
only 75 percent of what their white counterparts were (Smith,
1993). This growing wage gap across one's career is consistent with
the findings of Thomas, Herring, and Horton (1994: 608), who
attribute the phenomenon to a "cumulative effect of discrimination," which other researchers document as beginning with the
hiring process. Audits in which equally qualified blacks and whites
are sent to apply for the same job openings demonstrate that whites
receive more job offers by small, but important, margins (Ferguson,
1995). One counter to the cumulative discrimination effect may
have been identified by Javed Ashraf (1993), who found that wage

differentials between black and white workers tended to be lower in unionized environments than in those where collective bargaining was not present.

Data from the North Carolina Employment and Health Survey indicate that as the proportion of minorities on the job increases, hourly earnings fall. While Tomaskovic-Devey (1993: 57) attributes much of this to "human capital" differences, others might ascribe it to discrimination, since (as discussed earlier) the basic skills gap between whites and blacks has narrowed substantially. Ferguson (1995) points out that employers place greater value on the skills of white workers than they do on those of African American workers, possibly a discriminatory factor. If our society were moving universally and speedily in the direction of employment integration, one might feel secure in the thought that such discrimination would soon disappear. However, a review of forms filed by employers with the Equal Employment Opportunity Commission indicates a rise in the segregation of minority workers between 1982 and 1992, with the increase in segregation of African Americans the most pronounced. This finding supports the growing body of literature indicating that employers view and treat black workers differently than they do other workers (Rodgers, 1994).

In most instances affirmative action has had a more positive effect for women as a group, particularly white women, than for minorities. Women currently account for 24 percent of all lawyers, 19.4 percent of all doctors, and 8.3 percent of all engineers, compared to 5 percent, 7.6 percent, and 1.3 percent respectively in 1970. Further, women now hold 29.9 percent of all lower and middle managerial positions in private industry, up three times over 1966 levels—though the so-called glass ceiling effect has limited their proportion of senior managerial positions to 4 percent (Belsky and Berger, 1995).

Compared to men, women still earn less, despite both the cultural changes of the last quarter-century and governmental policies promoting gender equality. Women now earn 76.4 percent of men's wages, up from 62.5 percent in 1979. Younger women account for the closing of the gap; those aged twenty-five to thirty-four earn 83 percent of male wages, while those forty-five to sixty-four earn only 66 percent. The effect has been uneven across ethnic groups; African American women earn only 66 percent of male wages, and Hispanic women earn only 58 percent of the male total (Belsky and Berger, 1995). However, looking within ethnic groups, African American women have made more progress in wages relative to African American men than has occurred between white women and men. Their earnings differential decreased from 32.3 percent in 1967 to 12.8 percent in 1986, while no such trend was observed among the white population (Ashraf, 1993). On the other hand, with the exception of social work, the gap between men and women in predominantly female occupations is greater for African Americans than for whites. Black women in such situations earn 19.1 percent less than black men, while white women earn 6.9 percent less than white men (Kilburne, England, and Beron, 1994).

Looking at the wage gap between women by ethnicity and education, in 1989 African American women with fewer than sixteen years of education earned between 93 and 94 percent of equally educated white women; however, those with sixteen or more years of education exceeded their white counterparts by 1 percent (O'Neill and O'Neill, 1992). According to a Census Bureau report, this advantage experienced by well-educated African American women was not maintained; as of 1993, college-educated black women earned only ninety-five cents for every dollar earned by an equally educated white woman (Schulte, 1995). As of 1989, Hispanic women earned between 93 and 96 percent of what their equally educated white counterparts did. The best-compensated women in all education categories were Asian Americans; they exceeded white women by between 2 and 8 percent (O'Neill and O'Neill, 1992).

The nexus between education and income is compelling. Indeed, the Economic Policy Institute concluded that the expansion of the wage benefits of a college degree in the 1980s may have helped to widen the gap between African American and white workers, since blacks are underrepresented among college graduates. At the same time, shifts away from high-paying manufacturing jobs (in which blacks were overrepresented) to lower-paying jobs in the service industry left undereducated blacks with even less income (McClain, 1995). Still, there have been disparate effects of education within race. In 1969 African Americans with college degrees earned nearly three times as much as blacks who did not graduate from high school; fifteen years later, the advantage had dropped to about 2.25 times. On the other hand, the advantage of white workers with college degrees relative to those without increased by about 10 percent in the same period (Ashraf, 1993).

Isolating the comparisons to women aged twenty-five to thirty-four, college-educated white women earned 1.8 times more than high school–educated white women in 1970, while those with less than a high school diploma earned only 60 percent of those with only a diploma; by 1992 the differential for the college-educated had increased to 1.95 times more than the high school–educated, and those without a diploma gained ground on those with one, achieving 75 percent of their salary level. As with white women, African American women with college degrees increased their earning power slightly over the same period over African American women with high school diplomas (from 2.1 times in 1970 to 2.2 times in 1992), and the gap narrowed between those without a high school diploma and those with one (from 50 percent in 1970 to 70 percent in 1992) (National Center for Educational Statistics, 1994a).

Poverty

The same roller coaster effect that has been characteristic of college enrollments and wage differentials can also be found in the effort to alleviate poverty. In 1959 roughly two-thirds of African American children were in families at the bottom 20 percent of family income distribution, thirty-three times more likely to be there than in the top fifth. By 1989, nearly half of the black children were in the bottom 20 percent, eight times more likely to be there than at the top. By contrast, 18.9 percent of white children were in the bottom fifth and 18.3 percent were in the top fifth (Lichter and Eggebeen, 1993). A focus on the those living below the official poverty line tells a different story. By 1970, the proportion of African American children in poverty had decreased to about two in five, but by 1993, 60 percent were living in poor families (Schulte, 1995). Approximately one-third of the African American population consistently remains below the poverty line, compared to about a tenth of whites. In fact, the underclass—those Americans with little chance of escape from poverty—is about two-thirds black and about one-tenth Hispanic (*The Economist*, 1991). South Carolina provides a cogent example: in 1990, 72 percent of all children living in poverty were African American; unemployment for black males was 9 percent, compared to 3.3 percent for whites; and the African

American median income was only about half of what it was for whites (*The Economist*, 1994).

One explanation for the recent increase in poverty among African Americans is the rise in the proportion of families headed by single mothers, in a time when most families need two incomes to maintain a middle-class standard of living. According to the Census Bureau, approximately four out of five black families in poverty are headed by a single parent, and black children are three times more likely than whites to live in poor families headed by a single parent (Schulte, 1995). Approximately 45 percent of all single women heading households are African American or Hispanic (Caputo, 1993). The trend line is staggering. In 1950, 17.2 percent of African American families were headed by single women; by 1970, the proportion had risen to 28 percent, and by 1994 to 48 percent. (While a smaller share of white families are headed by women, the growth was of similar proportions—from 5.3 percent in 1950 to 17.3 percent in 1990.) In 1950, 16.8 percent of African American births were to unwed mothers, compared to 37.6 percent in 1970 and 66 percent in 1990. Similarly, the portion of births among white unwed mothers rose from 1.7 percent in 1950, to 5.7 percent in 1970, and to 16 percent in 1990 (Hacker, 1992; Schulte, 1995).

In 1973 the single largest category of recipients of Aid to Families with Dependent Children (AFDC) was separated or divorced women; by 1988, it was mothers who had never been married (Caputo, 1993). This has led to a considerable focus in recent years on the potential link between the rise in births to single parents (particularly among minority teenagers), the availability of welfare, and the growth in poverty. Several factors appear to argue against such a relationship. First, while births to young, single mothers skyrocketed, the rate of approximately eighty births per thousand unmarried black teens remained constant between 1970 and 1990 while it increased from eight births per thousand unmarried white teens in 1970 to twenty in 1990 (Schulte, 1995). Second, Richard Caputo (1993: 522) found "virtually no correlation between AFDC payments and poverty rates for either blacks or whites." Nor did he find any discernable trend in mean unemployment rates—which between 1981 and 1988 were 6.5 percent for whites and 15.5 percent for blacks, only slightly higher than the 6.2 and 14.1 percent means between 1973 and 1980).[6] Instead, he concluded that the increases in poverty during the 1980s had to do with working people earning less money. Also, contrary to the view of many that single parents are more often than not uneducated and happy to be on public assistance, the Census Bureau found that 62 percent of single parents in 1990 were high school graduates and worked at least part-time (Schulte, 1995).

The effects of poverty are seen in numerous statistics, one of which is the mortality rate. Although the national infant mortality rate reached an all-time low in 1989, baby deaths have become of particular concern; as we have recognized that our national rate is behind that of twenty other industrialized countries (Usdan, Delgado, and Swift, 1994) and that many of our communities rank with Third World nations. The rate among African Americans was 18.6 deaths per thousand births in 1989, more than twice the rate among whites. Data from the National Center for Health Statistics indicate that by nearly all measures, children born to African American women appear to be more at risk than those born to whites; the mothers are younger, come from lower income backgrounds, tend to have inadequate prenatal care, and are more likely to be without health insurance to pay for medical visits during infancy. Further— and of particular importance—they are more likely to deliver their babies prematurely and at lower birth weight (Hummer, 1993). In fact, if interventions had prevented the death of very small babies, the differential between black and white infant mortality rates would have been reduced by 25 percent (Overpeck, Hoffman, and Prager, 1992).

Beyond infancy, black death rates exceed mortality for all other ethnic groups in most categories, particularly under age forty-five. For example, for deaths by natural causes, African Americans between ages one and fourteen had a mortality rate of twenty-four deaths per 100,000 in 1988, compared with thirteen to seventeen for other ethnic groups; in the fifteen- to twenty-four-year-old age group their rate of forty-one exceeded the rates of fifteen to twenty-five for other groups. In the twenty-five- to forty-four-year-old group, black deaths from heart disease exceeded the next highest group, whites, by 2.6 times. Similarly, in the forty-five- to sixty-four-year-old group, the black death rate caused by heart disease was 426, compared to the next highest rate of 244, which was for whites. Further, among this same age group, the cancer death rate was 401 for blacks, compared to 289 for whites, the next highest group. Rates of death by HIV for all age groups was 3.6 times higher for African Americans, and 2.3 times higher for Hispanics, than for whites. For deaths caused by homicide, African Americans were also at the top: the rate for one- to fourteen-year-olds exceeded that of all other ethnic groups by three to four times, and among fifteen- to twenty-four and twenty-five- to forty-four-year-olds by as much as seven times (with whites and Asians having the lowest rates) (Kovar, 1992).[7]

One factor often thought to be reflection of the stress caused by poverty and lack of hope for a better future, as well as a contributor to increased dysfunction and mortality, is drug and alcohol abuse. While studies indicate that African Americans as a group are no more likely to consume alcoholic beverages than are whites (Morris, 1993), other studies reveal that there may be differences in levels of substance abuse, which typically can be explained by income and lifestyle factors. A nationally representative sample of high school seniors studied by Wallace and Bachman (1991) revealed that factors including educational values, religious commitment, and time spent in peer-oriented activities—so-called family values—strongly relate to drug use. Thus, black youth living in two-parent households with highly educated parents have a particularly low rate of drug use. Indeed, for young people, alcohol and drug use is generally lower than average among African Americans and Asian Americans, at intermediate levels among whites and Hispanics, and higher than average among Native Americans.

Wallace and Bachman's finding regarding youth appears to hold up for older people as well. Data from New York State confirm that black males in the lowest socioeconomic group are most likely to engage in substance abuse but that the higher the level of education, the fewer the number of substance abuse problems. For those earning less than $7,000 per year, African American males consumed 4.41 ounces of alcohol per day (averaging 24.5 alcohol-related problems), compared to 1.31 ounces consumed by equally poor white males (who averaged 6.5 alcohol-related problems). Similarly, black males in this group reported that they had used drugs an average of 8.5 times within the last thirty days, while white males in this group reported 1.3 drug uses. In the $15,000–$24,999 group, the substance abuse problems of African American males was only slightly higher than those for whites. At income levels of $25,000 and up, no difference in the incidence of substance problems among white and African American males is distinguishable.

However, problems begin to increase somewhat as African Americans reach the highest levels of education (Barr, Farrell, Barnes, and Welte, 1993). One might hypothesize that people at that level may find it difficult to deal with discrimination factors that they thought they had passed beyond. For example, in a set of focus groups that included forty-six African American and Hispanic faculty, called by the New Jersey Board of Higher Education to discuss how the climate on their campuses affects their professional lives, most stated that they were perpetually barraged with comments from their white colleagues that they owed their positions not to their talent but to affirmative action. The sessions also revealed that most felt exploited, under-appreciated, and isolated (Marcus, 1989). It is not uncommon to hear such concerns raised by other minority professionals also. To make matters worse, their money cannot always buy them the happiness that they have earned, as evidenced by the Federal Reserve Bank of Boston finding that in 1992 African Americans and Hispanics in the Boston area were rejected for mortgage loans 60 percent more often than whites of equal income and education (Rosen, 1995). A similar finding was reported in a national survey by five federal regulatory agencies released in 1995: except in the Chicago area, black applicants for mortgages were rejected twice as often as whites with similar incomes (Rubin, 1995).

THE CHALLENGE AHEAD

President Johnson originally believed that affirmative action would have a life of a few decades, that it would take that long to overcome the vestiges of our sorry history of *de jure* segregation. He may have been correct about the life span, but not about the cause of death. Affirmative action has proven to be extremely divisive, despite its positive intent. Its growing numbers of critics hold that it is "un-American" in its design and that it violates our cultural norms and constitutional protections, not just in theory but in practice.

While many argue that affirmative action has accomplished its goal of minority and female inclusion, the facts seem to tell a different story. Not only are the documented examples of reverse discrimination rare, but also, by nearly every socioeconomic indicator, African Americans as a group are still well behind whites— and discrimination cannot be ruled out as one of the important bases of the disparities. President Clinton was correct: the job of affirmative action is not complete. Indeed, one wonders how much greater the disparities might have been were it not for the policy of inclusion.

The controversy is likely to remain hot for some time to come, on-campus and off, as both sides seek to convince the great American center of the correctness of their positions. While supporters of the policy say that it is still necessary for clearing old debris off the road to the American Dream, opponents argue that it results in new debris being deposited there. At the moment, the latter group appears to have the edge in the minds of the public. In the next chapter, we will consider another intense controversy, about multiculturalism, which some assert is more dangerous to our national well-being than affirmative action.

NOTES

1. There was only enough money to fund 279 scholarships. Of the top 268, only three were awarded to minorities. The final eleven scholarships were given to minorities, to bring the proportion of minority students among the 495 qualified applicants to 5 percent.

2. The issue of minority scholarships made national news in December 1990, when Michael L. Williams, Assistant Secretary for Civil Rights in the Department of Education (ED), wrote to Fiesta Bowl officials informing them that their plan to establish minority scholarships at the two institutions whose football teams would be competing in its New Year's game was illegal. Following the resulting uproar among higher education officials and civil rights advocates, ED issued a policy forbidding colleges from using their own money for race-based scholarships but permitting the use of private donations and state appropriations designated for such purposes. With the furor at a steady pitch, ED Secretary Lamar Alexander told colleges in March 1991 that they could ignore the policy pronouncements until an in-depth review of the legal issues could be completed. The following December he proposed regulations that would prohibit minority scholarships unless they were intended to remedy documented past discrimination or were established by private donations; the regulations were not to be enacted until the Government Accounting Office (GAO) had studied the issue. In January

1994, after President Bush's defeat, the GAO study revealed that two-thirds of the colleges and universities offer at least one scholarship restricted to minority students but that only 5 percent of all scholarships awarded to undergraduates are so restricted. The following month, the new ED Secretary, Richard Riley, issued guidelines that minority scholarships are legal if they are designed to meet past discrimination or to promote diversity, a standard that most institutions can meet (Jaschik, 1994). However, the recent court rulings might obviate the policy.

3. The University of California action appears to fit the pattern described by Mari Matsuda and associates (1993: 14), who point to "an emerging and increasing virulent backlash against the extremely modest successes achieved by communities of color, women, and other subordinated groups in [their] efforts to integrate academic institutions . . . [by] polite and polished colleagues" who justify their actions by twisting words to try to portray "that the powerful have become powerless."

4. The reduction in minority enrollments was in total numbers; the experience of individual institutions may have been different. For example, in 1987 there were increases in African American enrollments at 18 percent of all institutions, while there were decreases at 13 percent. Similarly, Hispanic enrollments rose at 14 percent of the colleges and universities but fell at 9 percent (Birnbaum, 1988).

5. It should be noted that many of the Asian faculty were foreign-born. Since growth in faculty hiring typically comes from newly qualified Ph.D.s, a description of the 1989 Asian cohort is instructive: of the 5,150 doctorates awarded to Asians, 624 went to American citizens and 631 to holders of permanent visas (Orlans, 1992).

6. A recent analysis of nearly 2,000 able-bodied men from several ethnic groups in Los Angeles found not only a greater rate of unemployment among African Americans than whites (23.1 percent compared to 8.6 percent) but also that the rates were higher for darker-skinned African Americans than for those with lighter skin (27 percent compared to 20 percent). The differences held up at various educational levels; for example among those with thirteen or more years of schooling, unemployment among whites was 9.5 percent, among light-skinned African Americans it was 10.3 percent, and among dark-skinned African Americans, 19.4 percent. For those who had participated in job training programs, light-skinned African Americans had the lowest unemployment rate (11.1 percent), compared to 14.5 percent for whites and 26.8 percent for dark-skinned African Americans (Johnson and Farrell, 1995).

7. Typically, Asian Americans had the lowest mortality rates. Native Americans had the highest rates in certain categories; for example, the suicide rate among Native American youth exceeded that of other ethnic

groups by two to four times. Their rates of death by injury also exceeded other ethnic groups in certain age categories.

REFERENCES

Ashraf, Javed. "Differences in Returns to Education: An Analysis by Race." *American Journal of Economics and Sociology* v. 53 n. 3 (July 1993), pp. 281–290.

Ayres, B. Drummond, Jr. "University Regents in California Battle over Affirmative Action." *The New York Times.* July 21, 1995, pp. A1, A14.

Barr, Kellie E.M., Michael P. Farrell, Grace M. Barnes, and John W. Welte. "Race, Class, and Gender Differences in Substance Abuse: Evidence of Middle Class/Underclass Polarization among Black Males." *Social Problems* v. 40 n. 3 (August 1993), pp. 314–327.

Belsky, Gary and Susan Berger. "Women Could Be Big Losers if Affirmative Action Falls." *Money* v. 24 n. 8 (August 1995), pp. 20–22.

Birnbaum, Robert. "Administrative Commitments and Minority Enrollments: College Presidents' Goals for Quality and Access." *Review of Higher Education* v. 11 n. 4 (Summer 1988), pp. 435–457.

Caputo, Richard K. "Family Poverty, Unemployment Rates, and AFDC Payments: Trends among Blacks and Whites." *Families in Society: The Journal of Contemporary Human Services* v. 74 n. 9 (November 1993), pp. 515–526.

Card, David and Thomas Lemieux. "Changing Wage Structure and Black-White Wage Differentials." *The American Economic Review.* v. 84 n. 2 (May 1994), pp. 29–33.

Clinton, William J. "Excerpts from Clinton Talk on Affirmative Action." *The New York Times.* July 20, 1995, p. B10.

Commission on Minority Participation in Education and American Life. *One-Third of a Nation.* Washington, DC: American Council on Education and Education Commission of the States, 1988.

Darity, William, Jr. "The Undesirables, America's Underclass in the Managerial Age: Beyond the Myrdal Theory of Racial Inequality." *Daedalus* v. 124 n. 1 (Winter 1995), pp. 145–165.

Editors of *The Economist.* "America's Blacks, A World Apart." *The Economist* v. 318 (March 30, 1991), pp. 17–21.

———. "South Carolina, A Rebel Tamed?" *The Economist* v. 331 (June 11, 1994), pp. 23–24.

Editors of *The New York Times.* "Affirmative Action Will Be Examined in Senate." *The New York Times.* February 6, 1995, p. A15.

Ferguson, Ronald F. "Shifting Challenges: Fifty Years of Economic Change toward Black-White Earnings Equality." *Daedalus* v. 124 n. 1 (Winter 1995), pp. 37–76.

Gose, Ben. "Growth of Minority Enrollment Slowed to 2.6% in 1993." *The Chronicle of Higher Education.* March 17, 1995, p. A34.

Hacker, Andrew. "The Myths of Racial Division." *The New Republic* v. 206 n. 12 (March 23, 1992), pp. 21–25.

Hamilton, Charles V. "Affirmative Action and the Clash of Experiential Realities." *The Annals of the American Academy of Political and Social Science* v. 523 (September 1992), pp. 10–18.

Holmes, Steven A. "White House Signals an Easing on Affirmative Action." *The New York Times.* February 25, 1995, p. 9.

Hummer, Robert A. "Racial Differences in Infant Mortality in the U.S.: An Examination of Social and Health Determinants." *Social Forces* v. 72 n. 1 (December 1993), pp. 529–554.

Jaschik, Scott. "Minority Scholarships: A Chronology." *The Chronicle of Higher Education.* November 9, 1994, p. A30.

———. "Blow to Affirmative Action." *The Chronicle of Higher Education.* June 23, 1995a, pp. A21–A23.

———. "'No' on Black Scholarships." *The Chronicle of Higher Education.* June 2, 1995b, pp. A25, A29.

———. "U.S. Report Questions 'Bakke' Defense of Affirmative Action." *The Chronicle of Higher Education.* July 7, 1995c, p. A20.

Johnson, James H., Jr. and Walter C. Farrell, Jr. "Race Still Matters." *The Chronicle of Higher Education.* July 7, 1995, p. A48.

Kahlenberg, Richard. "Class, Not Race, an Affirmative Action That Works." *The New Republic* v. 212 n. 14 (April 3, 1995), pp. 21–27.

Kellough, J. Edward. "Affirmative Action in Government Employment." *The Annals of the American Academy of Political and Social Science* v. 523 (September 1992), pp. 117–130.

Kilbourne, Barbara, Paula England, and Kurt Beron. "Effects of Individual, Occupational, and Industrial Characteristics of Earnings: Intersections of Race and Gender." *Social Forces* v. 72 n. 4 (June 1994), pp. 1149–1176.

Kovar, Mary Grace. "Mortality among Minority Populations in the United States." *American Journal of Public Health* v. 82 n. 8 (August 1992), pp. 1168–1170.

Lichter, Daniel T. and David J. Eggebeen. "Rich Kids, Poor Kids: Changing Income Inequality among American Children." *Social Forces* v. 71 n. 3 (March 1993), pp. 761–780.

Locke, Michelle. "University Eyes End to Race-based Policies." *Philadelphia Inquirer.* July 21, 1995, pp. A1, A14.

Loury, Glenn C. "Incentive Effects of Affirmative Action." *The Annals of the American Academy of Political and Social Science* v. 523 (September 1992), pp. 19–29.

Marcus, Laurence R. "State-level Efforts to Improve Racial/Ethnic Harmony on Campus." Paper presented at the National Conference on Racial and Ethnic Relations in American Higher Education. Oklahoma City, June 1989.

Matsuda, Mari J., Charles R. Lawrence, III, Richard Delgado, and Kimberle Williams Crenshaw. *Words That Wound: Critical Race Theory, Assaultive Speech and the First Amendment*. Boulder, CO: Westview Press, 1993.

Maxwell, Nan L. "The Effect on Black-White Wage Differences of Differences in the Quantity and Quality of Education." *Industrial and Labor Relations Review* v. 47 n. 2 (January 1994), pp. 249–264.

McClain, John D. "Blacks' Academic Gains No Match for Bias, Market Forces, Study Says." *Philadelphia Inquirer*. April 30, 1995, p. A9.

Morris, Eugene. "The Difference in Black and White." *American Demographics* v. 15 n. 1 (January 1993), pp. 44–49.

National Center for Educational Statistics. *Mini-Digest of Educational Statistics 1994*. Washington, DC: US Department of Education, 1994.

O'Neill, Dave M. and June O'Neill. "Affirmative Action in the Labor Market." *The Annals of the American Academy of Political and Social Science* v. 523 (September 1992), pp. 88–103.

Orlans, Harold. "Affirmative Action in Higher Education." *The Annals of the American Academy of Political and Social Science*. v. 523 (September 1992), pp. 144–158.

Overpeck, Mary D., Howard J. Hoffman, and Kate Prager. "The Lowest Birth-Weight Infants and the US Infant Mortality Rate: NCHS 1983 Linked Birth/Infant Death Data." *American Journal of Public Health* v. 82 n. 3 (March 1992), pp. 441–444.

Purdum, Todd S. "President Shows Fervent Support for Goals of Affirmative Action." *The New York Times*. July 20, 1995, pp. A1, B10.

Rodgers, William M., III. "Racial Differences in Employment Shares: New Evidence from EEO-1 Files." Paper presented at the National Conference on Race Relations and Civil Rights in the Post Reagan-Bush Era. Minneapolis, MN, October 1994.

Rose, Tricia, Andrew Ross, et al. "Race and Racism: A Symposium." *Social Text* v. 13 n. 1 (Spring 1995), pp. 1–52.

Rosen, Jeffrey. "Is Affirmative Action Doomed? How the Law Is Unraveling." *The New Republic* v. 211 n. 16 (October 17, 1994), pp. 25–28, 30, 34–35.

————. "Affirmative Action: A Solution, Neither Color-blindness nor Quota-mongering." *The New Republic* v. 212 n. 19 (May 8, 1995), pp. 20, 22–25.

Rubin, James H. "Blacks Lead in Mortgage Rejection." *Philadelphia Inquirer.* July 19, 1995, p. C1.

Schrag, Peter. "Son of 187, Anti-affirmative Action Propositions." *The New Republic* v. 212 n. 5 (January 30, 1995), pp. 16–19.

Schulte, Brigid. "African American Family Income Hasn't Risen above the 1969 Level." *Philadelphia Inquirer.* February 23, 1995, p. A3.

Smith, James P. "Affirmative Action and the Racial Wage Gap." *The American Economic Review* v. 83 n. 2 (May 1993), pp. 79–84.

Taylor, William L. and Susan M. Liss. "Affirmative Action in the 1990s: Staying the Course." *The Annals of the American Academy of Political and Social Science* v. 523 (September 1992), pp. 30–37.

Thomas, Melvin E., Cedric Herring, and Hayward Derrick Horton. "Discrimination over the Life Course: A Synthetic Cohort Analysis of Earnings Differences between Black and White Males." *Social Problems* v. 41 n. 4 (November 1994), pp 608–628.

Tomaskovic-Devey, Donald. "The Gender and Race Composition of Jobs and the Male/Female, White/Black Pay Gaps." *Social Forces* v. 72 n. 1 (September 1993), pp. 45–76.

Usdan, Michael, Debra Y. Delgado, and Charlotte Swift. "A Healthy Future for Our Children." *Futures Research Quarterly* v. 10 n. 2 (Summer 1994), pp. 83–95.

Wallace, John M., Jr. and Jerald G. Bachman. "Explaining Racial/Ethnic Differences in Adolescent Drug Use: The Impact of Background and Life Style." *Social Problems* v. 38 n. 3 (August 1991), pp. 333–354.

Williams, John B. "Affirmative Action at Harvard." *The Annals of the American Academy of Political and Social Science* v. 523 (September 1992), pp. 207–220.

Wilson, Reginald. "Affirmative Action: Yesterday, Today and Tomorrow." *CUPA Journal* v. 40 n. 3 (Fall 1989), pp. 1–6.

Zapler, Michael. "Kentucky Lawmaker Sets off Affirmative Action Debate by Telling White Students They 'Lost' Scholarships." *The Chronicle of Higher Education.* October 12, 1994, p. A25.

Chapter 3

Identity Politics, Multiculturalism, and Political Correctness

As colleges and universities achieve greater diversity in their student bodies and faculty, increased incidence of intergroup politics and (possibly) tension can be anticipated, not simply due to the increased likelihood that someone will act against someone of another group, but also resulting from a predictable clash of ideas. This chapter discusses the issues regarding the diversification of our campuses and suggests that a curriculum that embraces multiculturalism and that is taught in an atmosphere encouraging free and open interchange is fundamental both to promoting intergroup understanding and to educating students for life in the twenty-first century.

IDENTITY POLITICS

We have lived with a mythology that America has always been a melting pot. It does not take deep reflection to realize that we have never melted racially. Even among those of European ancestry, the melting came rather late, has been incomplete, and has been attended by cultural conflict. After all, the European groups that settled here brought with them the biases and prejudices of their countries of origin. Religious conflict was present in New England in the seventeenth century. Ethnically related cultural conflict became part of the American landscape at least as early as the wave of Irish immigration that commenced in the 1840s. An argument is made by Benjamin Schwarz (1995: 65) that "America would have seen more conflict between white Americans of different ethnic and religious backgrounds (and classes) if these had not been muted by whites' common hatred and fear of black Americans."

"Our Sense of Who We Were"

Although there was a certain degree of assimilation among whites of different religious and ethnic backgrounds—for example, the old European languages were replaced by English, and people accommodated themselves to Anglo-Saxon–Protestant values—whites self-segregated according to ethnicity. Neighborhoods in most cities came to be known by the ethnic origin of the preponderance of their residents; groups set up their own schools and colleges; people patronized those purveyors of goods and services who were of similar background, etc. Ethnicity played a role in politics as well. As city populations diversified and the numbers of a given ethnic group grew, ward leaders who reflected the ethnicity of their neighborhoods began to take on the politically and economically dominant ethnic group, in most instances Anglo-Saxon–Protestants. Sometimes in order to defeat the entrenched powers, ethnic coalitions developed and supported multi-ethnic tickets, but the goal of each group was clear—to gain entrance of people from their own ethnic group into positions of power.

World War II seemed to alter our sense of who we were. The experience of having pulled together as Americans to defeat a foreign threat to our democracy caused us to identify more as Americans. The suburbanization that occurred in the post-war years did much to break down the ethnic identification of whites, as they moved next door to people who had come from different neighborhoods in the nearby city, and as intermarriage occurred.[1] This blurring of ethnic identity seemed to leave the cities—whose populations were declining as a proportion of the total American population—as the last bastion of ethnicity.

However, in the 1970s there was a re-emergence of the "hyphenated American," with many whites adopting a symbolic ethnicity grounded in nostalgia for the culture of the "old country" or in memory of the immigrant generation. However, because of the melting that had occurred, most of these hyphenated Americans carried "a portfolio of ethnic identities," which could be used differently as the situation changed (Nagel, 1994: 154).[2] While some scholars tie the revival of ethnicity and identity -based politics to the 1968 French intellectuals who posited that people view society in accordance with their own class-related experiences (Browder, 1994), it may have had more to do with the "black pride" movement, which helped African Americans replace their sense of second-class status with a positive self-identity. As blacks both celebrated their ethnicity and adopted the same tactics that white ethnics had used to gain political power a generation or two earlier, whites began again to think of themselves in ethnic terms.

The demographic changes that are transforming the face of America today exacerbate this phenomenon, as groups that have been subordinated politically, socially, and economically to a group declining in population seek power and influence. Since it takes more than just leaders and numbers to have a strong voice, groups seek to increase their "cultural capital" in the broader society, thus producing conflict with the dominant culture. Ordinary people, as "consumers" of culture, are drawn into a battle that they may not have initiated but which they cannot escape (Merelman, 1994).

While the emerging groups have much in common with the dominant groups, especially in terms of ideals and goals, their ability to open doors is reduced if they ignore differences between themselves and the dominant group. Indeed, some would contend that the emphasis, in pursuit of racial equality actually, on cultural similarities between whites and blacks served to protect the practices that impede real political and economic parity (Merelman, 1994). Thus, the emerging groups assert the positive difference of their experience, culture, and social perspective in order to define themselves; "liberation comes from positive self-definition of group differences" (Young, 1995: 199). But to expect a "comfortable accommodation" by the dominant group, which wants to retain its cultural influence, would be naive (Browder, 1994: 48).

Some see a way out of the conflict by changing the paradigm from a single, evolving culture, continually influenced by the cultures of new and growing groups, to a new pattern of cultural pluralism, which does not seek assimilation but values racial and ethnic difference and empowers the oppressed. Iris Young (1995: 204) posits that "the rejection and devaluation of one's culture and perspective should not be a condition of full participation in social life." Thus, by affirming and celebrating one's own ethnic identity, the Other no longer has "the impossible project of trying to become something one is not under circumstances where the very trying reminds one of who one is." She believes that this group consciousness would cause differences to be aired, thus mitigating intergroup conflict. But Arthur Schlesinger (1995: 226) disagrees. He believes that "the cult of ethnicity exaggerates differences, intensifies resentments and antagonisms, drives even deeper the awful wedges between races and nationalities." Benjamin Schwarz (1995: 67) is also skeptical. He has concluded that unless there is a common perception of "what it mean[s] to be an American, we are left with only tolerance and diversity to hold us together. Unfortunately, the evidence from Los Angeles to New York . . . shows that such principles are not so powerful as we had believed and hoped."

IDENTITY POLITICS: AFRICAN AMERICANS AND JEWS

In recent years, identity politics has played itself out between blacks and Jews, groups whose earlier unity did much to advance the cause of civil rights. The present breach is worth examining here since it plays a role in the current disquiet on our nation's campuses—as we saw earlier from the events at Kean College—and, in the view of some, including Henry Louis Gates (1992), may even be emanating from intellectual circles.

Paul Robeson, Jr. (1993), contends that the coalition of African Americans and Jews that resulted in mutually beneficial outcomes in the labor movement of the 1930s and the civil rights movement of the 1960s came about because both feared WASPs, non-Jewish white ethnics, and conservative Republicans more than they feared each other. The fruits of their cooperation included access to the middle class, something which took root more strongly for the Jews than for the blacks. Polls reveal that Jews are far less prejudiced against African Americans and more rarely subscribe to anti-black stereotypes than are non-Jewish whites and that (with the exception of economic stereotyping) African Americans are less hostile toward Jews than they are toward other whites. Indeed, the University of Kentucky's Doris Wilkinson (1994: 48) believes that "the existence of an authentic and consistent anti-Semitism among Americans of African descent across all social classes is questionable." Yet despite this general sensitivity and appreciation of each other—or perhaps because of it—tensions today are running high between the two groups.

A crack in the alliance developed in the early 1970s over affirmative action. While most African Americans saw the policy as the next logical step in the civil rights movement, some Jewish organizations saw it differently: as a threat to the civil rights achievements that had struck down the use of quotas, a tool that had been prominent in discrimination against Jews. Some Jews also saw it as a threat to their economic standing, since it appeared to give blacks an edge in competition for jobs.

The split also had bases in international politics. Many African Americans came to identify with the plight of the Palestinians in their quest for a homeland and were unhappy with Israel's inter-action with the apartheid government of South Africa. Jews saw a threat in such positions and were outraged when it was revealed that the American Ambassador to the United Nations, Andrew Young (one of the most prominent African Americans in the Jimmy Carter administration), had met with representatives of the Pales-tinian Liberation Organization. The furor led to Young's resignation and a bitter feeling in much of the black community.

Domestic politics also played a role. During Jesse Jackson's 1984 presidential campaign, mainstream blacks and progressives joined in support of his candidacy, while most Jews, concerned about Jackson's embrace of Yasir Arafat and his "Hymietown" comment, sided with traditional and conservative Democrats against him. Four years later, during the presidential primary campaign in his state, New York mayor Ed Koch ratcheted up the rhetoric by declaring that "Jews would have to be crazy to vote for Jesse Jackson" (Robeson, 1993: 172). According to Robeson (1993), the rebuke of Jackson by Jews and other white liberals revitalized the separatist movement within the African American community; white ethnic identification was pitted against black racial identifi-cation, and a small separatist minority among the black middle class abandoned the struggle for blacks as a group to enter into the melting pot, instead using grievances against "the Jews," a small and identifiable white ethnic group, as a foil for grievances against the broader white society.

Among these separatists was Louis Farrakhan, whose Nation of Islam published *The Secret Relationship between Blacks and Jews*, a book, without an identified author, that has been attacked both by reputable African American scholars and the American Historical Association for its inaccuracies and misrepresentation of history (Cudjoe, 1994; Winkler, 1995). During a 1991 speech at the University of Illinois, Farrakhan told the assembled fifteen thousand that the purpose of the book, which among its other contentions blames Jews for the slave trade and the horrors of American slavery, was to "rearrange a relationship" that "has been detrimental to us" (Gates, 1992: A19). Joining in the same vein of writing and teaching are prominent Afrocentrist academics, a group that Gates criticizes as "pseudo-scholars."

Michael Meyers (1994: 23–4), the Executive Director of the New York Civil Rights Coalition, believes that the anti-Semitic statements of black extremists should be no surprise, they have been around since he "was a lad in Harlem." He contends that such people will be around "as long as they can find a semi-deranged lost soul who needs the fix of racial bluster and rhetoric to boost his self-esteem." For such people, "the 'Jew' is shorthand for the white devil . . . the scapegoat." He is extremely critical of other African American leaders for not speaking out against this anti-Semitism, warning that "Jews are likely to remember these moral lapses on the part of most black leaders." He likens the "anger and depth of confusion that many Jews feel toward the black leaders' covenant with Louis Farrakhan" to how African Americans would shudder "if the Anti-Defamation League had made a pact with David Duke or George Wallace" (Meyers, 1994: 25).

Wilkinson (1994: 49) points out that "the dominant political and economic strata that have traditionally designated Jews as scapegoats have deliberately permitted racist and anti-Semitic sentiments to become grounded in the substance of the [American] culture." She sees the possibility of a political "set up," that anger within the black community is being intentionally misdirected at Jews to pit the two groups against each other, since "African Americans cannot conceivably benefit on any level from defaming Jews." Henry Louis Gates (1992: A19), however, views the set-up as perpetrated by a different set of players. He contends that it is the African American extremists who are behind a "top down" anti-Semitism that is really an attempt of "one black elite to supplant another" as the legitimate leaders of the African American community. Gates postulates, "The more isolated black America becomes, the greater their power. And what's the most efficient

way to begin to sever black America from its allies? Bash the Jews
. . . and you're halfway there."

From a sociopsychological perspective, Paul Berman (1994: 62)
builds on the work of French academic Vladimir Jankelevitch, who
has written about the relations between groups that are "almost the
same," that they become highly charged, since the resemblance
between the two threatens to obliterate what is special about each.
While relations between groups that are very different (that is,
between one group and the "Other") tend to be chilly, those that
are "almost the same" need to work up a rage against their "false
brothers" in order to defend their own uniqueness.

Berman contends that what makes African Americans and Jews
"almost the same" are their memories of catastrophe and their
dedication to liberalism as the protection against further catastrophe. Together, they have worked for a common good. However,
while liberalism benefited both groups, it had a more positive effect
for Jews than for blacks. When some Jewish groups opposed
affirmative action, blacks were hurt, sensing as a betrayal of the
black cause and a turning away from liberalism. Jews felt similarly
hurt when blacks sided with the Palestinians against Zionism. The
positions of each were sharply drawn to maintain values important
to each: blacks see affirmative action as a civil rights measure,
many Jews view it as quotas revisited; Jews assert the need for a
Jewish homeland as a necessity in the aftermath of the Holocaust,
many blacks perceive it as another intrusion on the rights of Third
World people. For the extremes in both groups, compromise becomes unthinkable. With self-identity woven into the groups'
positions, appeals for intragroup solidarity found receptive ears,
and the differences became magnified.

Berman's hypothesis that Jews and blacks are "almost the same"
has proven quite provocative. Arnold Eisen (1994) responds that
the two groups differ too much in history and too much in their
current situation. He sees the breach between old allies as the result
of their wanting different things for themselves and from each
other. African Americans seek the "practical, hands-dirtied, risk-
taking activism that some Jews displayed on their behalf" during
the civil rights movement (Eisen, 1994: 17). They point out that
Jews have "made it" while blacks have not and that Jewish liberalism "is all the less convincing when [it] grows comfortable in the
suburbs while the poor get poorer" (Eisen, 1994: 22). Jews, on the

other hand, want blacks to recognize the legitimacy of their concerns about the continuing perils of anti-Semitism during a period
of significant Jewish assimilation (Eisen, 1994: 17). He believes that
because neither group is receiving what it wants in the dialogue
with the other, each is less inclined to be responsive to the concerns
of the other, and the volume is raised—even among the legitimate
voices—regarding their differences.

While Jewish and African American elected officials have maintained their collaborative relationship in support of progressive
legislation and in reciprocal support of Jewish and black candidates
(conservatives are a greater threat to both than each are to the
other), those who would separate are making headway. Their
progress as can be seen in recent studies that indicate that blacks
are twice as likely as whites to hold anti-Semitic views and that
this feeling is most pronounced among younger and more educated
blacks (Robeson, 1993; Gates, 1992; Alexander, 1994).

One way that the current gap between many African Americans
and many Jews—indeed between many African Americans and
many whites—can be bridged would be to find common ground
that can reestablish the national commitment to help those who
have the least (who primarily are African American and Hispanic)
in a way that is seen as meaningful and fair. And there lies the nub
of the debate regarding identity politics (also known as the "politics
of difference") and multiculturalism. Are there basic values that
create enough common ground for all to stand on, or are group-
based histories and needs so different that common ground is an
unreasonable expectation? Indeed, can there continue to be one
nation if we focus on the many rather than on the one? Or does the
focus on the many who constitute our citizenry lead to a stronger
nation?

THE MOVE TO MULTICULTURAL CURRICULA

One of the most important roles of schools and colleges is to
enhance our society's capacity for democracy. Throughout most of
our history this has included the "Americanization" of the newly
arrived, not to "cleanse America of its ethnic minorities, [but to]
cleanse its minorities of their ethnicity" (Schwarz, 1995: 62). Further, educational institutions sought to minimize or neutralize
conflicts over race, religion, and ethnicity by ignoring them, hoping

that politics could be left outside the schoolhouse gate (Browder, 1994). In the mid-1980s, postmodernist thought, combined with the prospective demographic changes in the nature of the student body, provided impetus to bring into the curriculum a focus on groups, incorporating scholarship by and about people of color and women, including those from non-Western cultures. This touched a raw nerve among those who felt that the best way to deal with diversity in America is to promote the concept of the melting pot. The rancorous debate that raged in scholarly circles spilled over the ivy-covered walls of our colleges and universities into the broader society and became a prominent public policy issue. Major pieces were written in mass-market magazines, in such nationally read newspapers as *The New York Times*, the *Wall Street Journal*, and the *Christian Science Monitor*, and also in most local newspapers.

Purveyors of popular culture also jumped into the fray. For example, in Berkeley Breathed's comic strip *Outland* one Sunday in October 1991, an African American girl, Ronald-Ann, read to her classmates her essay, "The True Story of America." She said that Columbus was actually a black man whose three ships, built of African wood, were inspired by the grandeur of the African pyramids. She was interrupted by the strip's cockroach character, who said that the cutting of the trees had displaced generations of cockroaches and that the pyramids had been inspired by termite mounds; he called his version "cockro-centrism." Ronald-Ann replied, "Let's stick with the truth, shall we?" "Of course," he responded. She continued, "Thus, the brother Columbus sailed . . . , " only to be interrupted again by the cockroach, who added, " . . . with head lice." The strip was indicative of the controversy swirling around the effort to broaden the curriculum to include works by and about persons of different cultures—to shift from what has been called a "Eurocentric" curriculum toward a multicultural one. In this effort, scholars often tread over what other scholars see as "the truth," replacing it with material that may lead to a different conclusion. Some see this as liberating, others as an act akin to heresy.

David Abalos (1989: 1), a professor at Seton Hall University, describes the change as one intent on transforming our educational system and our people: "Multiculturalism is an attitude; it's a spirit of openness and celebration of inclusion that honors the history and culture of all peoples. It's not just tolerance; it's not begrudging acceptance; it's not stony silence and it's not expedient allowances. It's not the lie of behavior modification . . . based on external smiles that mask a condescending bias of the powerful toward their more naive and less wealthy neighbors."

While opinion within the American mainstream has never been monolithic, there is little question that we have been educated in accordance with the canons of the "Western tradition." Henry Giroux (1995: 136) captures the postmodernist view of such an approach: "Neither the curriculum nor the canon can be understood as expressions of the disinterested search for truth and knowledge. Such knowledge, more often than not, expresses the on-going process of negotiation and struggle among different groups over the relationship between knowledge and power, and between the construction of individual and social identity." Multiculturalism is an effort to broaden what we learn and to open our minds to streams of thought and expression beyond the conventional confines of Western tradition. According to James Banks (1995: 15), in order to teach in a liberating fashion "we must not only be aware of the knowledge produced, but must also understand that the knowledge producer is located within a particular social, economic, and political context of society."

Thus, no matter how well each of us may have been educated, we have been imbued with a culture-based point of view that is probably too narrow. Getting it right and teaching it right ought to be a goal of academics. In so doing, we may not only learn some totally new things but we may also gain better insights into things that we thought we knew. For example, a column in the *Philadelphia Inquirer* answers questions sent by elementary school children. In response to the youth who asked, "Who was the first American artist?" the column responded, "There were many American Indian artists who painted hides, created wood and stone sculptures and wove elaborate patterns with wampum beads." It then went on to the name that had popped into my mind (given my education in the schools and universities of Massachusetts) as the first American artist, John Singleton Copley. It cited him as "one of the earliest American artists of European heritage."

The interest in the quincentennial anniversary of Christopher Columbus's voyage provides another excellent example. For those who watched the PBS series on Columbus or who followed the seemingly ubiquitous "Year of Discovery" material, there were new insights on the man and the consequences of his life. Columbus's vision and bravery changed the course of world history and earned him a place of reverence meriting a national holiday and the naming of a country, cities, streets, and parks. But we have come to learn that he was probably a tyrant and that in opening up this "new world" to Europeans he brought the destruction of a thriving culture. Can the subject of Columbus ever be as simple as it was heretofore? Though it may tarnish a hero of Western civilization a bit, are we not better off knowing? (By the way, the Columbus quincentennial also taught us that a black explorer named Alonzo Pietro was the navigator of the *Nina*, one of the three ships.)

E. D. Hirsch launched an effort to help us get it right by proposing in his 1987 book, *Cultural Literacy*, the creation of a national core curriculum. He attempted to lay the groundwork for what would obviously be an undertaking of immense proportions with a sixty-three-page list of things that he believed literate Americans should know. It is quite a list, but it seems incomplete. Absent from that list are Boris Yeltsin, Tienanmen Square, and Saddam Hussein; one had not happened and the other two were not widely known when the list was put together. Mikhail Gorbachev, *glasnost*, and *peresvoika* had, but they are not there. Chuck Berry had also, but he is not there either (even though the song "Here We Go Round the Mulberry Bush" is). *Kwanza* is not there, nor is the term "leveraged buy-out." Nelson Mandela is not on the list, nor is the first president of Ghana, Kwame Nkrumah, who decolonialized his country more than three decades ago. Babe Ruth made the list but Henry Aaron, who surpassed him in total home runs, did not. Mrs. Malaprop is important enough to be included but Toni Morrison is not. Only six dates are listed: 1066, 1492, 1776, 1861–1865, 1914–1918, and 1939–1945. Should not 1929, the year that saw the Great Depression begin and with it a series of events that changed our views of the role of government, be included as well? What about the 1960s, or 1989, when the Berlin Wall fell and the Soviet Union and its sphere of influence began to disintegrate?

Despite the obvious flaws in the list approach, Hirsch's effort gathered momentum in a project undertaken by the National Center for History in the Schools, housed at UCLA. However, just as I found Hirsch's list to be lacking in persons of color, critics of the Center's proposed "United States History Standards" fault that curriculum for failing to provide "any indication that protesters, social reformers, feminists, or ethnic minorities ever did anything that was less than honorable," as well as for promoting the impression that "American history is one act of discrimination after another" (Fonte, 1995: A48).

The challenges of finding the truth are legion. I am reminded of a cartoon that appeared some years ago in *The Chronicle of Higher Education*, in which a matador is face to face with a bull, ready either to plunge his sword into the bull's spine or be gored by it. A man in the crowd has apparently said to his companion something like, "This is the moment of truth." The companion replies, "Yes, but is it the moment of relative truth, socialist truth, symbolic, ethnocultural, or postmodern-revisionist truth?" Perhaps it is not groups, acting as our surrogates, who can best find the truth and build it into a curriculum, but individual authors and faculty members. It is not as simple as merely adding female authors and authors of color to course plans. According to Paul Lauter (cited in Toma and Stark, 1995), a wider revision is required, one that reflects the growing heterogeneity of students and society. A curriculum centered around the exploration of differences should help students to understand social change, cultural fragmentation, and the forces of criticism, as well—presumably—as what Americans have in common.

Moving Beyond the Canon

While it is true that many individual faculty members sought to rid their curricula of negative racial and ethnic stereotypes in the late 1960s and early 1970s, the movement to *broaden* the curriculum began in the 1980s. In 1987, California instituted a new social studies curriculum for its public schools that included multiculturalism as one of its major features. As a result, for example, the ancient African civilizations of Cush and Mali are studied along with Greece and Rome. Students learn that Thomas Paine was not the only pamphleteer during the American Revolution; a woman, Mercy Otis Warren, also was a prominent producer of political material. Further, the curriculum no longer glosses over such tragedies as the suffering of Native Americans driven from their lands by white settlers. An important feature of California's approach is that it is intended both to impart understanding both of different points of view of different groups and also of values that unify people. Similar K-12 statewide efforts are underway in Texas, Florida, and Minnesota, (Chira, 1991).

Among the most controversial multicultural curriculum development projects occurred in the K-12 sector in the state of New York. In July, 1989 the New York Board of Regents was presented with a task force report entitled, "A Curriculum of Inclusion"; it cited the weak performance in school by large numbers of children whose heritage or backgrounds were not European. Based on its conclusion that this poor performance was the result of stereotyping and misinformation that "had a damaging effect on the psyche of young people of African, Asian, Latino and Native American descent," the task force recommended a movement away from a Eurocentric curriculum toward one that would assure that "all cultures receive equitable and accurate attention in the educational curriculum and members of all cultures experience excellence in the schools of New York State" (Commissioner's Task Force on Minorities, 1989: iii, 40). The report, which had a somewhat anti-Western tone, was viewed by many as extreme. Some attributed this to the involvement of the task force's chief consultant, Leonard Jeffries (McConnell and Breindel, 1990).

Nevertheless, the Board of Regents found merit in the report and directed the State Department of Education to undertake the development of a plan for a multicultural curriculum. On June 13, 1991, New York's Education Commissioner released a ninety-seven-page report on the social studies curriculum, entitled *One Nation, Many Peoples: A Declaration of Cultural Interdependence* (1991). That document, which would affect 731 school districts including New York City, noted that "the various peoples who make up our nation . . . seem determined to maintain and publicly celebrate much of that which is peculiar to the cultures with which they identify. . . . [R]ecognizing the interdependence of cultures in this multicultural nation, they now insist that their participation be recognized and that their knowledge and perspective be treated with parity" (New York State Social Studies Review and Development Committee, 1991: vii).

The report, much less strident than its predecessor, asserted that the social studies curriculum should "not be so much concerned with 'whose culture' and 'whose history' are to be taught and learned, as with the development of intellectual competence in learners, with intellectual competence viewed as having one of its major components the capacity to view the world and understand it from multiple perspectives. . . . Multicultural knowledge in this conception of the social studies becomes a vehicle and not the goal" (New York State Social Studies Review and Development Committee, 1991: vii).

Eight principles that would implement a multicultural approach in this curricular reform were recommended. The most pertinent included: that subject matter be culturally inclusive; that it represent diversity and unity within and across groups; that subject matter be set in the context of its time and place; that multicultural perspectives be infused across the entire curriculum, pre-kindergarten through grade twelve. Despite the less than unanimous support for the recommendations among the task force participants, much of the report was implemented.

To support such public school efforts, collegiate teacher education programs have begun to produce teachers who are prepared to teach in a multicultural fashion. For example, to satisfy a teacher certification requirement in California, Sacramento State University instituted a course called "Multicultural Education for a Pluralistic Society." The State University of New York at Plattsburg began to infuse its teacher training curriculum with multicultural concepts, as did the University of Maryland at College Park. In response to a state mandate, the University of South Dakota introduced into its teacher education program a mandatory course on race relations and prejudice. Going even further, the National Council for Accreditation of Teacher Education adopted an accreditation measure that requires multicultural perspectives to be infused throughout the teacher education curriculum, not just in one or two courses. Of the 132 universities evaluated in the early implementation of this accreditation requirement, about half met the standard (Nicklin, 1991).

Many colleges and universities have gone beyond teacher education. Major statewide efforts to assist college and university faculty across the state of New Jersey who wished to broaden their curricula were launched by the New Jersey Department of Higher Education; the Multicultural Studies Project, housed at Jersey City State College, was focused on infusing the curriculum with multicultural concepts; a companion effort, the New Jersey Project, centered at William Paterson College, supported the introduction into courses of scholarship about gender, class, and race, as well as scholarship by women. Also in New Jersey, Ramapo College, a four-year public institution, utilized state, federal, and private grants of nearly $5 million to make over its entire curriculum with international and multicultural concepts in order to become the "college of choice" for those seeking a "global education."

Efforts abound across the nation. For example, the University of Arizona introduced a series of humanities courses called "Critical Concepts in Western Culture." Each course focuses on a single theme, such as war, or love, or evil. In the course on evil, for example, students not only read traditional Western selections by such writers as Voltaire, Goethe, Camus, and Faulkner, but they also read Kiowan Indian mythology and view such films as Spike Lee's *Do the Right Thing* and one on a Yaqui Indian ceremony (Mooney, 1991).

Culture Wars on Campus

While the New Jersey and Arizona reforms have not met with great controversy, such has not been the case at other institutions, including among others the University of Pennsylvania, the University of Texas at Austin, Duke, and Stanford, which had been in the vanguard of the multicultural curriculum movement. Characteristic of the campus polemicism was the experience at the University of Oregon, where multicultural proponents sought to extend the distribution requirement to take one course, "Race, Gender, Non-European American," in place since 1988, to a second course. Opponents saw the bid as "extreme and greedy" (Leatherman, 1994: A15). A faculty committee appointed by the university's president recommended that students be required to take one course on contemporary American race relations and another on how race, class, and gender shape individuals and society, and that a special review panel examine all courses proposed to satisfy the requirement. Many on campus saw the recommendation as anti-intellectual, ideological, and costly; one faculty member commented that the faculty panel making the proposal was a "committee of right-thinking Ayatollahs." Another had a broader concern, that the debate "was about who's going to control the university's curriculum and who's going to control the university itself" (Leatherman, 1994: A17).

The University Assembly initially adopted the recommendation in 1993, on a close vote. The liberal student newspaper published the names and phone numbers of faculty who voted in the negative, calling upon students to ask them if they were racist; the conservative student newspaper replied by accusing its competition of McCarthyism. A month later the University Assembly acted to reconsider its action. In 1994, a second faculty committee offered a recommendation that students complete two courses from three areas, "American Cultures," "Pluralism and Tolerance," and "International Cultures." The courses were not restricted to a focus on American minority groups but could also include the experience of European Americans as well. The committee did not recommend the establishment of a review panel to examine the courses. This measure was adopted, with some opponents saying that they voted for it just to put the issue behind them and some multiculturalism proponents upset that students could graduate without having taken a course in race relations (Leatherman, 1994).

Robert Scott (1991), president of Ramapo College, which underwent its curriculum transition very smoothly, has cited several reasons for the furor on many campuses. Foremost, he says, is the historical faculty resistance to change in the college curriculum. Next is the prevailing belief that general education should be centered around the study of Western civilization and the "Great Books"; any effort to move away from such an approach is seen both as a movement away from quality and a challenge to traditional authority. Scott notes that those who speak against multicultural curricular approaches consider invalid the assumption that there is an equation between enhanced self-image among minority students and improved academic achievement; these critics argue that hard work and positive reinforcement is what is necessary, not a multicultural curriculum. He also cites the concern that proposals to sweep away the Eurocentric curriculum would have replaced it with one equally limited in ideology.

Some who believe that we should continue to base our curriculum on the canon of traditional Western thought argue that if we are to change what we teach, we will inevitably do so at the expense of important things currently being taught. This concern, however, rings hollow. I began my schooling in 1953 and received my bachelor's degree in 1969. During those sixteen years, most of my history courses ended with World War II, and I do not remember having read much literature written after the mid-1950s. It is unimaginable that today's history classes would ignore the civil rights movement, the assassinations that rocked our nation in the 1960s, Watergate and the Vietnam War, the Cold War and its end; or that today's literature classes would ignore Philip Roth, Maya Angelou, Toni Morrison, or Gabriel García Márquez. Have they stopped teaching the American Revolution or Shakespeare or Rousseau or Emily Dickinson in order to make room for the newer topics? I suspect not. As the world changes, so does the curriculum. It always has. Topics, themes, and writers who have stood the test of time still remain—that is what made them classics. As educators make room for the new, they need to assure that the best of the old is not lost. This has and will continue to be a challenge, but one that good academics can handle.

Leon Galis (1993), a professor at Franklin and Marshall, takes the cynical view that those who promote multiculturalism in education do so to make themselves feel good about participating in social change without tackling society's root problems. He believes that although multicultural proponents pay lip service to increasing tolerance and respect for others, they would rather mark a student paper down because it used the word "mankind" than dirty their hands by engaging in the real work of combatting discrimination. They are, he says, "motivated by a desire for moral purity on the cheap . . . , [in order] to pursue their careerist ambitions with a good conscience" (Galis, 1993: 100).

Others see grave danger in multicultural education. It is Diane Ravitch's (1990) belief that the United States has a common culture that is multicultural, formed by the interaction of its subsidiary cultures. She sees cultural pluralism as the organizing principle of our society and contends that pluralists seek a richer common culture. On the other hand are those whom she labels as "particularists," who insist that no common culture is possible or desirable. They believe that there are five cultures in America—African-American, Asian-American, European-American, Latino/Hispanic, and American Indian. Ravitch fears that particularism may very well be a bad idea whose time has come, that it is leading to a conversion to ethnocentric curricula in response to a misguided desire to give greater self-esteem to minority children.

Arthur Schlesinger, Jr. (1991: 45), fears that a curriculum based on multiculturalism will ultimately lead to the disintegration of the unifying American ethos. He does not believe that ethnic and racial themes should be magnified "at the expense of the unifying ideals that precariously hold our highly differentiated society together. The republic has survived and grown because it has maintained a balance between *pluribus* and *unum*." (His reference, of course, is to the national motto *E Pluribus Unum*—from many, one—which appears on the back of the dollar bill.) Julius Lester (1991) agrees. He believes that it is the responsibility of public education to say to its students, "Each of you comes from a different culture, but beyond that cultural identity, there is another one, and that is that we are all American citizens, and here are the concepts, ideals, experiences, hopes, and dreams which bind us together as Americans."

The National Endowment for the Humanities (NEH) recently took a step in the direction of seeking consensus on what it means to be an American. Through grants totalling $2 million, it commissioned twenty-seven organizations across the nation to establish a series of discussion groups and research projects linking scholars with the public to talk about common values and pluralism. The project was immediately criticized by Republican members of the House and Senate as attempting to push a "politically correct" agenda (Burd, 1995).[3] (Given the intention by the present Republican congressional majority to include in its budget-reduction efforts the phasing-out of NEH funding, this project might not have the time that such a massive endeavor would require.)

POLITICAL CORRECTNESS

Even though the cauldron continues to boil regarding whether multiculturalism should be the organizing principle for our democracy and our educational enterprises, there has been increasing recognition that our society benefits from our showing increased respect for one another, at least in our face-to-face interactions. Thus, we have learned to use language in such a way so as not to be offensive to others. However, given the involvement of the sensitive issues of race, ethnicity, and gender, what some view as simple civility others contend is a coerced infringement on freedom of speech, one that they have come to call "political correctness." Further, some argue that many who advocate multiculturalism in education—or even a socially progressive agenda—do so to be politically correct. They cite what they see as excesses, such as the attempt to remove *Huckleberry Finn* from a northern Virginia middle school because of its use of the word "nigger." On the other side of that particular debate were those who saw the book's removal not as censorship but as a push for responsibility (Oldaker, 1994).

The phrase "politically correct" was originally used by left-wing intellectuals as a way of making fun of their colleagues who seemed bound to match their behavior to their ideology, no matter how rough the fit. In the current debate, however, it is used as a counterattack by traditionalists who believe the pro-change group intentionally inhibits discussion on important issues by labelling as racist, sexist, or intellectually bankrupt anyone who disagrees with their viewpoint. The traditionalists view such an approach as being unfair, unwarranted, anti-democratic, and, in the academic setting, unscholarly. Even President Bush joined the debate. During his commencement address at the University of Michigan in May 1991, the president told the graduates (and the nation) that "political correctness . . . replaces old prejudice with new ones. It declares certain topics off-limits, certain expressions off-limits, even certain gestures off-limits. What began as a crusade for civility has soured into a cause of conflict and even censorship" (Bush, 1991: 32).

The issues regarding campus speech have become more confused by the excessive responses of some students to the ideas expressed by faculty members. Where that has occurred, the result has been a chilling effect on academic freedom. While the shouting-down of the likes of Brown student Douglas Hann during his nocturnal vitriolic diatribe against everyone different from himself would have been one thing—and within the rights (and, perhaps, responsibilities) of students—a number of incidents have made the press that have not been as clear-cut.

Take, for example, the New York University Law School moot court case that was to have focused on the rights of a lesbian mother but was temporarily postponed when students objected that arguments against the mother's position might offend gays. Or take the Harvard professor who was criticized for not providing a balanced view, because he read from a southern planter's diary but not from slave diaries (Seigenthaler, 1991). Stephen Thernstrom, one of the preeminent scholars of the history of race relations in America, has stopped offering the course called "Peopling of America" that he had co-taught at Harvard with Bernard Bailyn. He had been attacked in the *Harvard Crimson* for being "racially insensitive" because he had assigned a book that observed that some people view affirmative action as preferential treatment, and because he endorsed Daniel Patrick Moynihan's premise that poverty among blacks is the result of the disintegration of the black family. After a few semesters enduring charges of racism, Thernstrom cancelled the class; "It's like being called a Commie in the fifties. Whatever explanation you offer, once accused, you're always suspect" (Taylor, 1991: 34).

Donald Kagan, the Dean of Yale College, was the object of derision in the *Yale Daily News* and from several campus organizations as a result of a speech during new student orientation: he had cited his belief in the importance of Western thought and culture to American democracy. Rather than simply challenge his ideas, those who disagreed with him attacked him as "racist," "sexist," and "intellectually dishonest" (Goode, 1991: 9).

The student assaults against faculty have come not only from those at the liberal end of the political spectrum. Several years ago, the ultra-conservative *Dartmouth Review* unleashed an unrelenting barrage on a black faculty member because his teaching was thought by the editors of the *Review* to be too far to the left.

Academics Debate

College and university faculty have coalesced on both sides of the issue. Peter Drucker (1994: 58), one of the nation's preeminent scholars, sees an "attempt to beat academia into conformity of political correctness," "a purely totalitarian concept" that he likens to the attempts of American Stalinists in the late 1930s and the early 1940s to quell criticism of Soviet policies over the Hitler-Stalin Non-Aggression Pact. The National Association of Scholars, with twenty campus chapters and twenty-two state affiliates, has grown to some 2,500 members since its founding in 1987. It holds the view that the academy is controlled by "illiberal radicals," products of the 1960s who are using their tenured positions to promote a leftist social agenda. Its members accuse these faculty members of politicizing the curriculum with left-wing orthodoxies of "diversity" and "multiculturalism" (Magner, 1991) and charge them with employing McCarthyist tactics. Some assert that multicultural scholarship is based on myths and half-truths, or, as one critic put it, "a few scraps of truth amidst a great deal of nonsense" (D'Souza, 1991: 83). Others consider it even worse, a desperate—and surely self-defeating—strategy for coping with the educational deficiencies and associated social pathologies of young blacks (Kristol, 1991).

"Teachers for a Democratic Culture" was formed in response to the National Association of Scholars (Magner, 1991). Further, multiculturalists began to host their own national and regional conferences to discuss issues of multiculturalism as well as to respond to the attacks leveled upon it. They have called the furor over "political correctness" part of an organized conservative campaign to turn back gains made by women and minorities, partly in response to current economic uneasiness. They also assert that conservatives are in search of an enemy to fill the void created by the demise of the Soviet Union and communism (Heller, 1991); in this view, they "point to the tyranny of the politically correct as an ideological rallying cry to ward off the cultural threat posed by the 'enemy within'" (Giroux, 1995: 131). While some claim their more traditional colleagues are racist, sexist, and homophobic, others level against them charges of Orwellian thought-control: the traditionalists, they say, accuse the multiculturalists of McCarthyism in order to squash the spread of new ideas and are thus themselves the true McCarthyites (Spear, 1991). Henry Giroux (1995: 138) adds that "the battle against political correctness appears to be . . . a prescription for removing debate, cultural differences, and diverse theoretical orientations" from academe. Catharine Stimpson (1991: A40), one of the national leaders of the movement to make the curriculum more inclusive, concurs. She contends that those who attack political correctness are really engaged in "a scorched earth policy toward the truth, ostensibly in defense of the academy as the cathedral of truth" but really to uphold the old order. She asserts that they attempt to make their case by employing such tactics as sloppiness about facts, selective use of evidence, and the manipulation of fear.

We should recognize that "political correctness," like cultural conflict, has been a recurrent part of the scenery since America's earliest days. Roger Williams and Anne Hutchinson were banished to the frontiers of Rhode Island and Connecticut, respectively, because they did not agree with the politically correct religion of Massachusetts. People used the terms "Indian-lover" and once "Nigger-lover" to keep well-meaning whites from challenging the politically correct ideologies of their day. "America: love it or leave it" was used during the Vietnam War to stifle sentiment in opposition to the politically correct position that Americans should maintain a unified position in foreign policy. Today, efforts to get people to act in a politically correct fashion come from two directions at the same time: one side calling the other racist; the other side accusing the first of being radicals who would see our society destroyed in order to accomplish their socialist goals. Too many feel caught in the middle, reluctant to say anything.

THE ISSUES CONVERGE

An occurrence at Kean College after the February 1992 Leonard Jeffries visit gives us a vivid example of the convergence of identity politics, multiculturalism, and political correctness. Although the college is committed to a multicultural curriculum, it became apparent at a particular meeting of board of trustees that groups on campus understand multiculturalism differently. While there are those who take an all-embracing view, many in each of the different racial, ethnic, and religious groups believed multiculturalism to require a major focus on their own group; they assume the posture of particularist as they deprecate the contributions and understate the travails of other groups. At the same time, those who hold the most extreme positions make it difficult for others to show the way to common ground.

During the board meeting, a number of African American students were arguing about that history had been stolen from them, recounting the horrors of the Middle Passage and slavery. They asserted that they had never learned any of this in their American history courses at any level of their education, only when they took courses in the Africana Studies program did they gain an accurate understanding of this prologue to modern America. Several students also noted that Leonard Jeffries had asserted that a prominent role had been played by Jewish merchants in the slave trade. In response, members of the Jewish community denied that Jews had played such a role and pointed to their own historical persecution, which had culminated in the Holocaust. Debate ensued as to whether blacks or Jews had suffered more under their oppressors and whether the Middle Passage and slavery or the

Holocaust was worse. It seems self-evident that the perfect occasion had presented itself—what some would call a "teachable moment"—to induce both groups to appreciate the experience of the other, and to draw both together by discussing the common elements, outcomes, moral failures, etc., of both genocidal eras and what they shared with other genocides. However, given the heat of the argument and the intimidation that many felt, the moment passed; those who might have moved the discussion to a higher level remained quiet for fear of alienating, or becoming associated with, either group.

This example demonstrates what can happen when difference is allowed to reign over commonality, when particularism masquerades as multiculturalism. While everyone gains by multiculturalism, ethnocentric (or particularist) curricula can easily exacerbate the differences between groups. Aside from Native Americans (whose forbearers came here over twenty thousand years ago), blacks descended from slaves brought to America against their will, and also the descendants of those (mostly Mexicans) caught in the path of Manifest Destiny, we must readily acknowledge that most Americans are descended from people who came in search of a better life, in search of freedom or opportunity. The same holds true for today's immigrants. Most importantly, since at least the time of the American Revolution, most people who came here voluntarily (as well as most of those who are still coming) did so to become Americans. With respect to Native Americans, African Americans, and those Mexican Americans whose families lived in the Southwest when it was part of Mexico, there is no reason to believe that any of them seek anything other than what we commonly refer to as the American Dream. We need to keep returning to this point—what we have in common—at the same time that we discuss what makes us different.

The multicultural message is not quite grasped by some who endorse multiculturalism but do not understand that it must be all-embracing in order to endure. We need only to look at what has been happening in the former Yugoslavia and in the Russian Federation since ethnicity began to take precedence over national identity and, alas, over human beings.

Joan Wallach Scott (1991) believes that the conservative reaction to multiculturalism is anti-intellectual, in that it seeks to stem the critical thinking that is the basis for new ways to address the production and transmission of knowledge. She speaks of the commitment of intellectual activity in search of the truth—which she sees as an ever-receding horizon, not a fixed quantity that can ever be known. To Scott (1991: 36), the academy must be a place "where critical ideas are tried out, often in extreme, dogmatic and outrageous form . . . where, ideally, despite enormous differences, opinions are exchanged and ideas expressed." Divergent ideas must be permitted to coexist, so that "there is ultimately no resolution, no final triumph for any particular brand of thought or knowledge" (J.Scott, 1991: 43).

Scott is on target in her criticisms of conservatives who angrily charge "political correctness" against multiculturalists. Unfortunately, she falls a bit short in her analysis, since there are also some among the multiculturalists who deserve similar criticism; they, too, exhibit the frighteningly anti-intellectual traits that would muffle inquiry. Vartan Gregorian (cited in Peters, 1992: 178), president of Brown University, argues that coercion from any direction to invoke political correctness on college campuses should be heaved into the dumpster. He says that institutions of higher learning must foster free discourse and debate, putting an end to the pressure to "do the right thing, to say the right thing, to do politically the right thing." All who are engaged in the educational enterprise—whether teachers or students—must feel free to express their views and at the same time be willing to have their positions challenged. Name-calling and lobbing charges of anti-Americanism of one sort or another threaten that discourse. As Joan Scott (1991: 34) says, "There can be no democracy worthy of the name that does not entertain criticism, that suppresses disagreement, that refuses to acknowledge difference as inevitably disruptive of consensus, and that vilifies the search for new knowledge." The Carnegie Foundation's Ernest Boyer (cited in Peters, 1992) places the responsibility on educational leaders to make sure that robust discourse is fostered by defending free speech and denouncing censorship, but at the same time denouncing racism and sexism and giving voice to those who are least advantaged.

Our schools and colleges have historically served to help America evolve as a flourishing democracy. They still can, and they must. We would cheat our students if we were to maintain a solitary focus on the Western tradition when we know that there is so much worth learning from other traditions as well as from broadening our conception of what falls within the Western tradition itself. But to shift from one curricular approach that is too narrow to another (or to others) that may be equally narrow (or even more)—that is, to replace one canon with another—would also be to cheat our students. To be more practical, if we are to interact with the multitude of people on this planet, does it not make sense for us to understand their cultures so that we may be able to bridge any gaps that exist? Or, since our own nation is becoming increasingly populated with persons whose cultures differ from that which has predominated here, is it not logical that their cultures will have an effect on ours, just as ours will on theirs? If so, should we not know about their cultures? Further, as we learn more from other cultures, we can also gain greater insight into those things that we all have in common and begin to break down the stereotypes that cause us both to underestimate and overascribe. We can also begin to understand where the real differences exist and develop ways either to eliminate or accommodate the differences. There is no denying, however, that the road from here to there will not be smooth.

NOTES

1. This transition can be seen in my own experience. In the 1950s and 1960s in suburban Boston, where I grew up, ethnic identification was so strong that people spoke of children coming from "mixed" homes when one parent was an Irish Catholic and the other a Polish Catholic. However, if the Irish/Polish Catholic child married, for example, a French Canadian Catholic/Scotch Presbyterian, ethnic identities became more complicated. Last names and facial features no longer necessarily revealed an individual's ethnic identification. It was not uncommon for a person who felt comfortable making ethnic slurs (itself not an uncommon event) to be surprised at the offense taken by the person being addressed. Typically the offending party would respond with embarrassed "Oh, I didn't know you were Italian. You don't look Italian, and you have a German last name. I thought that you were German."

2. Thus, for example, many white ethnics can feel drawn to any number of the 765 parades (most of them ethnically oriented) that were held in New York City in 1990 (Browder, 1994).

3. In seeking to understand Republican opposition to the NEH project, one cannot overlook the fact that Sheldon Hackney, former president of the University of Pennsylvania, was the NEH's director.

Hackney's leadership at Penn had been the subject of criticism for ignoring free speech principles and appeasing minority students. He had failed to take disciplinary action against a group of African American students who had stolen a press run of the student newspaper because they disagreed with its content, whereas around the same time disciplinary proceedings were initiated against a white male student who had called several African American women "water buffalos." Hackney's confirmation hearing, as well subsequent NEH budget considerations, were dominated by his handling of those incidents (Zuckerman and Masci, 1993).

REFERENCES

Abalos, David. "Multicultural Education in the Service of Transformation." *Celebrating Diversity: Global Approach to Literature and World Culture, Conference Proceedings*. Montclair State College, March 10, 1989.

Alexander, Edward. "Multiculturalists and Anti-Semitism." *Society* v. 31 n. 6 (September/October 1994), pp. 58–64.

Banks, James A. "The Historical Reconstruction of Knowledge about Race: Implications for Transforming Teaching." *Educational Researcher* v. 24 n. 2 (March 1995), pp.15–25.

Berman, Paul. "The Other and the Almost the Same." *The New Yorker*. February 28, 1994, pp. 61–71.

Browder, Lesley H., Jr. "'Can We All Get Along?' The Politics of Diversity." *Leadership and Diversity in Education*, ed. Joel L. Burdin. Lancaster, PA: Technomic Publishing, 1994, pp. 36–54.

Burd, Stephen. "Humanities Endowment Approves Grants for 'National Conversation.'" *The Chronicle of Higher Education*. April 14, 1995, p. A34.

Bush, George. "Excerpts from President's Speech to University of Michigan Graduates." *The New York Times*. May 5, 1991, p. A32.

Chira, Susan. "Teaching History So That Cultures Are More Than Footnotes." *The New York Times*. July 10, 1991, p. A17.

Cockburn, Alexander. "Bush and P.C.—A Conspiracy So Immense . . . ," *The Nation* v. 252 n. 20 (1991), pp. 685–686.

Commissioner's Task Force on Minorities. *A Curriculum of Inclusion*. Albany, NY: New York State Department of Education, 1989.

Cudjoe, Selwyn R. "Time for Serious Scholars to Repudiate Nation of Islam's Diatribe against Jews." *The Chronicle of Higher Education*. May 11, 1994, pp. B3, B5.

Drucker, Peter. "Political Correctness and American Academe." *Society* v. 32 n. 1 (November/December, 1994), pp. 58–63.

D'Souza, Dinesh. "The Visigoths in Tweed." *Forbes* v. 147 (April 1, 1991), pp. 81–86.

Eisen, Arnold. "Limits and Virtues of Dialogue." *Society* v. 31 n. 6 (September/October 1994), pp. 17–22.

Fonte, John. "The Naive Romanticism of the History Standards." *The Chronicle of Higher Education.* June 9, 1995, p. A48.

Galis, Leon. "Merely Academic Diversity." *Journal of Higher Education* v. 64 n. 1 (January/February 1993), pp. 93–101.

Gates, Henry Louis, Jr. "Black Demagogues and Pseudo-Scholars." *The New York Times.* July 20, 1992, p A19.

Giroux, Henry. "Teaching in the Age of 'Political Correctness.'" *The Educational Forum* v. 59 n. 2 (Winter 1995), pp. 130–139.

Goode, Stephen. "All Opinions Welcome—Except the Wrong Ones." *Insight.* April 22 1991, pp. 8–17.

Heller, Scott. "Frame-Up of Multicultural Mvmt Dissected by Scholars and Journalists." *The Chronicle of Higher Education.* November 27, 1991, pp. A15–A17.

Hirsch, E. D. *Cultural Literacy: What Every American Needs to Know.* Boston: Houghton Mifflin, 1987.

Kristol, Irving. "The Tragedy of Multiculturalism." *Wall Street Journal.* July 31, 1991, p. A10.

Leatherman, Courtney. "The Minefield of Diversity, How Debate over Expanding a Multicultural Requirement at the U. of Oregon Got Ugly." *The Chronicle of Higher Education.* June 15, 1994, pp. A15, A17–A18.

Lester, Julius. "Whatever Happened to the Civil Rights Movement?" *Second Thoughts about Race in America,* ed. Peter Collier and David Horowitz. Lanham, MD: Madison Books, 1991, pp. 3–9.

Magner, Denise K. "Gathering to Assess Battle against 'Political Correctness,' Scholars Look for New Ways to Resist 'Illiberal Radicals,'" *The Chronicle of Higher Education.* October 30, 1991, pp. A17–A19.

McConnell, Scott and Eric Breindel. "Head to Come. Is 'White Nationalism' the Problem?" *The New Republic.* January 8 and 15, 1990, pp. 18–21.

Merelman, Richard M. "Racial Conflict and Cultural Politics in the United States." *Journal of Politics* v. 56 n. 1 (February 1994), pp. 1–20.

Meyers, Michael. "Black/Jewish Splits." *Society* v. 31 n. 6 (September/October 1994), pp. 23–27.

Mooney, Carolyn J. "Amid the Continuing Debate over 'Political Correctness,' University of Arizona Courses Seek to Explore the Middle Ground." *The Chronicle of Higher Education.* May 29, 1991, pp. A9–A10.

Nagel, Joane. "Constructing Ethnicity: Creating and Recreating Ethnic Identity and Culture." *Social Problems* v. 41 n. 1 (February 1994), pp. 152–176.

New York State Social Studies Review and Development Committee. *One Nation, Many Peoples: A Declaration of Cultural Interdependence*. Albany: NY State Department of Education, 1991.

Nicklin, Julie L. "Teacher-Education Programs Face Pressure to Provide Multicultural Training." *The Chronicle of Higher Education*. November 27, 1991, pp. A1, A16–A17.

Oldaker, Lawrence L. "Coping with 'Hate Speech' in Educational Settings." *Leadership and Diversity in Education*, ed. Joel L. Burdin. Lancaster, PA: Technomic Publishing Company, 1994, pp. 76–85.

Peters, Ronald M., Jr. *The Next Generation, Dialogues between Leaders and Students*. Norman, OK: University of Oklahoma Press, 1992.

Ravitch, Diane. "Multiculturalism: E Pluribus Plures." *The Key Reporter* v. 56 n. 1 (1990), pp. 1–4.

Robeson, Paul, Jr. *Paul Robeson, Jr. Speaks to America*. New Brunswick, NJ: Rutgers University Press, 1993.

Schlesinger, Arthur, Jr. "Report of the Social Studies Syllabus Review Committee, A Dissenting Opinion." New York State Social Studies Review and Development Committee. *One Nation, Many Peoples: A Declaration of Independence*. Albany: NY State Department of Education, 1991, pp. 45–47.

————. "The Disuniting of America: Reflections on a Multicultural Society." *Campus Wars, Multiculturalism and the Politics of Difference*, ed. John Arthur and Amy Shapiro. Boulder, CO: Westview Press, 1995, pp. 226–234.

Schwarz, Benjamin. "The Diversity Myth: America's Leading Export." *The Atlantic Monthly* v. 275 n. 5 (May 1995), pp. 57–67.

Scott, Joan Wallach. "The Campaign Against Political Correctness, What's Really at Stake?" *Change* v. 23 n. 6 (1991), pp. 30–43.

Scott, Robert. "Multiculturalism." Invited Address: Organization of African Unity Lecture Series on Multiculturalism. Ramapo College, September 26, 1991.

Seigenthaler, John. "Politically Correct Speech: An Oxymoron." *Editor and Publisher* v. 126 n. 10 (March 6, 1993), pp. 48, 38.

Spear, Thomas. "Attacks on 'PC' Are New McCarthyism." *Christian Science Monitor*. April 24, 1991, p. 19.

Stimpson, Catharine R. "New 'Politically Correct' Metaphors Insult History and Our Campuses." *The Chronicle of Higher Education*. May 29, 1991, p. A40.

Taylor, John. "Are You Politically Correct?" *New York Magazine.* January 21, 1991, pp. 32–40.

Toma, J. Douglas and Joan Stark. "Pluralism in the Curriculum: Understanding Its Foundations and Evolution." *Review of Higher Education* v. 18 n. 2 (Winter 1995), pp. 217–232.

Wilkinson, Doris. "Anti-Semitism and African Americans." *Society* v. 31 n. 6 (September/October 1994), pp. 47–50.

Winkler, Karen J. "Historical Group Issues Statement on Role of Jews in Slave Trade." *The Chronicle of Higher Education.* February 17, 1995, p. A15.

Young, Iris Marion. "Social Movements and the Politics of Difference." *Campus Wars, Multiculturalism and the Politics of Difference,* ed. John Arthur and Amy Shapiro. Boulder, CO: Westview Press, 1995, pp. 199–225.

Zuckerman, Jill and David Masci. "House Panel OKs Arts Funding, Sidesteps Obscenity Issue." *Congressional Quarterly* v. 51 n. 26 (June 26, 1993), p. 1667.

Chapter 4

Campus Climate

That all is not well with race and intergroup relations in higher education can be seen in the frequent reports in the media about incidents of "ethnoviolence" and insulting behavior on our college campuses. Hundreds of episodes are documented each year; here are a few examples:

- At the University of Michigan, a speech code was adopted in response to the distribution of flyers declaring "open season" on blacks, the broadcast of racist jokes on the campus radio station, and the hanging of a Ku Klux Klan uniform in a dormitory window (Gibbs, 1992).

- At William Paterson College (NJ), several nights after their dorm room door was spat upon by white students, two black students were awakened by "wild kicking" on their door and found racial slurs written on an African American flag that the roommates had placed on the door (D'Aurizio, 1993).

- At the University of Massachusetts at Amherst, a black resident assistant was beaten by a white visitor to the dormitory, and feces were smeared on his door; in response, a group of black students rampaged through the twenty-two story residence hall (Elfin and Burke, 1993).

- At the University of North Carolina at Chapel Hill, a sign appeared in a dormitory bathroom that read, "This bathroom is no longer desegregated. No niggers allowed except for housekeepers" (Sanoff and Minerbrook, 1993:57).

- At Montclair State University (NJ) and the University of Delaware, white fraternities displayed Confederate flags; at the latter, the African American student who led a protest received death threats, and her dormitory was the object of a bomb scare (Florio, 1994; *Philadelphia Inquirer*, 1995).

- The retired founder of the Tacoma campus of Evergreen State University (WA) gave a lecture in which she said that "the white student role [on the Tacoma campus] is as place holders" until minority students could enroll (Monaghan, 1995: A38).

INCIDENTS WIDESPREAD

Incidents like these are not limited to issues of black and white but are also frequently aimed at members of other ethnic and religious groups, and toward women and gays, as well. For example, the Anti-Defamation League (1995) reported a 17 percent increase in 1994 over the previous year in reported incidents of anti-Semitism on college campuses, the seventh consecutive annual increase; at Bates, Colby, and Bowdoin colleges (ME), alone, there were twenty-one anti-Semitic incidents. Ruth Sidel (1994), who interviewed over a hundred students from seventeen colleges and universities, tells of the removal of mezuzas from the doors of Jewish students at Barnard, and of the Native American student at the University of Washington on whom flour was poured as he left a shower, so that he could "know what it's like to be white" (Sidel, 1994: 114). She also cites the experience of an Asian American student of Filipino heritage, born in this country, whose treatment by his fellow students at Tufts led him to conclude that he will "spend the rest of [his] life proving that [he's] an American" (Sidel, 1994: 137).

Episodes of harassment or discrimination are ubiquitous on college campuses, so much so that they typically do not get reported unless someone asks. For example, at Princeton University, an institution that has no reputation for serious intergroup problems of the sort that has been associated with other campuses, a study conducted by three students in 1992 revealed 108 anecdotes of racial or religious harassment or discrimination (Sidel, 1994).

Verbal harassment takes different forms. Sometimes students use such tactics as screaming epithets out of dorm windows or scrawling slurs on bulletin boards or bathroom walls, to intimidate, humiliate, insult, and demean minority students in order to impede their enjoyment of campus life and convince them that their presence is unwelcome (Jones, 1991). Sometimes they make cruel remarks not necessarily meant to be heard by the target. For example, an African American student on her first day at Tufts was walking in the dining hall with a white student whom she had known since she was four years old when she overheard someone say, "Look at that nigger bitch with that white boy" (Sidel, 1994: 5). In that same vein is the freedom some students feel, having assumed that everyone in their ethnic group shares their prejudices, to make derogatory comments about persons of other groups. For example, a white student told me of numerous instances of other white students referring to African Americans as "niggers" in normal conversation. One one occasion, in the gym, he was waiting for a turn to get into a basketball game when a white student standing beside him (whom he did not even know) commented in admiration about one of the players: "Look at that nigger's moves!" The student who recounted the episode said that, rather than causing a scene, he remained silent and took a few steps away from the offending student, hoping that no one would think that he was prejudiced.

Some students make remarks based on stereotypes or generalizations, not meaning to be offensive but making the person to whom they are speaking feel uncomfortable. An African American student at the University of Wisconsin–Madison experienced three such incidents in his first week of school: he was asked by one white student if he were on an athletic scholarship; another white student asked to touch his hair; and a third white student, upon their first meeting, extended his hand, saying, "What's up, bro?" On the same campus, a Native American student was asked if she lived in a tepee (Sidel, 1994: 152). Similarly, I was told by a Hispanic student, whose accent caused other students to assume that he was a poor city kid but who had in fact grown up in a working-class suburb, that he was asked how he was able to avoid problems with gangs in his neighborhood. An African American student told me of the surprise of many white students in her dorm that she knew who her father was, that she grew up in a two-parent household (with both of her biological parents), and that her family had never lived with her grandmother.

Sometimes the problem is not stereotypical assumptions but unexpected noninteraction, that is, white students frequently treat their black friends from high school like strangers once at college (Sanoff and Minerbrook, 1993). An African American student at a northern New Jersey college told me about a white student who, while not one of her closest friends, had been part of the same social circle in the suburban high school that both had attended in the southern part of the state. Although she had not expected that they would "hang together" in college, she felt hurt that she would be ignored whenever her friend was in the presence of other white students.

Often, interracial difficulties on campus extend beyond student-to-student interaction. Grayson Noley (1991: 110) has found that "minority students may not find the institution to be quite as 'user friendly' " as white students do. Black males in particular are routinely subjected to racially or ethnically based disparate treatment by institutional officials. For example, security guards would ask them for identification to enter their own residence halls, or question them when they were posting flyers on bulletin boards, while permitting others to enter (or post flyers) at will (Elfin and Burke, 1993; Sidel, 1994). I was told by a student who was well known on campus as a member of student government that, to the amazement of everyone sitting in the lobby of his girlfriend's dorm, a guard who had seen him "tons of times before" had stopped him and asked for an ID. A student at another campus told me about the "cafeteria ladies" who flashed their smiles as they served the white students but snarled as he came through the line, particularly if he were talking to a white female student. I have myself witnessed bookstore staff with eyes glued to groups of African American male students, and I have heard complaints from black students and those of Indian subcontinental heritage that staff in college offices interact with them very defensively, as if they were expecting the students to be hostile.

Not all racism on campus is blatant. As Katherine McClelland and Carol Auster (1990) found at a predominantly white liberal arts college (and as may well be the case at many institutions), even where the racial climate is calm on the surface, with students interacting with each other every day without overt conflict, significant tensions hide beneath. Evidence is the social distance between groups. Many point to "the subtle manifestations of attitudes and preconceptions shaped by white race consciousness that materially affect institutional practices and interpersonal relations" on campus (Brown, 1990). For example, African American and other minority students are typically called upon to represent the views of their entire ethnic group (Sanoff and Minerbrook, 1993), like the student at Vassar who was asked by her professor, "So what's the black perspective?" (Sidel, 1994: 165). A Hispanic student told me of having been asked what Puerto Ricans thought about the matter being discussed in class; she took herself out of the spotlight by indicating that she was Dominican. Further, many faculty routinely make it clear to students of color that they do not expect the students to make it through the curriculum (Turner, 1994; Brown, 1990). An African American student majoring in engineering complained to me that she had been told by an Asian instructor that she would probably pass his course but that women do not do well in mathematics and blacks do not get good preparation in high school, and so she would be best advised to change majors. Another African American, majoring in accounting at a different college, told me that he was never called on by the instructor in several accounting classes. A third described comments written on a paper that she had written for a history class essentially expressing the faculty member's surprise that she had done so well. A student who appeared with me on a television program on campus racial climates noted that on her campus, black students knew to avoid certain professors (if they could), because they would never receive a grade higher than C. Darryl Brown (1990: 323) believes that this "daily repetition of subtle racism and subordination in the classroom and on campus can ultimately be, for African Americans, more productive of stress, anxiety, and alienation than even blatant racist acts."

STUDENT PERCEPTIONS

That students are not blind to the state of intergroup relations was readily demonstrated by the emergence of issues of racism, sexism, and homophobia throughout a leadership symposia involving two hundred students at the University of Oklahoma in 1990. However, that such issues were not discussed more than they were during the symposia (Peters, 1992), may indicate a tendency of many students to see intergroup relations as better on their campuses than in society in general. For example, in 1989 the Higher Education Research Institute (HERI) at UCLA undertook a follow-up study of the national sample of college freshmen it had surveyed four years before. They found that only 12 percent of students at four-year institutions thought that "racial discrimination is no longer a problem in America" and that one-quarter saw consider-able racial conflict; the proportion rose to one in three among university students. Focusing on intergroup relations on campus, slightly more than two-thirds thought that "students of different ethnic origins communicate well with one another." Students at Catholic colleges reported the best intergroup communication (82 percent). Consistent with the discussion in an earlier chapter regarding differences in perceptions, African American students were more critical of the campus climate than were other students (seeing more racial tension and lower levels of commitment to diversity), although whites who had entered college expecting to become involved in campus protest, along with white women, also saw higher levels of racial tension.[1] Also congruent with that earlier discussion, white students' perceptions of racial tension increased as the proportion of African American enrollment increased (al-though there was a negative association between white perceptions of racial tension and proportions of Hispanic enrollment); in contrast, minority students saw decreased racial tensions when minority enrollments were higher (Hurtado, 1992).

HERI's findings regarding positive intergroup communication appear to be at odds with the results of other surveys, but some of these are targeted to specific institutions or subsets of students (for example, student leaders). Further, some of the other studies use focus groups or are anecdotal. Also, one cannot discount that responses in surveys may be influenced by recent events; thus, when the surveys were taken may account for some of the differ-ence.

In a poll of 703 students at seven Massachusetts colleges and universities, commissioned by the *Boston Globe* in September 1993, 60 percent of the students reported that racial tensions were present at their institutions; among seniors and minority students the situation seemed worse, with 75 percent indicating the exist-ence of the problem. Forty-nine percent of the 550 editors of student newspapers surveyed by *US News and World Report* the previous spring had reported that race relations on their campuses were fair or poor, and 71 percent (85 percent at the institutions enrolling more than ten thousand students) reported at least one racial incident on their campus in the past year. The student editors at 37 percent of the campuses (53 percent among those at the large campuses) thought that blacks on campus found white students to be "aloof and hostile," while 24 percent (33 percent from the large campuses) said that white students were physically afraid of black students (Elfin and Burke, 1993). Even at the liberal arts college studied by McClelland and Auster (1990), where there had been no interracial confrontations, only 55 percent of the black students and 69 percent of the white students characterized race relations as friendly.

Effect of Hostile Environments

The feelings generated by such campus climates are intense. Said the student who was the target of the incident cited earlier at William Paterson College, "I felt that I was nothing, that I didn't deserve to be getting a college education. . . . No one has the right to make you feel inferior" (D'Aurizio, 1993: A14). A Chapel Hill student lamented, "I can be Mr. UNC . . . and still walk down the street and get called 'nigger'" (Sanoff and Minerbrook, 1993: 64). An African American student who was a resident assistant in her dorm told me that she had been well received by the two black students on her floor and by several of the white students but that most of the white students and the half-dozen Asians on the floor treated her as if she had been hired only to serve the black students and never utilized her as a resource despite her outreach efforts; in fact, they were never more than polite to her. Sanoff and Minerbrook (1993) heard from their focus group of black students at Chapel Hill that the students felt like outsiders. Turner's (1994: 356) study of the University of Minnesota and several smaller, two-year institutions revealed that students of color view their campus as "intimidating, lonely and exclusionary" and often feel themselves like "a guest in someone else's house," never being able to "relax and put our feet up on the table."

Further, stress among African American students is often generated within the racial group. Some students, particularly if they are upper-middle-class or do not use urban black English, are urged to "act more black" (Sanoff and Minerbrook, 1993; Sidel, 1994). While some are called on to be more accepting of the campus climate (McClelland and Auster, 1990), pressures are levied on others to become more militant about it (Sanoff and Minerbrook, 1993). There are also tensions between those who have become extremely politicized and the large numbers who reject identity politics (Sidel, 1994). As one African American student at a New Jersey college said to me, "Some of my friends became real political. They're all upset with me because I'm not. I just want to study and have a good time while I'm here. But I do have to admit that the way things are done around here tempts me to become active."

Asian Americans report similar problems regarding campus climate. A student from Brown spoke of "the scars that the words 'ching' and 'chang' left on my being" (Stern, 1990: 1). A student from the University of Washington reported the strain that came from perceptions of Asian students as "the compromising, sell-out minority . . . all lumped together and stereotyped as rich (Sidel, 1994: 113). A student whose parents came here from Taiwan when she was an infant told me of the pressure that she felt to work hard in school. While she considered the job that helped her to meet her college expenses to be an acceptable break from her studies, she felt guilty whenever she partied during the week with her non-Asian (or as she called them, "regular American") friends. She knew that some of the other Asian American students thought less of her for socializing with whites, while some whites thought that she should be sticking with the Asians.

Hostile environments on college campuses have many outcomes. High school students with options may decline an offer of admission from an institution known to have had recent problems in favor of one that they believe will be more welcoming. The University of Massachusetts learned this lesson when minority enrollments declined substantially in the aftermath of a series of intergroup problems that occurred in 1986–1987 (Oteri and Malaney, 1990). Rutgers University had the same experience in 1995, subsequent to serious racial disquiet prompted by remarks by the university's president, who had wondered publicly whether disadvantaged black students have "the genetic hereditary background" to get higher SAT scores (Nordheimer, 1995b: B5).[2] The number of high-achieving African Americans accepting a $20,000 undergraduate scholarship declined from 130 in 1994 to 86 in 1995. The effect was also felt at the graduate level, as indicated by the statement by the Graduate School of Management's minority affairs coordinator, who said, "I've had a hard time trying to recruit students since February," when the president's remarks became known (Associated Press, 1995b: S8).

Numerous researchers have demonstrated the effect that a feeling of connectedness with the college community has on student retention and graduation rates. They point to the difference in perception among minority and white students regarding the campus climate as an important factor in the outcomes gap that exists between the groups (Crosson, 1988). In their longitudinal study of a large university at which nearly half of the enrollment was composed of students of color with strong SAT profiles, Smedley, Myers, and Harrell (1993) found that the typical, chronic role strains and life events stresses experienced by students were, for minority freshmen, exacerbated by social climate stresses such as racism, interracial and within-group stresses, conflicts between academic expectations and readiness to compete, etc. As a result, their psychological distress substantially exceeded that felt by white freshmen. Further, since these status-related pressures "pose additional demands on students' coping resources," they represent "an additional source of academic vulnerability" (Smedley, Myers, and Harrell, 1993: 446). Similarly, a study undertaken at Princeton (subsequent to the study at that university discussed earlier) revealed that "persistent stereotyping and bias is both a severe impediment to [the] academic success [of minority students], as well as a deterrent to healthy, unforced, unstructured association with members of other races on campus" (Sidel, 1994: 86).

Issues of Self-Segregation

In an effort to make things better for themselves in the face of an unwelcoming atmosphere, minority students have sought refuge in such "supportive niches" as ethnically oriented resource and cultural centers, ethnic studies departments, student service programs intended to provide support to minority students, a specific set of tables in the dining commons or the student union, etc.— places where, as a student at the University of Minnesota said, "you can feel comfortable . . . [and] feel a sense of community" (Turner, 1994: 361–62). The *US News and World Report* survey reported self-segregation by African American students at 75 percent of the institutions, 90 percent at those that enroll more than ten thousand students, and it found that the degree of self-segregation was significantly related to the number of racial incidents that had occurred on the campus (Elfin and Burke, 1993), indicative of the defensive nature of the self-segregation.

Just as many minority students feel hurt by the conditions that they experience on campus, some well-intentioned white students who want to improve intergroup relations feel hurt at the rebuff they perceive in minority self-segregation. This sentiment has been expressed to me by numerous students. One university senior said that she wished that she had been able to get to know better a particular African American woman who had been in many of her major classes. She said that based on their brief conversations before and after class and the comments that each made during class, the two seemed to have a lot in common; however, when the class ended, the two went their separate ways. Once, when the first student asked the second if she wanted to get some coffee, the second declined, saying that she had to meet her friends. A little later, the first student saw the second sitting in "the black part of the cafeteria." She did not ask again, nor did the African American woman ever return the invitation.

For other white students, it is resentment, not hurt, that they feel, either because they do not understand the reasons that prompt minority students to seek these "supportive niches" or because they see a double standard that would frown on white separation but condones minority separation. One Chapel Hill student in the racially integrated focus group conducted by Sanoff and Miner-brook (1993: 64) spoke for many in expressing his belief that African American students are saying by their self-segregation that they are "going to do [their] black thing, and if you don't understand it—and if you can't be with it—screw you." This same sentiment has been stated to me by white students on many campuses. Two are illustrative: "If they want to be with other blacks, why didn't they go to Howard?" "How long do you think that it would take for the administration to close down a white cultural center? We'd be branded *racists* and thrown out, but they can have a black cultural center and even get money from my tuition to help pay for it."[3]

The concern of white students about minority self-segregation must also be placed in the context that many whites (particularly at four-year institutions) question whether most of the minority students are even qualified to be enrolled. Many make the assumption that all minority students are the beneficiaries of special admissions programs, which some see as antimeritocratic. The students in Sanoff and Minerbrook's (1993) white focus group, for example, expressed a deep resentment regarding their perception that lower-qualified blacks were being admitted over higher-achieving whites. A review of editorials in student newspapers undertaken by *US News and World Report* (Elfin and Burke, 1993) indicates a more ambivalent position on the part of white students, who understand the validity of programs that bring to campus students whose family and educational experiences may have handicapped their precollegiate academic performance, but who also object to "unqualified" students in their classrooms. Nevertheless, the outcome is the same: white students think that minorities are there by the grace of policy or for compassion, or for some reason other than achievement or right.

For an element of the campus community, notably the so-called angry white males, institutional policies intended to foster diversity have instead increased alienation. Some of these students, particularly those from modest economic circumstances, see unfair advantage being accorded through preferential programs. As one student—the first in his family to go to college—put it, "You know what affirmative action means to me? It means that even with a 3.9, I have less of a chance of getting into med school than someone with a 3.4 who's lucky enough to be a 'victim'—whatever that means." A student at a large urban university expressed similar emotion. "I guess you could say I'm mad. All they ever do around here is lecture me about how I have to care about people who would blow my brains out if they could get away with it. Nobody gives a damn about me" (Dziech, 1995: B1). Ironically, some of these students criticize their institutions for diversity-related programs despite the fact that some of those programs made their own attendance possible. For example, a low-income student at elite Columbia presumably supported the scholarship program that permitted him to attend but complained that another diversity effort, the university's orientation program, seemed to point an accusing finger at him because there was no one in his background "who was a slave, or Japanese, or affected by the Holocaust" (Sidel, 1994: 139).

The feelings of some white males come out when incidents appear to them to be handled in such as manner as to favor minorities or women. For instance, at the University of Pennsylvania in the early 1990s, anti-harassment policies permitted formal charges to be dropped against accused violators if they agreed to engage in programming on ethnic or sexual harassment. Such an offer was turned down by the student who made the national press for calling several African American women "water buffalos." A conservative columnist for the *Daily Pennsylvanian*, who had written that Martin Luther King should not have a holiday named for him (due to purported adultery and plagiarism), was informed that charges would be dropped against him if he agreed to meet with thirty-one of his accusers. On the other hand, no actions were initiated against the African American students who stole a press run of the student newspaper in protest of the conservative columnist (Bernstein, 1993). Further, even after the campus harassment policy was significantly altered in conformity with legal concerns, the Student Activities Council withdrew eligibility for funding to a campus magazine (that actually received no money from the council) because it published a tasteless piece of satire regarding conditions in Haiti (Shea, 1995a). Episodes such as these leave a campus that believes that it is trying to do the right thing exposed to the anger of white males.

Desire for Positive Relations

Despite an angry attitude, even the white male student from Columbia cited above was hopeful that the college experience would bring people closer together, confident that "people's beliefs will change as they meet different people, see different groups" (Sidel, 1994: 143). This is characteristic of the belief of most students, both majority and minority, that it is important to have positive relationships with people of all races. A 1992 HERI survey of more than 213,000 first-year students from across the nation found that 42 percent believed that the goal of "helping to promote racial understanding" was "essential" or "very important"; only one-third of entering students had held such sentiments the year before, and the previous high of 38 percent had been recorded in 1990 (Collison, 1993). An even higher proportion (76 percent) of the respondents in the *Boston Globe* (1993) survey thought it important to maintain strong relationships with people of other groups. The McClelland and Auster (1990) study of the liberal arts college found a similar openness: all of the black students and nearly all of the white students surveyed said that they would be close friends with a person of the other race and would be roommates of a person of the other race. However, getting there seems a bit lopsided. African American students participating in the integrated focus group at Chapel Hill point out that blacks are the ones who are expected to go the extra mile; those who make friends with whites are expected to come onto the "turf" of the whites, but the whites do not reciprocate with their black friends (Sanoff and Minerbrook, 1993).[4] That reality is in keeping with the conclusion reached by McClelland and Auster (1990) that black students are more willing to associate at intimate levels with whites than whites are with blacks, a finding that they came to as a result of the differences they found regarding acceptability of interracial dating, serious romantic involvement, and marriage.

Yet, while students say that they want friendships with people of other groups, the path is not an easy one; those traveling it can easily be thrown off course. Princeton University found that students from all groups "appear to feel that there are too few 'safe' spaces within the university in which discussions on race can take place among different ethnic and racial groups without accusations, hostility, and recriminations" (Sidel, 1994: 86). In the same vein, Sanoff and Minerbrook's (1993: 61) white focus groups indicated that "discussions about race can be a dicey proposition except among close friends. . . . Nerve endings lie close to the surface and . . . tolerance for dissent is in short supply." Many are afraid to express their opinions for fear of offending or, even worse, being branded a racist.[5] Similarly, 55 percent of those polled by the *Boston Globe* (1993) said that they were consciously being careful about what they said in and out of class so that they would not offend anyone. One African American student told me that outside of discussions that occurred in a few classes, she had not had a conversation about race with anyone white, except in the most superficial manner when the white students "were trying to show how liberal they were." She said that "everyone—black and white— tries to be so 'PC,' that they don't say what is on their minds." That it is difficult to initiate and sustain dialogue on matters of race is apparent from the experience at Iowa State, where, according to the editor of the student newspaper, a campus rally for unity was held in the aftermath of a racial skirmish, "but all the blacks clustered together and all the white clustered together" (Elfin and Burke, 1993: 52).

INSTITUTIONAL LEADERSHIP
AND CAMPUS CLIMATE

A student who participated in the University of Oklahoma symposium series offered that until recently he had paid very little attention to the problems of bigotry and ethnic separation at his university. He said that he assumed "that other people, especially the college administration, would solve the problem" (Peters, 1992: 38). This sentiment in favor of top-down solutions was shared with me by a student at a northern New Jersey college who told me about fighting (usually verbal, but physical on at least one occasion) that sometimes occurred when several white women (who had been drinking) made disparaging remarks to a group of Puerto Rican women; she thought that the administration should do something about it. Slightly more than two out of five college students in HERI's longitudinal survey believed that their administrations are doing something about it; they saw their institutions having placed a priority on creating a diverse, multicultural environment on campus (Hurtado, 1992).

However, many believe that an obvious commitment on only 40 percent of the campuses is insufficient, and even then they see the changes to improve the climate for minority students as being extremely fragile. (Indeed, Mildred Garcia, president of the American Association of University Administrators, sees "a frontal attack on programs that better people of color" [Phillip, 1995: 10].) Some assert that institutional leaders are simply not sensitive to intergroup dynamics on campus, ignoring fundamental issues and not acknowledging the relevance of race except in the most blatant and intentional incidents, often focusing only on offensive behavior by students and slow to react to such conduct by colleagues (Brown, 1990). Further, they contend that higher education leadership has not demonstrated that it is up to the challenge of opening the minds of its students on matters of race and ethnicity. Benjamin Barber (cited in Harvey, 1991: 116) levies sharp criticism at college administrators who "wring hands and rue the social crises of higher education . . . but hesitate when faced with hard decisions and prefer to follow rather than challenge the national mood." As a result, many simply tolerate hateful speech, sending a message of tacit approval in a way that encourages more hateful speech (sometimes from those who had been reluctant to express their views) to the detriment of the targeted groups (Lange, 1990). Official tolerance may even be more harmful in colleges and universities than when it occurs in the broader society, since students are dependent on the institution to provide a community that supports intellectual development and self-definition (Matsuda, 1993). Not only does tolerance appear to contradict the institution's goals of inclusion and knowledge-based behavior as well as the ethics that it espouses, but also there is harm that can have a lifelong effect on all involved: perpetrators learn that expressing their hateful views will be unfettered by authority, and victims view institutional inaction as really taking sides with the haters.

Shelby Steele (1995: 186), on the other hand, sees university leaders as too sensitive, capitulating to the politics of difference as a means of handling their "white guilt." Rather than working with African American students regarding that group's "real needs," they go along, according to Steele, with whatever the black students put on the table, thus creating a pattern of demand and concession. White students become increasingly alienated in such a situation both because they see racial appeasement and because they are typically excluded from the discussions.

Too often, institutional leaders believe or hope that they will never have to respond to incidents of bigotry and, thus, are unprepared to act if an incident occurs, giving the incident an opportunity to mushroom. Further (and sadly), many see ethnic and racial explosions as simply public relations, rather than human relations, problems, and act accordingly (Stern, 1990). This focus on incident rather than climate may be understood if Russell Adams (1994) is correct that today's college and university administrators are not steeped in and do not have a passion for the civil rights tradition; thus, they have a "don't rock the boat" mentality when it comes to human relations. Moral imperative does not appear to be the driving force for college presidents, according to Robert Birnbaum (1988: 448), a former college president. He asserts that "by and large, presidents do not initiate either social or educational movements. They respond to them," spurred to action by political pressure (from within and without, but more from without). Thus, in a period of retreat from enforcement of civil rights legislation and a rethinking of the validity of official efforts focused on race, ethnicity, or gender, it is not surprising that university presidents have not universally risen to the challenge.

The criticisms are not directed solely at administrators; faculty also take a substantial amount of heat. Adams (1994), noting that most colleges take a laissez-faire posture regarding low levels of interaction among students of different racial and ethnic groups, contends that no one is doing a good job at teaching students how to live together. Despite the fact that two of every three students believe that most faculty are sensitive to the issues of minority students (Hurtado, 1992), some argue that this sensitivity is not always translated into action. In fact, William Harvey (1991: 116) asserts that faculty "silence is deafening on the subject of racism." Not only do they fail to speak out against attacks against minority students and the campus climate that spawns hostile acts, but they also do not decisively assure that the curriculum focuses on issues of American race relations and racial history, or denounce racism as an unacceptable base for thought and action. Harvey (1991: 125) contends that "as long as the critical academic responsibility of providing the truth, in its totality to all students is ignored, it is unrealistic to expect any fundamental change in racial intolerance."[6]

These criticisms, while rightly aimed in too many instances, are not totally fair, if levied across the board. A Carnegie Foundation study several years ago indicated that 48 percent of the presidents of research and doctoral granting universities acknowledged that "racial intimidation/harassment" was a moderate-to-major problem on their campuses (Gibbs, 1992). Many presidents and faculty have sought to make things more congenial to positive intergroup relations on their campuses. Some have responded to the rising tide of incivility by establishing speech codes (most of which may have been well intended but find themselves in conflict with the First Amendment, as will be discussed in the next chapter). Many have supported the development of courses that take a multicultural perspective. Some have implemented speakers programs intended to improve intergroup understanding. Some have incurred the wrath of students for "trying to ram diversity down their throats," as one Tufts student reported (Sidel, 1994: 196). Other presidents, for example Thomas Kean (1994: A23), former New Jersey governor and now the president of Drew University, have sought to address issues of hate speech head-on, invoking their role as a moral leader. In response to the incidents of hate speech that have frequented our campuses, Kean says, "I still believe in freedom of speech, but this kind of thing cannot go unanswered. . . . When we allow a demagogue to blame all our troubles on some race or religious group, the hate spreads like some slow poison through the veins of society." Kean told students interested in inviting Louis Farrakhan to speak at Drew that he would not try to stop them, but that he would be among those picketing the event if it were to occur. The students decided not to invite the Nation of Islam leader.

With unsettling social and economic conditions a characteristic of today's America, with students bringing their prejudices to campus, and with many campus leaders taking a reactive rather than proactive posture on intergroup harmony, the fragile calm that existed on campuses has given way to an increasing number of incidents. Some white students have deliberately set out to intimidate minority students, physically and psychologically. Some have simply acted, perhaps unknowingly, in ways that convey prejudicial attitudes. Similarly, campus structures, again perhaps unconsciously, have exhibited institutionally racist features. At the same time, administrations and faculty have not universally focused on the need to improve intergroup harmony.

In response to what they see as a hostile environment, as well as to the political appeal of the extreme (sometimes including members of their own faculty), some African American students have invited speakers to campus whose presence sends a message that cannot be ignored, even when the speech turns out to be milder than had been expected. Others angry about the conditions that they confront on a daily basis and needing to feel group solidarity, may reject the message of the hate speaker but support the legitimacy of the invitation.

CAMPUS CLIMATE AT KEAN COLLEGE

While on many levels (including student government), interactions between black, Hispanic, and white students at Kean have been exemplary, the pilled threads of the national campus climate tapestry are apparent on that campus. Consistent with the belief among college students that intergroup relations are generally better on-campus than elsewhere, one Kean student told the trustee subcommittee (1994: 21) that "there is some tension but it is not obvious here as it is at other places." However, as on other campuses, members of the college community were aware that all was not perfect. In fact, the trustee subcommittee (1994: 19) was told that "there have been problems at the institution before the [Muhammad] speech."

Some of the problems were the result of the clandestine graffiti writers who turned men's room walls into outlets for their racist thoughts. Some were the result of attitudes ranging from coldness to outright hostility from white working-class students who saw their own uncertain futures made more uncertain by upwardly mobile minorities. Thus, in the aftermath of the first Jeffries visit, an African American student told me that Jeffries had released some of the anger that he had felt regarding his campus experience: "There have been people, here, in my face since day one. So what if they are offended by Dr. Jeffries. I don't agree with a lot of what he says, but he should be able to speak. Now they know what it feels like."

The need for "supportive niches," then, was operative at Kean. As has occurred elsewhere, white students at Kean have not readily understood the pattern of self-segregation among minorities. A white woman told me that she had come to Kean because she believed in integration and wanted to have a multiracial, multiethnic college experience. She lamented that a better description of what she found was a set of parallel experiences by race and ethnicity. She had expected that some "Neanderthal" white students would want to remain aloof from persons of other groups, but she never expected that African American or Hispanic students would want to isolate themselves from whites like her who wanted to make America a more cohesive society.

White student resentment over the self-segregation, increasing solidarity, and display of cultural difference by blacks at Kean can be seen in the concern of many whites over a greeting among the African American students: a student walks up to a group of friends, raises his hand, and says, "Hotep"; and the group repeats the greeting in unison. More than one white student (and several white faculty members) told me that they thought that this was intended to be threatening to whites (as *sieg heil* would be threatening to Jews); the black students, on the other hand, said that it was simply an African greeting and nothing to be concerned about. Further, a number of white students claimed to have heard black students late at night yelling from residence hall windows "Kill Whites! " and "Kiwi!", purportedly an acronym for the former epithet. A white female student wrote about the incidents in the campus newspaper, alleging that her complaints to campus police had been ignored. A subsequent investigation by the county prosecutor's office found that there was no reason to believe that such taunts had been occurring, that what the students heard was most likely "skeewee," a call used by the members of one of the college's African American sororities; but there is little question that intergroup sensitivity was high (Trustee Subcommittee, 1994: 20–1).

Pressures on students of color from within their own ethnic groups were also manifest at Kean. For example, a student government leader who is African American told me that after the 1992 Jeffries speech but prior to the Muhammad visit, the extremists tried to get him to join them in disavowing the governance system as racist, and that the more moderate black students attempted to persuade him to attack the extremists (though none were willing to do so themselves). He acknowledged that this might be the price paid by someone in a leadership position; but his own words had fallen on deaf ears.

Regarding leadership from the top, a small, integrated group of students who spoke with me after a board of trustees meeting concurred with one among their number who asked, "Isn't the administration supposed to make sure that race relations are better than this?" With few exceptions, most on campus were upset with the president and the board for what they perceived as a lack of moral leadership since the first Jeffries speech, and for waiting nearly two weeks before issuing a statement in condemnation of Muhammad's remarks. One faculty member, identified in the trustee subcommittee report as a minority, commented, "the main problem is that the administration didn't react immediately." Another member of the college community was paraphrased by the trustee subcommittee as saying, "The response to hate speech needs to be strong and vigorous—this was not apparent in the kind of generic response made by the administration. There was no moral outrage . . . " (Trustee Subcommittee, 1994: 17). Many on the faculty and staff, however, expressed their own moral outrage at Muhammad's speech. An integrated group of faculty and staff circulated a letter calling on the college community to pull together to oppose bigotry of all sorts. The president of the faculty senate told *The New York Times* that the outrage was also shared by 99 percent of the African Americans on campus (Nordheimer, 1993, B6).

There was apparent consensus among the twenty-eight people interviewed by the trustee subcommittee that administrative handling of events after the 1992 speech by Leonard Jeffries was largely responsible for Muhammad coming to campus. Tensions regarding this issue were never resolved, and when the president introduced a new speakers policy at the same time that she announced that Jeffries would return for another speech, some members of the African American community took umbrage. As one student indicated to the subcommittee, the students "were angry that the president . . . associated the guidelines for speakers on campus with the October visit" of Jeffries (Trustee Subcommittee, 1994: 5). Thus, Muhammad was invited.

The trustee subcommittee heard from a number of people regarding identity politics, which had intensified after the 1992 Jeffries speech. Given the status of black-Jewish relations, it is no surprise that a member of the college's minority community felt that "in the past the Jewish/Black alliance was much stronger—obviously not so today" (Trustee Subcommittee, 1994: 19). I heard from both administrators and faculty from both groups that in private conversation they largely agreed with persons from the other group about the nature of the problems and the solutions, but that they were constrained from public agreements or any but the most tepid joint public statements, due to the pressures from those at the extreme. A similar comment was made to the trustee subcommittee (1994: 22) by a minority faculty member who "knows that some individuals have painfully worked through these issues on a one to one basis." I also heard from some who said that they had never before at Kean had to act in ethnic solidarity but now felt compelled to do so for reasons of group consciousness. They were speaking not just of the very real issues of racism and anti-Semitism but of influence in campus politics as well.

Since the Jeffries visit, some have mistakenly sought to marginalize the campus turmoil as simply an argument between a group of Jewish faculty and a group of black students, a theme that some advanced to the trustee subcommittee. There were, however, indications that Jews were the surrogates for all whites. Not only did the debate in the student newspaper, in both commentary pieces and letters, reveal an increasing gap between whites and blacks, but, African American students I had conversations with after board of trustee meetings often used the terms "Jew" and "white" interchangeably.[7]

Identity politics was also evident within the Hispanic community, as Hispanic speakers both from the college community and off-campus came before the board of trustees on several occasions to support the nation's first Latina president of a four-year college. Their message was that the faculty response to the Muhammad speech had been orchestrated to embarrass the president: that several of the most vocal members of the affronted Jewish faculty were also members of the faculty/staff union (which was battling the president over a number of policy and procedural matters), and African American faculty saw an opportunity to replace the president with one of their own. Any previous alliances with the college's African American community appeared to have evaporated; as one faculty member told the trustee subcommittee (1994: 19), "there is polarization between . . . Blacks and Hispanics."

Not only was the identity politics felt on campus, but it was also played out in the media. For example, the head of the Concerned Black Personnel told *The New York Times* that the only objectionable thing that she heard from Muhammad was his use of profanity. An African American columnist from the student newspaper said that he was untroubled by the remark because "they were not directed at me." The assistant director of the Africana Studies program offered that Jews were part of "a white power structure on campus that operates in a covert fashion covered up by the jargon of academia." In the same newspaper account, the head of the Jewish Faculty and Staff Association contended that Kean had "become a hotbed of anti-Semitism in recent years" (Nordheimer, 1993, B6). Further, the Hispanic concern that the college's president was being made a scapegoat was the subject of an op-ed piece in the *Bergen Record*, a major northern New Jersey newspaper (Perez, 1994).

Kean had a set of vulnerabilities to serious intergroup problems: economic uncertainty in the broader society, felt by students both in their futures and in losses in services prompted by budget reductions; intergroup tensions lurking below a calm surface, and a community that did not look deep enough to assure an embracing campus climate; a president who did not exert effective moral leadership; an administration that was unprepared to respond quickly to incidents; a group of minority students who felt increasingly alienated, urged on by a few extremist faculty and advisors; a group of white students who felt that multiculturalism was not working the way that it was intended; intensifying identity politics; and the inability of anyone to pull things back to center once events precipitated previously hidden tensions.

It is reasonable to ask whether circumstances as they unfolded at Kean fostered or retarded discussion. Tensions were brought to the surface—and the boiling pot was kept boiling—by the heat generated by outside speakers who brought messages of hate (and the manner in which those events were handled). Unfortunately but predictably, hate began to reproduce itself; the trustee subcommittee (1994: 19) was told that "more hate groups have come out of the closet" since the Muhammad speech.

Was the college unwise in permitting the controversial speeches to occur? Could Kean have minimized its problems by precluding Muhammad from speaking, since the campus had yet to heal from the visit of Leonard Jeffries nearly two years before? Could the disruptive aftermath of Muhammad's speech have kept Louis Farrakhan from being given a forum? The next chapter addresses the issues that swirl around such questions.

NOTES

1. In their study of students at Grinnell College, Kent McClelland and Christopher Hunter (1992) found a difference in perception among white and minority students regarding what constitutes racial harassment. White students (males more so than females) are more likely to rely on the account of the incident given by the putative harasser than on that of the victim. Further, they are more accepting of apologies (though turned off by justifications or excuses). An example can be seen in the statement of one University of Oklahoma student who referred to a bottle-throwing incident as simply "some guys having a good time, drinking, and having a little fun"; he appeared indignant that feelings focused on the targets (Peters, 1992: 33).

2. President Francis Lawrence's remarks had been made in November 1994 in a meeting with faculty at the university's Camden campus. Word of the conversation reached the main campus in New Brunswick

in February and sparked immediate student protests and calls for Lawrence's resignation (Nordheimer, 1995a). Lawrence quickly and repeatedly apologized for his comments, which he said did not represent his true feelings. Much of the nation learned of the affair during its first week as the result of a sit-in by African American students during half-time of a basketball game between Rutgers and the University of Massachusetts, causing a postponement of the remainder of the game (Carvagal, 1995). While most of the demonstrations against Lawrence included white students, many whites were upset with the protests and began to fling racial epithets at minority students and to make insulting phone calls to the African American students leading the protests. This prompted Lawrence to write an open letter to the university community urging students to end divisive attacks and to come together in the spirit of healing (Associated Press, 1995a). The protests continued throughout the semester.

3. While that student would be correct that most campuses would not appreciate centers or groups focused on whiteness (such as the white student center that Temple University closed down), some institutions do permit groups comprised solely of white students to explore issues related to overcoming white racism. At Temple's crosstown neighbor, the University of Pennsylvania, for example, an African American student was turned away from a meeting of "White Women Against Racism" because she was not white. She was informed by the director of the university's women's center that the group's goal of helping participants deal with their own racism could not be achieved in the presence of persons of color. The African American student felt that it was wrong to deny her the opportunity to join the meeting because of her race (Shea, 1995a). To avoid such situations, colleges and universities should be careful to make distinctions between offerings that may appeal to one group more than another or that prohibit persons not of a specific group; the latter should fall outside of the officially sanctioned realm.

4. These findings seem to be consistent with the 1992 People for the American Way survey of fifteen- to twenty-four-year-olds revealing that 70 percent "had a close personal relationship with a person of another race." At the same time, many still held ethnically based stereotypical perceptions (Collison, 1992).

5. Such a concern is also raised regarding discussions in class. The president (a white female) of the student government at Barnard spoke of the reluctance of many students to express their opinions in class discussions, in papers, or on exams for fear of receiving a lower grade (Sidel, 1994).

6. Stassen (1995) offers insight from the social-psychological literature. First, white faculty, even those who are sympathetic to and suppor-

tive of African American students, have some degree of negative affect toward them as a result of their socialization in American society. Second, the racial attitudes of well-intentioned white faculty are neither totally positive nor negative. Third, how the person views the context plays a critical role in determining how these ambivalent attitudes shape behavior. Thus, it appears that institutional leaders, both in the administration and the faculty, will need to be skillful in motivating faculty colleagues to rise to the challenge that Harvey sets forth.

7. During the 1994–95 academic year, Kean experienced a rash of anti-Semitic graffiti. Even though the college responded by launching an investigation to find the culprit, its spokesperson sought to downplay the matter by unnecessarily characterizing the Jewish group that brought it to the attention of the media as a "very small group in New York City that is very militant" (*The Chronicle of Higher Education*, 1995: A15).

REFERENCES

Adams, Russell. "Hate Speech on Campus." Paper presented at the QEM Biannual Conference. Washington, DC, July 15, 1994.

Anti-Defamation League. "ADL Special Summary Report: 1994 Audit of Anti-Semitic Incidents, Overview." New York: Anti-Defamation League, 1995.

Associated Press. "At Rutgers, Bias Incidents Follow Protests over President's Remarks." *Philadelphia Inquirer*. February 23, 1995, p. S7.

————. "Rutgers Minority Recruiting Down," *Philadelphia Inquirer*. May 29, 1995, p. S8.

Bernstein, Richard. "Play Penn." *The New Republic* v. 209 n. 5 (August 2, 1993), pp. 16–19.

Birnbaum, Robert. "Administrative Commitments and Minority Enrollments: College Presidents' Goals for Quality and Access." *The Review of Higher Education* v. 11 n. 4 (Summer 1988), pp. 435–457.

Brown, Darryl. "Racism and Race Relations in the University." *Virginia Law Review* v. 76 (1990), pp. 295–335.

Carvagal, Doreen. "Protest against President Halts Basketball Game at Rutgers." *The New York Times*. February 8, 1995, p. B1.

Collison, Michelle N.-K. "Young People Found Pessimistic about Relations between Races." *The Chronicle of Higher Education*. March 25, 1992, pp. A1, A32.

————. "Survey Finds Many Freshmen Hope to Further Racial Understanding." *The Chronicle of Higher Education*. January 13, 1993, pp. A29, A32.

Crosson, Patricia H. "Four-Year College and University Environments for Minority Degree Achievement." *The Review of Higher Education* v. 11 n. 4 (Summer 1988), pp. 365–382.

D'Aurizio, Elaine. "Campus Speech Codes, Policing Bias, Many NJ Colleges Try to Control Language of Hate." *Bergen Record.* June, 2, 1993, pp. A1, A14.

Dziech, Billie Wright. "Coping with the Alienation of White Male Students." *The Chronicle of Higher Education.* January 13, 1995, pp. B1–B2.

Editors of the *Philadelphia Inquirer.* "Confederate Flag Dispute Widens at U. of Delaware." *Philadelphia Inquirer.* May 8, 1995, p. B2.

Editors of the *Boston Globe.* "Mass. Students Upbeat amid Sobering Problems." *Boston Globe.* September 12, 1993.

Editors of *The Chronicle of Higher Education.* "'In' Box." *The Chronicle of Higher Education.* January 13, 1995a, p. A15.

Elfin, Mel and Sarah Burke. "Race on Campus." *US News and World Report.* April 19, 1993, pp. 52–56.

Florio, Gwen. "Campus Polarized after Confederate-flag Flap." *Philadelphia Inquirer.* November 28, 1994, pp. S1, S9.

Gibbs, Annette. *Reconciling Rights and Responsibilities of Colleges and Students: Offensive Speech, Assembly, Drug Testing and Safety; ASHE-ERIC Higher Education Research Report No. 5.* Washington, DC: The George Washington University, 1992.

Harvey, William B. "Faculty Responsibility and Tolerance." *Thought and Action, the NEA Higher Education Journal* v. 7 n. 2 (Fall 1991), pp. 115–136.

Hurtado, Sylvia. "The Campus Racial Climate, Contexts of Conflict." *Journal of Higher Education* v. 63 n. 5 (September/October 1992), pp. 539–569.

Jones, Charles H. "Equality, Dignity and Harm: The Constitutionality of Regulating American Campus Ethnoviolence." *Wayne Law Review* v. 37 (1991), pp. 1383–1432.

Kean, Thomas. "The Way to Handle Hatemongers, Confront Their Ideas Forcefully." *Bergen Record.* May 22, 1994, p. A23.

Lange, Ellen E. "Racist Speech on Campus: A Title VII Solution to a First Amendment Problem." *Southern California Law Review* v. 64 (1990), pp. 105–134.

Matsuda, Mari J. "Public Response to Racist Speech: Considering the Victim's Story." *Words That Wound: Critical Race Theory, Assaultive Speech and the First Amendment,* ed. Mari J. Matsuda, Charles R. Lawrence, III, Richard Delgado, and Kimberle Williams Crenshaw. Boulder, CO: Westview Press, 1993, pp. 133–136.

McClelland, Katherine E. and Carol J. Auster. "Public Platitudes and Hidden Tensions, Racial Climates at Predominantly White Liberal Arts Colleges." *Journal of Higher Education* v. 61 n. 6 (November/December 1990), pp. 607–642.

McClelland, Kent and Christopher Hunter. "The Perceived Seriousness of Racial Harassment." *Social Problems* v. 39 n. 1 (February 1992), pp. 92–107.

Monaghan, Peter. "Charges of Bias against Whites Erupt at Evergreen State Branch." *The Chronicle of Higher Education*. February 24, 1995, p. A38.

Nordheimer, Jon. "Divided by Diatribe, College Speech Ignites Furor over Race." *The New York Times*. December 29, 1993, pp. B1, B6.

———. "At Rally Students Seek Resignation of Rutgers President." *The New York Times*. February 2, 1995a, p. B4.

———. "Rutgers Leader Disavows Linking Race and Ability." *The New York Times*. February 1, 1995b, p. B5.

Noley, Grayson. "Fear, Higher Education and Change." *Thought and Action, the NEA Higher Education Journal* v. 7 n. 2 (Fall 1991), pp. 105–114.

Oteri, Lisa A. and Gary D. Malaney. "Racism on Campus—The Negative Impact on Enrollment." *College and University* v. 65 n. 3. (Spring 1990), pp. 213–226.

Perez, Miguel. "In Search of a Scapegoat." *Bergen Record*. March 9, 1994, p. A24.

Peters, Ronald M., Jr. *The Next Generation, Dialogues between Leaders and Students*. Norman, OK: University of Oklahoma Press, 1992.

Phillip, Mary-Christine. "Fiscal Reality Hits Higher Education's Ivory Tower . . . Hard." *Black Issues in Higher Education* v. 11 n. 26 (February 23, 1995), pp. 8–14.

Sanoff, Alvin P. and Scott Minerbrook and Associates. "Students Talk about Race, at Chapel Hill, N.C. Racial Tension Runs High. A Special Report." *US News and World Report*. April 19, 1993, pp. 57–64.

Shea, Christopher. "Sore Relations Again at Penn." *The Chronicle of Higher Education*. March 24, 1995a, pp. A39–A40.

Sidel, Ruth. *Battling Bias, The Struggle for Identity and Community on College Campuses*. New York: Viking, 1994.

Smedley, Brian D., Hector F. Myers, and Shelly P. Harrell. "Minority Status Stresses and the College Adjustment of Ethnic Minority Freshmen." *Journal of Higher Education* v. 64 n. 4 (July/August, 1993), pp. 434–452.

Stassen, Martha L.A. "White Faculty Members and Racial Diversity: A Theory and Its Implications." *The Review of Higher Education* v. 18 n. 4 (Summer 1995), pp. 361–391.

Steele, Shelby. "The Recoloring of Campus Life: Student Racism, Academic Pluralism and the End of a Dream." *Campus Wars: Multiculturalism and the Politics of Difference*, ed. John Arthur and Amy Shapiro. Boulder, CO: Westview Press, 1995, pp. 176–187.

Stern, Kenneth S. *Bigotry on Campus: A Planned Response*. New York: American Jewish Committee, 1990.

Trustee Subcommittee (Patricia Weston Rivera, Chair). *Report of the Subcommittee*. Union, NJ: Kean College Board of Trustees, June 1994.

Turner, Caroline Sotello Viernes. "Guests in Someone Else's House: Students of Color." *The Review of Higher Education* v. 17 n. 4 (Summer 1994), pp. 355–370.

Chapter 5

Regulating Speech on Campus

Colleges and universities face an existential crisis when they are forced to grapple with issues of hate speech and other verbally or symbolically expressed intolerance. The issues came directly to the fore at Kean College after Khalid Abdul Muhammad's November 1993 speech. The campus (and the rest of the New Jersey higher education community) was split between those who thought Muhammad should have been prevented from speaking; those who disagreed with what he said but who would defend to the death his right to say it; those who believed that he should have been required to present his views in a debate format that would subject them to immediate scrutiny; and those who supported both his unabridged right to speak and also his views. That there was no consensus view is understandable, given the historic tension between the First and Fourteenth Amendments and the racial divisions in our society.

Deeply ingrained in higher education is the principle of academic freedom, which incorporates the concepts of freedom of inquiry and freedom of expression. As John Seigenthaler (1993: 48) of the Vanderbilt University's Freedom Forum First Amendment Center posits, "the academy should be an open forum—a place where learning [is] fostered and knowledge revered, but where ignorant, unpleasant, objectionable, offensive points of view might be exposed for what they [are], or rejected in debate for what they [are], but never suppressed or banned or sanctioned punitively." At public institutions, academic freedom rests on the First Amendment protection of freedom of speech. While not necessarily a legal requirement in the independent sector, the principle is strong also in most private institutions, where it is supported by a long tradition of commitment to the value of the inquiring mind. Indeed, the centrality of freedom of expression to higher education has been recognized by the Supreme Court, in *Sweeney v. New Hampshire*, 354 U.S. 234 (1957). Thus, the intellectual reaction to an incident of hateful speech on campus is that, distasteful as it may be, it falls under the protection of academic freedom or the First Amendment.

The gut reaction is often very different, since most on college campuses view hate speech as antithetical to the goals of higher education and the mission of their institutions. As Andrew Altman (1995) states, the slurs and epithets that constitute hate speech involve treating someone as a moral subordinate, taking their interests and lives as inherently less valuable than those who belong to the speaker's group. This runs counter to the idea of people as free and equal, and, according to Altman, it is one of the primary wrongs that has prevented Western democracies from living up to their ideals. In fact, the argument can be made that a college or university that fails to protect its students from being treated as moral subordinates (based on such characteristics as their race, ethnicity, religion, gender, etc.) is denying them equal protection under the law and is thereby violating the Fourteenth Amendment of the Constitution.

Kean College professor Michael Israel (1994) perceives a no-win situation in which colleges and universities often find themselves: by ignoring hate speech they leave it uncontradicted and its victims feeling abandoned, but by responding to it they seemingly give it legitimacy as a viewpoint worthy of debate. Others, including Lawrence (1990: 436), see a broader dilemma for colleges seeking to deal with hate speech: "By framing the debate as we have—as one in which the liberty of free speech is in conflict with the elimination of racism—we have advanced the cause of racial oppression and have placed the bigot on the moral high ground, fanning the flames of racism." Thus, higher education—along with the rest of American society—must grapple with the clash between civil liberties and civil rights. As Richard Delgado (1991) notes, this is a predicament that is embedded in our society, since we both want and fear liberty and equality.

LIMITATIONS ON FREE SPEECH:
INVITED SPEAKERS

In the aftermath of Khalid Abdul Muhammad's November 1993 speech, Kean College found itself in a maelstrom. After what many felt was an unconscionable ten days without speaking out, President Elsa Gomez learned that there was little, if anything, that she could say to assuage those who felt maligned by Muhammad or to assure others that her condemnation of his remarks was not intended to have a chilling effect on free speech on campus.

As she considered how to restore calm to her campus, state-level policy makers pondered initiatives that might be appropriate for future occasions. The chairman of the New Jersey State Board of Higher Education, Stephen B. Wiley, himself a prominent attorney, had a member of his law firm research the law concerning campus speech. He was informed that Muhammad and others with similar messages of hate could not be barred from speaking at public campuses and perhaps not from private colleges, nor could they be required to deliver their remarks in a debate-like setting (Bren, 1993). Some months later, faced with the prospect of a return visit by Muhammad or his former employer, Louis Farrakhan, President Gomez asked the state's attorney general whether any content-based restrictions can be imposed on speakers invited by college-affiliated groups. She was told that while student-sponsored speaking engagements can be regulated "so that campus activity is not disrupted and reasonable college rules are followed, . . . [the rules] may not infringe upon first amendment rights by restricting speakers because of the content of the expected speech" (Poritz and Brown, 1994). The legal advisories to Wiley and Gomez were both in keeping with a large body of First Amendment judicial findings.

The First Amendment states that "Congress shall make no law . . . abridging the freedom of speech." Subsequent to the Civil War, this protection against governmental intrusion into the area of free expression was extended to the state (and thus local) level by the Fourteenth Amendment. Freedom of speech is one of America's defining characteristics. It is intended to be a strong, anti-majoritarian protection. Constitutional scholar Gerald Gunther (1995: 112–3) cites the opinions of famed Supreme Court Justices to demonstrate that protecting the right of the minority to express its views is fundamental to our democracy. Oliver Wendell Holmes, for example, held that "if there is any principle of the Constitution that more imperatively calls for attachment than any other it is the principle of free thought—not free thought for those who agree with us but freedom for the thought that we hate." Louis D. Brandeis Branders stated that the First Amendment rests on a belief "in the power of reason as applied through public discussion," thus barring "silence coerced by law—the argument of force in its worst form." Contemporaries William O. Douglas and John Marshall Harlan also spoke eloquently about the First Amendment; the former stated that a "function of free speech [is] to invite dispute. . . . Speech is often provocative and challenging. That is why freedom of speech [is ordinarily] protected against censorship or punishment." The latter noted both "that the air at times [seeming] filled with verbal cacophony is . . . not a sign of weakness but of strength," and that "we cannot indulge in the facile assumption that one can forbid particular words without also running the substantial risk of suppressing ideas in the process."

Defamation, Obscenity, and Incitement

Nevertheless, the Supreme Court has acted to limit speech in certain instances—defamation, obscenity, incitement to lawlessness, and "fighting words" (*Perspective*, 1991).[1] But even those restrictions are rather narrow. In *Cantwell v. Connecticut*, 310 U.S. 296 (1940), a religious freedom case, the Court held that the use of "epithets or personal abuse is not . . . safeguarded by the Constitution." It revisited the matter a decade later in response to an Illinois law that sought to punish speech that "portrays depravity, criminality, unchastity, or lack of virtue in a class of citizens of any race, color, creed, or religion" (*Beauharnais v. Illinois*, 343 U.S. 250 [1952]). In that case, the Court upheld the conviction of a man arrested for distributing literature calling on Chicago's white population to unite against the "rapes, robberies, knives, guns and marijuana of the negro." Justice Felix Frankfurter's opinion ruled that since "an utterance directed at an individual may be the object of criminal sanctions we cannot deny to a state power to punish the same utterance directed at a defined group." Beauharnais's pamphlet fell outside of political speech because his characterizations of African Americans amounted to group defamation. However, this concept of anti-defamation protection was narrowed in *Milkovich v. Lorain Journal Co.*, 497 U.S. 1 (1990), a case in which a newspaper was sued by an individual whom the paper had accused of perjury. The Court ruled that a reasonable fact-finder must be able to conclude that the defamatory statements imply "an assertion of fact" and are not simply "'rhetorical hyperbole' which has traditionally added much to the discourse of the Nation."

Few would claim that racial, ethnic, religious, and gender stereo-typing has added anything of a positive nature to our national discourse. Most such stereotyping is clearly defamatory to the targeted group (e.g., that Jews are greedy; Italians are gangsters; Mexicans are lazy; women are weaklings) and is thought by those who use it to be factual. However, if legally challenged, it could probably be argued to be "rhetorical hyperbole." Thus, it is unlikely that a defamation action against such expressions would be suc-cessful in today's world, or that a Khalid Abdul Muhammad could be constrained from calling Jews "murderer[s] . . . from the beginning," as he did at Kean, despite the defamatory nature of the remark.

There are those who contend that racially or ethnically offensive material is also obscene. Indeed, there were many in the Kean College community who felt that certain books (for example, The Nation of Islam's *The Secret Relationship between Blacks and Jews*) that were sold at speeches or ethnically related cultural events were not simply factually incorrect and bad scholarship but defamatory and obscene, and thus should be banned. Here, the fate of an Indianapolis ordinance that banned the sale of pornographic ma-terial that degrades women is instructive. In *American Booksellers Association, Inc. v. Hudnut*, 598 F. Supp. 1316 (S.D. Ind, 1984), a federal judge, affirmed by the Supreme Court (aff'd. mem., 475 U.S. 1001 [1986]), concluded that "in seeking to ban speech directed to the general public because it is highly offensive to many, the Ordinance violates established . . . precedents which preclude the banning of speech simply because its contents may be socially or politically offensive to the majority."

Regarding incitement to lawlessness, what may appear to most people as fitting that definition may not qualify for restriction. In *Brandenburg v. Ohio*, 395 U.S. 444 (1969), the Court, in unanimously overturning the conviction of a member of the Ku Klux Klan whose anti-black, anti-Semitic speech advocated illegal actions, deter-mined that a state may not forbid "advocacy of the use of force or of law violation except where such advocacy is directed to inciting or producing imminent lawless action and is likely to incite or produce such action." Muhammad advocated at Kean College the unquestionably illegal act of mass murder—i.e., that white South Africans should be given twenty-four hours to get out of town or "we kill everything white that ain't right," and that wheelchair bound South African whites should be pushed off cliffs. In this view, such statements cannot be restricted (nor are they actionable) unless they have the immediate effect of actually inciting listeners to lawless action—which they did not, in fact, do.

Could Muhammad have been precluded from speaking at Kean in the first place on the basis of earlier speeches in a similar vein advocating illegal activity, or could future appearances be prohibited there or elsewhere on the basis of his call for lawless behavior at Kean? *Molpus v. Fortune*, 432 F. 2d. 916 (5th Cir. 1970), suggests not. In that instance, students at a state university had been prohibited from inviting a speaker who had previously disrupted a faculty meeting and had threatened a campus police officer during a student protest. The Fifth Circuit Court of Appeals upheld the order of a federal district court judge who ruled that the university could not bar the speaker, based on the speaker's earlier remarks and actions, unless there appeared to be a reasonable probability that illegal action would result from the proposed appearance; lacking such probability, the speaker did not constitute a clear and present danger to the university and could not be banned.

Fighting Words

Much of the current focus on how speech may be legally restricted utilizes the "fighting words" doctrine of *Chaplinsky v. New Hampshire*, 315 U.S. 568 (1942). At issue in that case was whether calling someone "a goddamned racketeer" and "a damned fascist" was protected or actionable speech. By today's standards those are rather mild insults, but for the times they were quite provocative. The Court held that there is no constitutional safeguard for words that "by their very utterance inflict injury or tend to incite an immediate breach of the peace." Nevertheless, in all of the years since the *Chaplinsky* ruling, the Court has not used the "fighting words" principle to uphold a conviction in which speech was at issue. In fact, subsequent decisions have narrowed the doctrine's reach. During the emotion-charged days of the Vietnam War, the Burger Court ruled in *Cohen v. California*, 403 U.S. 15 (1971), that to fall outside of constitutionally protected territory offensive words must be directed specifically at an individual. In that case, the offending "fuck the draft" epithet could not be taken as a personal insult, since it was a general statement regarding public policy, not an insult aimed at anyone in particular. The next year, in *Gooding v. Wilson*, 405 U.S. 578 (1972), the Court ruled in favor of a black war protester who called the police officer who arrested him a "white son of a bitch"; the insult did not constitute "fighting words," since offending words must be contextually evaluated and there is no constitutional bar to language that might be expected in a given circumstance. Thus, since during his speech at Kean Muhammad did not stand in anyone's face, directing to an individual a remark that would ordinarily provoke an immediate violent response, there were no "fighting words." Further, since he set the context for his speech, at the outset by stating, "It's going to be a rough ride. . . . I didn't come here to take no prisoners," audience members who might have been provoked to violent reaction had ample warning of what was coming and could have chosen to leave.

Another restriction to the "fighting words" doctrine arose in *R.A.V. v. St. Paul, Minnesota*, 505 U.S. 377, 112 S.Ct. 2538 (1992), a symbolic-speech case in which a teenager was arrested for burning a cross on the lawn of an African American family that had moved into a previously all-white neighborhood. (Prior to the cross incident, the tires on the family's car had been slashed, its windows had been broken, and the family had been subjected to a series of racial epithets.) R.A.V. was charged with violating a St. Paul city ordinance that prohibited the display on public or private property of any symbol (such as a swastika or a burning cross) that "arouses anger, alarm, or resentment in others on the basis of race, color, creed, religion, or gender." The Minnesota Supreme Court held that the burning of a cross was "deplorable conduct that the City of St. Paul may without question prohibit. The burning of the cross is itself an unmistakable symbol of violence and hatred based on virulent notions of racial supremacy." However, the U.S. high court held that the ordinance was invalid since it targeted certain, but not all, "fighting words" (only those that dealt with race, color, creed, religion, or gender). Speaking for the Court, Justice Antonin

Scalia stated that "the government may not regulate use based on hostility—or favoritism—towards the underlying message expressed," and that "the First Amendment does not permit . . . special prohibitions on those speakers who express views on disfavored subjects." He suggested that the city could ban cross burnings through laws against arson, property damage, and terrorism, but not through content-based speech prohibitions.

The *R.A.V.* ruling has proven to be rather controversial, since the cross burning was not a symbolic speech act that occurred in a public forum or on property owned by the cross burner but a terrorist act that occurred on property owned by the victim. Matsuda and Lawrence (1993), among others, find it unfathomable that local governments can prohibit littering or arson on people's lawns but may not criminalize racially motivated acts such as burning a cross on someone's lawn. They lament that the Court's decision, without due regard for history or context, elevates cross burners to the level of an unpopular minority that must be defended against the power of the state.

It is not easy to meet the "fighting words" standard—that is, to fall outside of constitutional protection by having made an insulting statement. Nadine Strossen (1990: 524) of the American Civil Liberties Union posits that to meet the "fighting words" criteria, the language in question: "(1) must constitute a personally abusive epithet, (2) must be addressed in a face-to-face manner, (3) must be directed to a specific individual, and (4) must be uttered under circumstances that the words have a direct tendency to cause an immediate violent response by the average recipient." The latter is a particularly difficult standard to meet in today's world, since the average recipient of a slur tends to suffer in silence or utter an offensive retort rather than react violently. Further, given *R.A.V.*, any rule that seeks to apply the "fighting words" doctrine as a means to control speech must be generally stated, not defined specifically in relation to race, color, creed, religion, or gender.

Time, Place, and Manner

Finally, we come to the question of whether a college such as Kean must provide a forum for any of its student groups or others in the college community who wish to host speakers representing organizations or espousing viewpoints that are contrary to the mission and goals of the institution. Since it was his appearance at Kean that brought Muhammad to national prominence, few on the campus (including most of the students who voted to sponsor the event) knew how vitriolic he would be.² But if the college had known how divisive Muhammad's speech would be and how long and deeply the campus, both as a public entity and as a community of scholars, would suffer, could the event have been prohibited? Several Court rulings lead to a negative conclusion.

In *Healy v. James*, 408 U.S. 169 (1972), Central Connecticut State College was required to recognize a student organization affiliated with Students for a Democratic Society, despite the fact that the college president believed that the organization's philosophy was contrary to the important institutional principle of academic freedom. The Court concluded that there was no compelling reason why "First Amendment protections should apply with less force on college campuses than in the community at large." The following year, in keeping with the *Healy* finding that the institution "has the inherent power to promulgate rules and regulations . . . [and to] protect itself and its property," the Court held that the University of Missouri could promulgate reasonable rules regarding the time, place, and manner in which speech could be exercised but could not prohibit speech based on its content. That case, *Papish v. Board of Curators*, 410 U.S. 667 (1973), concerned an attempt to stop the distribution of a student newspaper that contained an obscene headline. As the federal judge stated in *Auburn Alliance for Peace and Justice v. Martin*, 684 F. Supp. 1077 (M.D. Ala. 1988), such rules permit institutions to prohibit "a speech or demonstration in the reading room of the library." Similarly, "a public university does not violate the First Amendment when it takes reasonable steps to maintain an atmosphere conducive to study and learning by designating the time, place, and manner of verbal and especially non-verbal expression" [*Shelton v. Trustees of Indiana University*, 891 F. 2d. 165 (7th Cir. 1989)]. However, in accordance with *Clark v. Community for Creative Non-Violence*, 468 U.S. 288 (1984), time, place, and manner restrictions cannot be a subterfuge for barring the speech; institutional policies must "leave open ample alternative channels for communication of the information."

Widmar v. Vincent, 454 U.S. 263 (1981), a case involving another campus of the University of Missouri, produced a ruling by the Court that although universities do not need to recognize student organizations or to permit them a forum, once they do, they may not make determinations with regard to the viewpoint of the organization. At issue in *Widmar* was whether it was proper to deny the use of university facilities to a religiously affiliated student organization on the basis of separation of church and state. The Court held that "having created a forum generally open to student groups, a state university may not practice content-based exclusion of religious speech when that exclusion is not narrowly drawn to achieve a state interest."

This stream of cases indicates that institutions like Kean College need not recognize any given campus organization, nor permit any that it does sanction to invite speakers to campus. However, if it provides official recognition to one, it must recognize all that comply with its rules regarding campus organizations, without reference to viewpoint. Further, if it permits any organization to invite speakers, it must permit all to do so, irrespective of the viewpoint of the organization or the content of the particular speech. It may, however, have rules regarding the time, place, and manner of such events, so long as the rules are uniformly enforced and do not abridge First Amendment freedoms. Thus, it is clear that it is not possible for a public college to bar a speaker such as Khalid Abdul Muhammad, even if it believes that the message is contrary to the mission and goals of the institution and even if it has reason to believe that it would suffer serious emotional disruption and sustained intergroup hostility in the aftermath.[3]

CAMPUS SPEECH CODES

It is not only outside speakers who have stirred emotions on college campuses. The increasing (or at least more open) intergroup insensitivity and intolerance that characterizes most institutions, as well as the all-too-frequent acts of ethnoviolence, produce an atmosphere discomforting to members of targeted groups and to those who empathize with them. In the aftermath of offensive or intolerant incidents, a number of colleges and universities have adopted regulations that they believed would protect the rights of those being victimized, prevent further acts from occurring, and result in a positive learning environment for all members of the campus community. Oldaker (1994) found that over a five-year period more than two hundred colleges and universities adopted anti–hate crime regulations to combat verbal and physical assaults in residence halls. Michael Olivas (1992) surveyed university attorneys at a public and a private institution in each state as well as in the District of Columbia and Puerto Rico; additionally, he reviewed policies from fifty other colleges and universities. He found that nineteen (including multi-institutional systems such as the University of California) had racial harassment policies, only five of which existed prior to 1988. Charles Jones (1991) cites a study by Henry McGee, who examined the racial harassment policies of twenty public and twenty private colleges and universities, finding a wide range of policy positions—all the way from the protection of free expression as an overriding value to the prohibition of conduct that "annoys" another person or group.

From their inception, these rules, commonly referred to as "campus speech codes," have been extremely controversial. Some observers are concerned that they are a throwback to the days when most students were under the age of majority (at that time, twenty-one years old) and colleges and universities acted *in loco parentis* to regulate student behavior (Delgado 1991). Some lament that victims "have given up on the option of dealing with the problem [of intolerance] through debate as simplistic and unworkable," thus such a solution could have the effect of incubating hate speech and prejudice by pushing them underground (Seigenthaler, 1993: 38). There are distributive justice concerns: how to assure that rules intended to protect targeted groups do not find their greatest use *against* those groups (Hodulik 1991). There are apprehensions regarding arbitrary enforcement (Strossen 1990). There are also legitimate worries regarding what the rules can reasonably accomplish and how to assure that members of the community know what is and is not covered. One of the major concerns continues to be the chilling effect that such codes might have on academic discourse. The debate often comes down to an issue of how to balance the protections of the First Amendment with those of the Fourteenth, or of which should prevail—civil liberties or civil rights. Before discussing the apparent conflict among constitutional protections (which is the heart of the matter), an examination of several prominent campus speech code cases is useful.

The first, *Doe v. University of Michigan*, 721 F. Supp. 852 (E.D. Mich. 1989), had its origin in a policy that arose in response to a series of well publicized incidents that rocked the Ann Arbor campus in 1986 and 1987; they included the distribution of flyers declaring "open season" on blacks (referring to them as "saucer lips, porch monkeys, and jigaboos"), the broadcast of racist jokes on the student radio station, and the display of Ku Klux Klan regalia in a residence hall window during a demonstration held in protest of the aforementioned incidents. Harold Shapiro, the university's president at the time, sought to quell the disquiet by issuing a statement that expressed outrage over the incidents, "reaffirming the University's commitment to maintaining a racially, ethnically, and culturally diverse campus" (Siegel, 1990: 58). However, his words did not assure members of the legislature, who held a hearing at which forty-eight people testified their disapproval of how the university was handling the racially tense situation. In the aftermath of two formidable threats—the first to reduce state support (which came from the chair of the legislative committee that prepares higher education budgets), the second by a campus group openly considering initiating a class action suit that would force the university to improve intergroup atmosphere on campus—the university implemented a six-point plan that included a racial harassment policy (Siegel, 1990).

The 1988 policy divided the university into three speech zones: public areas, where only physical acts would be restricted; residence halls, where room leases would govern speech and conduct, and educational facilities (including libraries), where the university sought to regulate speech that either "stigmatizes or victimizes an individual on the basis of race, ethnicity, religion, sex, sexual orientation, creed, national origin, ancestry, age, marital status, handicap, or Vietnam-era veteran status," or that resulted in "a hostile learning environment." In order to give guidance to the university community, the administration promulgated a booklet describing the intentions of the policy. *What Students Should Know about Discriminatory Harassment by Students in the University Environment* included a number of illustrations of potential policy violations. Some were noncontroversial, such as "Racist graffiti written on the door of an Asian student's study carrel," or "A black student is confronted and racially insulted by two white students in a cafeteria." Others left room for considerable disagreement as to whether they should be actionable (even though all might rather that they not occur); for example, "Your student organization sponsors entertainment that includes a comedian who slurs Hispanics," thus making the group guilty of harassment; or "a male student makes remarks in class like 'Women just aren't as good in this field as men,' thus creating a hostile learning atmosphere as female classmates." (Although the interpretive statement was subsequently withdrawn by the university as containing "inaccuracies," it played an important role in the court case.)

Some of the concerns cited earlier regarding speech codes became real when the University of Michigan sought to implement its policy. For example, the fear that such policies might tend to punish those in whose name it was established proved to be the case, as more than twenty whites charged blacks with racist speech; the only two times that sanctions were invoked against racist speech involved speech by or on behalf of African Americans (Strossen 1990). On several occasions, actions were taken against students for remarks that they made in class: a student in a social-work class was punished for stating that he thought homosexuality to be a disease that could be psychologically treated; a business student was sanctioned for reading a homophobic limerick as part of a public speaking exercise; a dental student had charges brought against him by a faculty member for a saying that he understood that "minorities had a difficult time in the course and that . . . they were not treated fairly."

The speech code was challenged by a psychology graduate student who contended that it had a chilling effect on his ability to explore and to discuss in the classroom setting his "controversial theories positing biologically-based differences between sexes and races [which] might be perceived as 'sexist' and 'racist' by some students" and thus be actionable under the policy. He told the federal district court that "some arguments will no longer be tolerated. Rather than encouraging her maturing students to question each other's beliefs . . . the University has decided that it must protect its students from what it considers to be 'unenlightened' ideas." Federal Judge Avern Cohen concurred with his position and invalidated the policy. While acknowledging that the university had a need and right to address the issue of intergroup incivility, the judge felt that its policy went too far by prohibiting speech in instances of "disagree[ment] with the ideas or messages sought to be conveyed." He was concerned that there had been no consideration, for example, of "the possibility that the limerick [cited above] was protected speech." This reach into the classroom was improper, thus rendering the policy "overbroad."

Judge Cohen also found Michigan's speech code to be impermissibly vague, that it did not "give adequate warning of the conduct which is to be prohibited and . . . set out explicit standards for those who apply it." The policy's use of words such as "stigmatize" and "victimize," which "are general and elude precise definition," lead to confusion on the part of students regarding what is meant and what would cause such a condition. Thus, there was no way for a student to determine what was sanctionable speech and what was protected speech. "The terms of the Policy were so vague that its enforcement would violate the [Constitution's] due process clause." Even if there were common understanding, the court held, "the fact that a statement may victimize or stigmatize an individual does not, in and of itself, strip it of protection under the accepted First Amendment tests."

Thus according to *Doe*, a campus speech policy may be neither overbroad nor vague. However, the judge did not empty the university's arsenal of anti-intolerance measures, citing precedents permitting the regulation of the time, place, and manner of speech within constitutionally acceptable boundaries, the application of sanctions against discriminatory conduct, and the ability to prohibit "racial and ethnic epithets, slurs and insults" if they fit into the categories of "fighting words," inciteful speech, and other constitutionally unshielded categories. As Charles Jones (1991) indicates, the decision has three important implications for institutions seeking to mount a constitutionally permissible regulation: first, policies must be carefully drafted to overcome the vagueness problem; second, policies need to be clear as to whether guilt is to be measured by intent alone or in combination with the severity of the offending conduct, and; third, policies may incorporate the concept, left untouched by the court, of differential speech zones on campus.

The University of Wisconsin sought to mount a campus speech policy that it believed would meet these criteria. It, too, was spurred to action by a series of high-profile racial incidents, many of them initiated by student fraternities. For example, one fraternity had advertised its "Fiji Island Party" by placing a large caricature of a black man on its front lawn. Another fraternity party had served watermelon punch and fried chicken in a "Harlem room."

Also, an African Languages and Literature class had been disrupted by members of another fraternity who entered the room uttering racial epithets. The policy adopted by the Board of Regents in June 1989 was narrowly drawn to conform to the requirements of the "fighting words" doctrine and to apply to nonacademic situations only. Sanctions would be applied to speech that was racist or discriminatory on the basis of ethnicity, religion, gender, sexual orientation, etc., if it was directed at an individual, intended to demean that person on the basis of one of the protected characteristics, and meant to create a hostile or intimidating campus environment.

According to Laurence Weinstein (1990: 7), a member of the university's Board of Regents, the board sought "to create an environment that would give each student . . . equal access to campus educational opportunities" while not "tread[ing] on the student's First Amendment rights of free speech." The board believed that its rules would not prevent the exchange of ideas or chill classroom discussion (since classrooms were excluded from coverage by the policy), nor would it constrain artistic expression (since the policy did not prohibit societal commentary). Only harassing speech of one student toward another was prohibited. To invoke sanctions, the university would have to prove intent on the part of the offending student, a requirement not easily met but also not very different from stipulations in other laws. Punishments would depend on the severity of the offense, and students would be entitled to due process. While the rules could not stop a fraternity or any other person or group from repeating two of the three offensive acts cited above, Laurence argues that the mere enactment of the policy made a strong symbolic statement that would affect attitudes and would make the university more "user-friendly."

Patricia Hodulik (1991: 1442-3) reviewed the thirty-two complaints filed in accordance with Wisconsin's policy during its first eighteen months. Thirteen were dismissed by student affairs officers because they were found not to violate the rules; two others were dismissed after hearings. Among the complaints dismissed were an art exhibit that some thought to be offensive to Catholics, a student's reference to a group of student senators as "rednecks," a statement by a Libyan to a Zionist that Libyans would destroy Zionism, and a cartoon regarding abortion that appeared in the student newspaper, offending some Christians. Discipline was imposed in ten cases; among them were an incident where a woman was called a "fucking cunt" and a "fucking bitch," an episode in which a black residence hall employee was called "a piece of shit nigger," and another involving the use of e-mail to send a message to an Islamic professor that read "Death to all Arabs!!! Die Islamic scumbags!" The most serious offenses (leading to seven probations and one suspension) involved violations of other university rules or state laws, which could have served as the basis for punishment (for example, prohibitions against physical violence and underage drinking); the other transgressions, however, (typically involving the use of epithets) could not have been the subject of official sanction if there had been no anti-harassment regulation. In keeping with the intent of the policy, no sanction was invoked as the result of discussion in class or expressed opinion, and as Hodulik found, there was little to suggest that the policy had a chilling effect on the free exchange of ideas. Finally, concerns that the policy would be used against the very people it was intended to protect proved groundless (in contrast to the Michigan example), as only one complaint against women or minority group members was found to be within the scope of the rules (that action against a white woman). Further, in each of the ten cases where discipline was imposed, the person harassed was a woman or a minority group member.

Despite the fact that Wisconsin's policy appeared to be working as intended, it could not withstand legal scrutiny. In *UWM Post v. Board of Regents of University of Wisconsin,* 774 F. Supp. 1163 (E.D. Wis. 1991), the court found the regulation of speech to be overbroad, based on content (that is, of a racist, antiethnic or religious group, sexist, homophobic, etc.) rather than on "fighting words." "It would be improper," said the court, "to expand the Supreme Court's definition of fighting words to include speech which does and speech which does not tend to incite violent reaction" (a premise that the Supreme Court would utilize the following year in *R.A.V.*).

Around the time that the University of Wisconsin's policy was invalidated, George Mason University also found that its attempt to sanction students for behavior that was racially and sexually offensive was impermissible [*Iota Xi Chapter of Sigma Chi Fraternity v. George Mason University,* 773 F. Supp. 792 (E.D. Va. 1991)]. In that instance, a fraternity's fund-raising event for charity, an "ugly woman contest," had members dressing as caricatures of women; one wore blackface, a black wig and curlers, and pillows to exaggerate the female figure. Sanctions were placed on the fraternity and its members for a period of two years. Basing its decision on the Supreme Court ruling in *Texas v. Johnson*, 491 U.S. 397 (1989)—the case in which the Court had held that such a publicly offensive act as burning the American flag was constitutionally protected free speech—the court ruled that the university could not punish the fraternity because it found the message to be offensive. It noted that the "First Amendment does not recognize exceptions for bigotry, racism, and religious intolerance or matters some deem trivial, vulgar, or profane."

These decisions appear to leave colleges and universities in a difficult position. If they mention race, ethnicity, religion, gender, etc. in their codes of student conduct, they may well have a policy that is not content-neutral and that is overbroad, thus violating the First Amendment. If they are not so specific (providing for sanctions against certain speech or behaviors without clearly defining how the policy is violated), they risk having a policy that is vague, thus again violating the First Amendment. The more specific they get, the less content-neutral they may become. Further, a reliance on the "fighting words" doctrine may require a series of immediate, violent responses to face-to-face insults in order to sanction others who would use those same inciteful words, but if no violent response were to occur on a given occasion, no "fighting words" would have been uttered. In any event, much of the speech that offends (such as Muhammad's speech at Kean, the display of the Klan uniform in opposition to the protest at Michigan, the Fiji Island party and the Harlem room at Wisconsin, and the ugly woman contest at George Mason) is protected speech.

HOSTILE ENVIRONMENTS

In the face of such stringent First Amendment restrictions, a logical question is whether there might be another approach, one where the First Amendment is not at the heart of the defense. Civil rights proponents believe that the body of law deriving from the Fourteenth Amendment provides such a basis. Adopted during Reconstruction to assure that states did not remove the rights accorded to African Americans under the Constitution, the Amendment prohibits any state from "deny[ing] to any person within its jurisdiction the equal protection of the laws." The "equal protection clause" has served as the basis for the major Supreme Court decisions that have torn down *de jure* segregation and that seek to eliminate the racially disparate effects of *de facto* segregation.

Critical Race Theory

"Critical race theorists" believe that because racism is so endemic to American life, one must view with skepticism claims that neutrality, objectivity and color blindness characterize the experience of racial and ethnic minorities. Based on a viewpoint that racism has contributed to the race-based group advantage and disadvantage that characterizes our society, they argue that the goal of eliminating racial oppression (as part of the broader goal of ending all forms of oppression) requires a contextual and historical analysis of the law (Matsuda, Lawrence, Delgado, and Crenshaw, 1993). Since racism is a class harm and "the ubiquity and incessancy of harmful racial depiction are the source of its virulence," racist speech cannot be viewed as an individual harm (to be judged in accordance with the First Amendment). It must be viewed as a group harm (to be judged in accordance with the Fourteenth Amendment), since that is the sole way of addressing the source of the problem (Delgado, 1991: 384). Henry Louis Gates (1993: 40) interprets this group of legal scholars as simply saying, "Rather than trying to fashion neutral laws to further our social objectives, why not put our cards on the table and acknowledge what we know" about what caused the condition that we are trying to fix?

One critical race theory scholar, Stanford University's Charles R. Lawrence III (1990), utilizes the decision in *Brown v. Board of Education*, 347 U.S. 483 (1954), to argue that colleges and universities can, indeed must, regulate racist speech. In that landmark case, the Court unanimously held that "education is perhaps the most important function of state and local governments. . . . In these days, it is doubtful that any child may reasonably be expected to succeed in life if he is denied the opportunity of an education. Such an opportunity . . . is a right which must be made available to all on equal terms." In his first major written opinion as Chief Justice, Earl Warren relied on a finding that officially condoned racial separation generates in African Americans "a feeling of inferiority as to their status in the community that may affect their hearts and minds in a way unlikely ever to be undone." Thus, Lawrence (1990: 439) holds that the Court found segregated schools to be unconstitutional "primarily because of the *message* segregation conveys. . . . Segregation serves its purpose by conveying an idea." He also notes that the decision "requires the affirmative disestablishment of societal practices that treat people as members of an inferior or dependent caste, as unworthy to participate in the larger community."

The public accommodations provisions of the Civil Rights Act of 1964, which not only prohibit racially separate restaurants, hotels, drinking fountains, swimming pools, etc., but also ban the signs (that is, the symbolic speech) that once indicated whether the area was open or closed to persons of a certain race, are cited by Lawrence as evidence that the Court and Congress meant to ban "free expression" of a racist nature. In *Heart of Atlanta Motel v. U.S.*, 379 U.S. 241 (1964), the Court, in upholding the public accommodations provisions, rejected the argument that private discriminators were protected by First Amendment speech and association rights. Two decades later, in another situation where race was the determining factor, the Court again gave preference to equal protection over free expression, this time in the form of religious liberty. In *Bob Jones University v. U.S.*, 461 U.S. 574 (1983), at issue was whether the university's tax-exempt status was jeopardized by its religiously based prohibition against interracial dating among its students. In ruling against the university, the Court determined that irrespective of the burden that might accrue to the institution as it sought to exercise its beliefs in accordance with the First Amendment, there was "a fundamental overriding interest in eradicating racial discrimination in education."[4]

Thus, Lawrence (1990: 449) concludes that "if we understand *Brown* . . . correctly, and if we understand the necessity of disestablishing the signs and symbols that signal blacks' inferiority, then we should not proclaim that all racist speech that stops short of physical violence must be defended." In fact, he asserts that "*Brown* may be read as regulating the content of racist speech," if such speech results in the state of inferiority (actual in the eyes of the law, or perceived in the hearts and minds of the targeted group) that the Court was seeking to remedy.

Analogizing from Legal Protections
in the Workplace

A review of the law regarding hostile workplace environments, where restrictions against content-specific expression have been required, lends credence to such a conclusion. Three federal statutes, Title VII of the Civil Rights Act of 1964, the Equal Employment Opportunity (EEO) Act of 1972, and Title IX of the Education Amendments of 1972, are important to this line of argument. The latter protects college students from being "excluded from participation in, be[ing] denied the benefits of, or be[ing] subjected to discrimination under any educational program or activity receiving Federal financial assistance" on the basis of sex;[5] the other two are more specifically related to employment and extend protections more broadly than on the basis of gender. Title VII, which became applicable to higher education with the enactment of the 1972 EEO Act, prohibits discriminatory hiring and other employment practices, including activities "that would deprive or tend to deprive any individual of employment opportunities or otherwise adversely affect his status as an employee, because of such individual's race, color, religion, sex, or national origin." The provision has been implemented through *Guidelines* of the Equal Employment Opportunity Commission (EEOC), which place upon an employer "an affirmative duty to maintain a working environment free of harassment," including limiting speech or behavior that "(1) has the purpose or effect of creating an intimidating, hostile or offensive working environment; (2) has the purpose or effect of unreasonably interfering with an individual's work performance; or (3) otherwise adversely affects an individual's work performance."

Title VII protection against a hostile work environment need not be limited to actions directed at the employee, as an optical company learned in a suit brought by a Hispanic employee for the firm's practice of segregating patients according to national origin [*Rogers v. E.E.O.C.*, 454 F. 2d. 234 (5th Cir. 1971), cert. denied, 406 U.S. 957 (1972)]. When the Supreme Court took up the matter of conditions in the workplace, it determined that isolated instances of offensive behavior by an employer or by fellow employees are not sufficient grounds for a finding that a work environment is hostile. In *Meritor Savings Bank v. Vinson*, 477 U.S. 57 (1986), it ruled that in matters of sex discrimination, an employer is responsible for having created a "hostile or abusive working environment" if the harassment is so severe or pervasive that it alters the conditions of the victim's employment. Similarly, minorities are protected against a work environment "so heavily polluted with discrimination as to destroy completely [their] emotional and psychological stability [*Risinger v. Ohio Bureau of Workers Compensation*, 883 F. 2d. 475 (6th Cir. 1989)]. The employer is also liable for failing to correct an ongoing situation in which he or she has no role other than preventing the reoccurrence of harassment by some employees against members of protected groups [*Bohen v. City of East Chicago*, 799 F. 2d. 1180 (7th Cir. 1986)].

Title IX has also been the basis of a hostile environment finding. A medical resident demonstrated that her residency program was so contaminated with sex discrimination as to retard her ability to be successful [*Lipset v. University of Puerto Rico*, 864 F. 2d. 881 (1st Cir. 1988)]. However, given the plaintiff's dual status as an employee and a student, it is unclear whether a finding in her favor would have been accorded solely on the basis of her being a student.

These cases lead to the conclusion that an employer has an affirmative responsibility to have its employees remove from the workplace such otherwise protected items as offensive posters or pictures of nude people and of persons engaged in sex acts, if there are individuals who find that they interfere with their ability to work effectively. The employer must also assure that employees are disciplined if they repeatedly tell offensive jokes or make sexually suggestive or racially offensive comments, again speech that is otherwise protected. Here, content-neutrality does not apply. It is the content that has the effect of denying equal employment opportunity, and thus it is the content against which the law protects.

If the content of speech may be regulated when it results in the denial of equal employment opportunity based on race, ethnicity, religion, gender, etc., is there not an analogous basis for the prohibition of a hostile environment in the training grounds for employment i.e., colleges and universities? Charles Jones (1991: 1412), for one, believes so. He argues that the Supreme Court consciously chose to interpret the Fourteenth Amendment to require more than mere formal equality in the educational context.

Brown, he says, also underscores the right to equal dignity and respect as well. Thus, if hate speech becomes so pervasive on a campus that it "constitutes such a harm that it interferes with the intangibles constituting the kind of educational quality to which African-Americans and other minorities have equal entitlement," a hostile environment exists such that the institution is required to act.

A strong case can be made that hate speech results in a hostile campus environment and has the effect of maintaining its targets in a subordinate status by conveying notions of superiority of the speaker and the inferiority of the victim, often in a terrifying way. Annette Gibbs (1992) notes that such acts erode sense of self, create fear, and restrict the movement of those targeted. Jones (1991) argues that campus ethnoviolence subordinates and stigmatizes members of minority groups, causing them to lose the full benefit of academic institutional life. Charles Lawrence provides a cogent example in his reaction as an African American to an incident at his university: two white freshmen, upset at the statement made by a black student that Beethoven had had a black parent, defaced a poster picturing the composer by transforming his likeness into the caricature of a black person. Lawrence said that the message to the student on whose door the altered poster was placed was, ". . . you and all your African-American brothers and sisters are all Sambos. It's a joke to think that you could ever be a Beethoven . . . could ever be anything more than a caricature of a real genius" (Matsuda, Lawrence, Delgado, and Crenshaw, 1993: 8). In acknowledging that they, too, are more cautious and less visible after receiving hate mail, "walk[ing] more quickly to our cars and glanc[ing] more often over our shoulders as we jogged the trails around our campuses," Lawrence and his colleagues—all highly regarded faculty members at prestigious institutions—underscored that it is not just students who can fall prey to terrorism (Matsuda, Lawrence, Delgado, and Crenshaw, 1993: 7).

Mari Matsuda (1993: 18) contends that acts of hate speech place "a psychic tax on those least able to pay," hitting at the emotional place where the target will feel the most pain. She points to studies that show victims experience "physiological symptoms and emotional stress ranging from fear in the gut to rapid pulse rate and difficulty in breathing, nightmares, post-traumatic stress disorder, hypertension, psychosis, and suicide" (Matsuda, 1993: 24).[6] If victims identify with the community that tolerates acts of racist speech, they succumb to the idea that there may be some truth in the contentions of their inferiority; if they reject an identification with the community in the aftermath of such occurrences, they become "stateless people" (Matsuda, 1993: 25).

Jones (1991) asserts that when the harm caused by group vilification exceeds the value to society from the exercise of free speech, institutions of higher learning must act to protect the learning environment so that it facilitates the progress of minority students. Matsuda and her colleagues believe that those targeted by haters at colleges and universities need to know that their institutions stand behind them (Matsuda, Lawrence, Delgado, and Crenshaw, 1993). Thus, limitations to free expression may be required to preclude the existence of a hostile environment and to given meaning to equal educational opportunity.

BALANCING FREE SPEECH AND EQUALITY

While, in theory, grounding a campus speech code on the concepts of equal protection and the prevention of a hostile environment may have validity, there has yet to be a legal test of this approach. Further, given the fundamental relationship between teaching, learning, and speech, there must be some consideration of First Amendment principles, a point that is recognized by the critical race theorists. They suggest that a narrow approach be taken in constructing such a policy in order to respect First Amendment values. Actionable speech would need to meet a three-pronged test: first, it must convey a message of racial superiority; second, it must be directed against a historically oppressed group; third, it must be persecutory, hateful, and degrading (Matsuda, Lawrence, Delgado, and Crenshaw, 1993). Even narrowly drawn, such rules would have the effect of stemming some prejudicial speech, as those who might have spoken intolerantly accede to the what they see as official authority acting in accordance with its legitimate responsibility (Delgado, 1991). For those not deterred by the rules, sanctions would be levied. An example of how such a code would work is cited by Richard Delgado (1991: 380): four men yell at a woman at a bus stop, "You spick whore," their intention being to humiliate and terrorize her based on her ethnic identity and gender. A punishment would be warranted in such a situation, despite claims of free speech, since the incident would meet the three-pronged test. Such rules, the critical race theorists contend, would not have a chilling effect on free expression, because the four individuals in question could express their views of Hispanics or women in a different manner that did not have the effect of intimidating or subordinating the individual or the historically oppressed group.

Ellen Lange (1990: 121–22) would apply Title VII principles. Derogatory slurs or other verbal or physical conduct against members of protected groups "would constitute harassment when [it]: (1) [h]as the purpose or effect of creating an intimidating, hostile, or offensive educational environment; (2) has the purpose or effect of unreasonably interfering with an individual's academic performance; or (3) otherwise adversely affects an individual's educational opportunities." To protect freedom of inquiry, such a policy would not be applicable in the classroom, nor (for jurisdictional purposes) would it apply to the conduct of students off of the campus.

While Lange would make every incident actionable (in the knowledge that students of color confront harassing situations all the time), John Shapiro (1990) would provide sanctions only in instances where the harassment is so severe or pervasive as to create a hostile environment. In accordance with his model, single incidents by individual students would violate the policy only if a hostile environment were to arise out of a series of individual acts. In order to satisfy concerns regarding excessive breadth and vagueness, he would specify what conduct would be unacceptable; most isolated jokes or derogatory statements would not rise to the impermissible level. Borrowing from the "fighting words" doctrine, he would stipulate that the perpetrator must intend to insult the victim and must address the statements directly to the victim. Statements generally directed to the university community or to the public at large, even if intentionally derogatory, would not be actionable.

Jones (1991) would take a more proscriptive approach but would be careful in the regulation of activities in which there is not a direct, hateful communication. For example, a fraternity's "mock slave auction" would not be prohibited unless it is a repeated occurrence or is staged in an area where students of color could not avoid being offended. Lawrence (1990) would go further, prohibiting, for example, racist posters and graffiti in dorms, classrooms, and bathrooms, in the belief that students should find safe haven in their dormitories and other common areas on campus. He would also depart from the premise that speech should be protected in certain public forums (such as a street or a park) if the offended party may reasonably avoid the speech by walking away or looking in another direction. He wonders why minority students should have to risk confronting assaultive speech every time they leave their dorm room.

A number of observers thought Stanford's policy to be one that meets constitutional standards, balancing the protections of the First and Fourteenth Amendments. The first section states the university's policy on free expression, noting that students must learn to "tolerate even expression of opinions which they find abhorrent." The second section affirms the university's policy against discrimination. The third section cites the conflict between the principles of free expression and anti-discrimination in certain instances, concluding that "protected free expression ends and prohibited discriminatory harassment begins" when the expression of an opinion becomes "personal vilification" of someone protected by the anti-discrimination policy. The fourth section defines "personal vilification" as speech (verbal or symbolic) that is intended to insult or stigmatize an individual on the basis of one of the characteristics noted in the anti-discrimination policy, that is addressed directly to those insulted or stigmatized, and utilizes insulting or "fighting words" as defined in *Chaplinsky* or "commonly understood to convey direct or visceral hatred or contempt for human beings on the basis of characteristics specified in the anti-discrimination policy" (Grey, 1992: 497). Altman (1995) points out that while slurs and epithets do not capture all speech-act wrongs, prohibiting more would run the risk of overinclusiveness.

Civil libertarians contended that the Stanford policy falls short, arguing that campus speech codes underpinned by a Fourteenth Amendment orientation would not meet the content-neutrality test of the First Amendment (Strossen , 1990). The weight of the rulings in the University of Michigan and University of Wisconsin cases, reinforced by *R.A.V.*, leans in their direction. Indeed, a California Superior Court judge recently struck down the Stanford policy, but on a somewhat different basis: a 1992 California statute that forbids universities from restricting speech that would be protected off-campus.

Stanford was unsuccessful in its argument that its First Amendment right to prohibit unacceptable speech on its property would be abridged by the application of the law to its code (Associated Press, 1995). Robert J. Corry, one of the nine students who brought the suit against the university, lauded the decision, contending that "students should not live in fear that what they say could get them expelled" (Shea, 1995b: A32). Stanford President Gerhard Casper, despite his contention that "a ban on insulting, fighting words based on group characteristics is not likely to have a chilling effect on almost all relevant speech," decided not to appeal the ruling, given the expense that would be incurred in a lengthy legal battle (Shea, 1995c: A40).

For policies that incorporate an anti-discrimination orientation to be upheld in the judicial arena, conditions on the campus would have to be, as Thomas Grey (1992: 490) notes, "widespread and serious enough to go beyond what the courts judge must be tolerated as part of life's ordinary rough and tumble." Since just as strong a case could be made regarding the overbreadth, vagueness, and content-specific nature of a workplace code extended to non-workers as has been made against campus speech codes, it is probably a safer approach for institutions to follow a set of principles that might more readily pass constitutional muster. The University of Michigan and University of Wisconsin cases tell us that campus rules cannot be overbroad or vague and must not have a chilling effect on the free flow of ideas in the academic setting. Generally aimed speech, including cat-calls from windows or offensive signs displayed in acceptable areas, as well as speech that makes a political statement such as a protest demonstration or wearing a Confederate flag or Nazi insignia, is protected. Further, such troublesome occurrences as fraternity parties based on insensitive or bigoted themes may not be prohibited, nor can student groups be constrained from bringing to campus speakers known to deliver messages of hatred. However, William Kaplin (1992), a scholar of higher education law, notes that an institution may forbid a sign that reinforces a discriminatory practice by a campus organization. Thus, a fraternity may be prohibited from posting a sign on its front door that reads, "no blacks allowed," since it is actually engaging in discriminatory behavior rather than expressing an opinion. (Institutions need to be careful here, since there may be a fine line between opinion and behavior: a sign that reads,

"If we had our way, no blacks would be allowed," might very well have the same effect as the banned sign yet would clearly state an opinion.)

Institutions may punish "fighting words," narrowly defined to mean face-to-face intentional provocations. Similarly, incitements to violence may be prohibited, but distinctions must be made between whether the provocateur is simply stating an opinion that supports violence or is actually inciting people to be violent. Institutions have the right to enact reasonable restrictions on the time, place, and manner of speech, and accordingly may require student groups inviting speakers to follow certain procedures to assure compliance. However, they must be even-handed and con-tent-neutral in the application of the rules.[7] Thus, for example, a college may prohibit students from having a demonstration in a classroom building, in a library, or in an office building, but not based on the subject of the demonstration. (Recall that in *Doe* the judge let stand the use of differentiated speech zones on campus.) Further, as Kaplin (1992) indicates, speech that occurs in private areas of the campus (for example, residence halls, designated study carrels, and, perhaps, other study areas) may be regulated if it infringes on the privacy interests of persons legitimately in those private places. Certain behaviors that extend beyond speech may also be regulated, even if expressing an opinion; students may be disciplined in instances where institutional or personal property is defaced or damaged (spray painting, setting fire to doors, "trashing" a room, etc.), or for physical assaults.

Punishing Actions

Colleges and universities may seek to foster a positive learning environment by placing sanctions against harassment of all sorts. However, given the Court's ruling in *R.A.V.*, many concur with Georgetown University counsel Lawrence White (1994: A48) that "the safest hate-speech code may be one that makes no mention of the very groups it is designed to protect"; that is, that campus rules should be content-neutral, not singling out any particular subjects for punishment (for example, anti-harassment stipulations should bar all harassment, not just that which is racially, ethnically, religiously, or sexually related).

The University of Pennsylvania changed its speech code in compliance with *R.A.V.* (Gose, 1994: A30). Its previous policy had barred racial harassment, defined as "any verbal or symbolic behavior . . . that insults or demeans the person or persons to whom the behavior is directed." The revised policy states that "the university condemns hate speech, epithets, and racial, ethnic, sexual, and religious slurs. . . . However, the content of student speech or expression is not by itself a basis for disciplinary action. Student speech may be subject to discipline when it violates applicable laws or university regulations or policies."

However, while behavior regulations should be generally stated and evenly applied, an institution may provide stiffer punishments if the victim is targeted as a result of being a member of a protected class. In *Wisconsin v. Mitchell,* 508 U.S. 476 (1993), the Supreme Court upheld the sentencing of an African American convicted of aggravated battery against a white youth. After viewing the film *Mississippi Burning,* Mitchell exhorted a group of black youth to attack a white passer-by in revenge for the treatment accorded to blacks during the period depicted in the film. In accordance with a statute that enhances penalties whenever a defendant "intentionally selects the person against whom the crime is committed . . . because of race, religion, color, disability, sexual orientation, national origin or ancestry of that person," Mitchell received a seven-year sentence rather than the two-year term that would have been invoked had bias not been a factor. Chief Justice Rehnquist, speaking for a unanimous Court, noted a difference between the unconstitutional statute in *R.A.V.* (which was specifically directed at expression) and the one at issue in this case, which was aimed at conduct not protected by the First Amendment. *NAACP v. Claiborne Hardware Co.*, 458 U.S. 886 (1982), established that the First Amendment does not protect violence. *Tison v. Arizona,* 481 U.S. 137 (1987), made note of the principle "deeply ingrained in our legal tradition . . . that the more purposeful is the criminal conduct, the more serious is the offense, and therefore, the more severely it ought to be punished." While *Dawson v. Delaware,* 503 U.S. 159 (1992), precludes a defendant's abstract beliefs, no matter how obnoxious, from being taken into consideration in determination of guilt, evidence concerning how one's beliefs or associations directly relate to the crime may be considered at sentencing [*Barclay v. Florida,* 463 U.S. 939 (1983)]. In

Mitchell, the Court referred to evidence provided by Mari Matsuda and others that "bias motivated crimes are more likely to provoke retaliatory crimes, inflict distinct emotional harms on their victims, and incite community unrest." Rehnquist concluded that "the State's desire to redress these perceived harms provides an adequate explanation for its penalty-enhancement provision." He rejected Mitchell's argument that the statute had an overbroad, chilling effect. For such a condition to occur, the Court "must conjure up a vision of a Wisconsin citizen suppressing his unpopular bigoted opinions for fear that if he later commits an offense covered by the statute, these opinions will be offered at trial to establish that he selected his victim on account of the victim's protected status." Rehnquist thought such a hypothesis to be "simply too speculative."

The constitutionality of enhanced penalty provisions in response to bias-related victim selection provides colleges and universities the opportunity to make a specific statement of institutional resolve in codes of student conduct.[8] Thus, using the anti-harassment example cited earlier, while harassment may be generally prohibited, specific references to harassment based on race, ethnicity, etc., should not be made. However, the code may clearly state that there will be enhanced penalties in instances where it can be demonstrated that the victim of a code violation was targeted as a result of racial, ethnic, or other specified bias.

A Broader Challenge

While enhanced penalties for bias-related activity have their value, they can only be invoked after the hatred has been spewed and someone has been injured. Further, a whole range of offensive and hurtful speech, although unjust and immoral, remains protected. The best way to preclude such damage is for the offense not to have occurred in the first place. However, our experience makes it plain that injurious speech will not go away on its own. The commitment of our major societal institutions (including government, religion, education at all levels, service organizations, etc.) to teaching tolerance and understanding, and to promoting intergroup harmony, is required if the slur is not to be uttered, the offensive sign is not to be posted, and the insensitive event is not to be scheduled.

NOTES

1. In addition, there are also certain restrictions on the media; for example, there are words considered too profane for broadcast over the public airwaves. Also, there are prohibitions against the publication of certain confidential information, such as the names and addresses of rape victims or of children involved in certain legal matters.

2. As discussed in the opening portion of this book, the president's office was informed that Muhammad was a speaker who could be expected to deliver anti-Semitic remarks in keeping with the ideology of the Nation of Islam.

3. It is a generally held principle that the First Amendment does not apply to independent colleges and universities unless they voluntarily comply. Public institutions must honor that constitutional provision, since their actions are taken as actions of the state. An unsuccessful bill, the "Collegiate Speech Protection Act of 1991," introduced by U.S. Representative Henry Hyde, would have accorded First Amendment protections to speech on independent college campuses. It had support of the ACLU but was opposed by private higher education (Michelman, 1992).

Notwithstanding, free-speech clauses in state constitutions may bind private institutions in those states to the same requirements. For example, two cases based on state constitutional provisions, *Princeton University v. Schmid*, 455 U.S. 100 (1982), which overturned Princeton's exclusion of a non-student for distributing political literature, and a similar state court case involving Muhlenberg University in Pennsylvania, *Commonwealth v. Tate*, 495, Pa. 158, 432 A. 2d, 1382 (1981), may extend the *Widmar* principle to private higher education. Evan Siegel (1990) argues that although both *Schmid* and *Tate* involved non-students, "certainly those same protections [to exercise free speech irrespective of content] should extend to the smaller class of individuals with whom a [private] college or university voluntarily associates." However, this seems to be an area of law that is not finally resolved. Harvard University law professor Randall Kennedy (1994: B2) holds that independent institutions are not bound, nor should they voluntarily bind themselves, to follow First Amendment rulings. He contends that while "the First Amendment or something like it is essential to the democratic process[,] [i]t is not essential . . . to the inculcation of political, moral , or religious values that various sorts of [private] colleges may want to protect and preserve."

4. The ACLU's Nadine Strossen (1990) draws a distinction between actions and words in this instance. She argues that at issue in *Bob Jones* was whether the government, through its provision of a tax exemption, should contribute to the institution's racially discriminatory *practices*, not

its advocacy of ideas that the government thought offensive. Thus, if the university did not bar or otherwise punish interracial dating (including by permitting vigilantism against interracial dating to go unpunished), it was free to express its views on interracial dating.

5. The Court's decision in *Grove City College v. Bell*, 465 U.S. 555 (1984), affirmed the interpretation that federal financial aid to students constituted aid to a college. However, the Court took a narrow perspective in ruling that compliance with Title IX need not be extended beyond the particular program that received the federal money, rather than to all programs at the institution. Several years later, Congress reinstituted the broad sweep of Title IX when it enacted the Civil Rights Restoration Act.

6. Richard Delgado (1993) believes that the psychological harm caused to individuals by the racist behavior of others should be recognized by a tort for racial insults. Currently, victims have few means of coping with the harms caused by such insults. Their sense of helplessness would be relieved if they were able to threaten and institute legal action. Michael Israel (1994: 20) argues for a "tort of outrage," where damages would be recognized for a victim who has been put in fear by persons or groups drawing on a history of intimidation, like that of the Ku Klux Klan or by the Nazis in the Holocaust.

7. Some institutions have sought to discourage vitriolic speakers by assessing the costs of security to the student group offering the invitation. Such practices, if applied even-handedly, would probably be upheld. However, if utilized only when the institution disagrees with the content of the speaker's remarks, they would be improper. For example, if one student group is assessed security costs for Khalid Abdul Muhammad's visit but another is not for a speaker invited to respond to Muhammad's speech, the rule would be found to have been arbitrarily applied, and thus unconstitutional. In some instances, colleges have required that the sponsoring group secure a bond that would cover damages in the event of violence. Again, if not uniformly applied, such a rule would be seen as an attempt to chill free expression.

8. It should be noted that the Omnibus Anti-Crime Act (P.L. 103–322), enacted into law on September 13, 1994, included a provision requiring the U.S. Sentencing Commission to develop enhanced penalties for federal crimes in instances when the victim was targeted as a result of being a member of a protected class. Proposing the measure shortly after the *Mitchell* decision was announced, Representative Charles Schumer articulated the prevailing view that "hate crimes take on the cherished American notion that we can all live together harmoniously" (Idelson, 1993: 2563).

REFERENCES

Altman, Andrew. "Liberalism and Campus Hate Speech." *Campus Wars: Multiculturalism and the Politics of Difference*, ed. John Arthur and Amy Shapiro. Boulder, CO: Westview Press, 1995, pp. 122–134.

Associated Press, "Court Overturns Stanford Code on Bigoted Speech." *The New York Times*. March 1, 1995, p. B8.

Bren, Vicki L. "Memorandum to Stephen Wiley, Re: Free Speech on College Campuses—Kean College." December 28, 1993.

Delgado, Richard. "Campus Antiracism Rules: Constitutional Narratives in Collision." *Northwestern University Law Review* v. 85 n. 2 (1991), pp. 343–387.

———. "Words That Wound: A Tort Action for Racial Insults, Epithets, and Name Calling." *Words That Wound: Critical Race Theory, Assaultive Speech and the First Amendment*, ed. Mari J. Matsuda, Charles R. Lawrence, III, Richard Delgado, and Kimberle Williams Crenshaw. Boulder, CO: Westview Press, 1993, pp. 93–111.

Editors of *Perspective, the Campus Legal Monthly*. "First Amendment on Campus: Four Exceptions." *Perspective, the Campus Legal Monthly* v. 6 n. 1 (January 1991), pp. 1–2.

Gates, Henry Louis, Jr. "Let Them Talk: Why Civil Liberties Pose No Threat to Civil Rights." *The New Republic* v. 209 n. 12–13 (September 20 and 27, 1993), pp. 37–49.

Gibbs, Annette. *Reconciling Rights and Responsibilities of Colleges and Students: Offensive Speech, Assembly, Drug Testing and Safety; ASHE/ERIC Higher Education Research Report No. 5*. Washington, DC: The George Washington University, 1992.

Gose, Ben. "Penn to Replace Controversial Speech Code. Will No Longer Punish Students for Insults." *The Chronicle of Higher Education*. June 29, 1994, p. A30.

Grey, Thomas C. "Civil Rights vs. Civil Liberties, the Case of Discriminatory Verbal Harassment." *Journal of Higher Education* v. 63 n. 5 (September/October 1992), pp. 485–516.

Gunther, Gerald. "Good Speech, Bad Speech—No." *Campus Wars: Multiculturalism and the Politics of Difference*, ed. John Arthur and Amy Shapiro. Boulder, CO: Westview Press, 1995, pp. 109–113.

Hodulik, Patricia. "Racist Speech on Campus." *Wayne Law Review* v. 37 (1991), pp. 1433–1450.

Idelson, Holly. "House Hate Crimes Measure Would Increase Sentences." *Congressional Quarterly* v. 51 n. 38 (September 25, 1993), p. 2563.

Israel, Michael. "Hate Speech and the First Amendment." Unpublished manuscript shared with members of Kean College Board of Trustees, 1994.

Jones, Charles H. "Equality, Dignity and Harm: The Constitutionality of Regulating American Campus Ethnoviolence." *Wayne Law Review* v. 37 (1991), pp. 1383–1432.

Kaplin, William A. "A Proposed Process for Managing First Amendment Aspects of Campus Hate Speech." *Journal of Higher Education* v. 63 n. 5 (September/October 1992), pp. 517–538.

Kennedy, Randall. "Should Private Universities Voluntarily Bind Themselves to the First Amendment? No!" *The Chronicle of Higher Education.* September 21, 1994, pp. B1–B2.

Lange, Ellen E. "Racist Speech on Campus: A Title VII Solution to a First Amendment Problem." *Southern California Law Review* v. 64 (1990), pp. 105–134.

Lawrence, Charles R., III. "If He Hollers Let Him Go: Regulating Racist Speech on Campus." *Duke Law Review* v. 1990 n. 3 (June 1990), pp. 431–483.

Matsuda, Mari J. "Public Response to Racist Speech: Considering the Victim's Story." *Words That Wound: Critical Race Theory, Assaultive Speech and the First Amendment*, ed. Mari J. Matsuda, Charles R. Lawrence, III, Richard Delgado, and Kimberle Williams Crenshaw. Boulder, CO: Westview Press, 1993, pp. 17–51.

Matsuda, Mari J. and Charles R. Lawrence, III. "Epilogue: Burning Crosses and the R.A.V. Case." *Words That Wound: Critical Race Theory, Assaultive Speech and the First Amendment*, ed. Mari J. Matsuda, Charles R. Lawrence, III, Richard Delgado, and Kimberle Williams Crenshaw. Boulder, CO: Westview Press, 1993, pp. 133–136.

Matsuda, Mari J., Charles R. Lawrence, III, Richard Delgado, and Kimberle Williams Crenshaw. "Introduction." *Words That Wound: Critical Race Theory, Assaultive Speech and the First Amendment*, ed. Mari J. Matsuda, Charles R. Lawrence, III, Richard Delgado, and Kimberle Williams Crenshaw. Boulder, CO: Westview Press, 1993, pp. 1–14.

Michelman, Frank. "Universities, Racist Speech and Democracy in America: An Essay for the ACLU." *Harvard Civil Rights—Civil Liberties Review* v. 27 n. 2 (Summer 1992), pp. 339–369.

Oldaker, Lawrence L. "Coping with 'Hate Speech' in Educational Settings." *Leadership and Diversity in Education*, ed. Joel L. Burdin. Lancaster, PA: Technomic Publishing Company, 1994, pp. 76–85.

Olivas, Michael. "The Political Economy of Immigration, Intellectual Property and Racial Harassment, Case Studies on the Implementation of Legal Change on Campus." *Journal of Higher Education* v. 63 n. 5 (September/October 1992), pp. 570–598.

Poritz, Deborah T. and William C. Brown. "Letter to Elsa Gomez Re: Constitutionality of Content-Based Restrictions on Speakers at State Colleges." D.O.L. No. 94-80057. March 16, 1994.

Seigenthaler, John. "Politically Correct Speech: An Oxymoron." *Editor and Publisher* v. 126 n. 10 (March 6, 1993), pp. 38, 48.

Shapiro, John T. "The Call for Campus Conduct Policies: Censorship or Constitutionally Permissible Limitations on Speech." *Minnesota Law Review* v. 75 (1990), pp. 201–238.

Shea, Christopher. "Stanford Anti-harassment Policy Violates Rights of Free Speech, Cal. Judge Rules." *The Chronicle of Higher Education.* March 10, 1995b, p. A32.

————. "Stanford Gives Up Legal Battle to Keep Its Hate Speech Code." *The Chronicle of Higher Education.* March 24, 1995c, p. A40.

Siegel, Evan G. S. "Closing the Campus Gates to Free Expression: The Regulation of Offensive Speech at Colleges and Universities." *Emory Law Journal* v. 39 (1990), pp. 1351–1400.

Strossen, Nadine. "Regulating Speech on Campus: A Modest Proposal." *Duke Law Journal* v. 1990 n. 3 (June 1990), pp. 484–573.

Weinstein, Laurence A. "Policing Prejudice." *AGB Reports* v. 32 n. 1 (January/February 1990), pp. 6–11.

White, Lawrence. "Hate Speech Codes That Will Pass Constitutional Muster." *The Chronicle of Higher Education.* May 25, 1994, p. A48.

Chapter 6

Dealing with Hate Speech

Speakers carrying messages of hate do not simply arrive on campus seeking a forum. They are invited by disillusioned and angry students. Some of these students came to college as a means of escaping a life dominated by race-based discrimination but found an environment more hostile than they had expected, one replete with hateful words and deeds that make them fighting mad. Others enrolled to achieve or to protect their economic security but concluded that all the breaks were being given to someone else, causing their emotions to simmer. Assuming that such students want to avoid the consequences associated with physically or verbally striking back, venting frustration may be difficult. Indeed, there may not even be a specific culprit to strike back against. The African American student may find the chilliness so pervasive, the prejudice so subtle, the graffiti so anonymous, that "white society" takes the blame. Similarly, for the angry white male, striking out against an individual who may have received some preference does not stop the "system" from pursuing such policies.

Students of all persuasions (those who are angry as well as those who are not) tend to seek "supportive niches" to help them to cope with the pressures of collegiate life, both in response to their environments and as a means of facilitating common interests. Sometimes, particularly when students are intellectually charged by politicized faculty, these supportive niches provide the critical mass that radicalizes them. It only takes some precipitating event for a group composed of like-minded, angry students to decide that it is time to send a loud message, to strike back in a way that is academically legitimate: inviting a speaker to campus to deliver a message that cannot be ignored—what Russell Adams (1994) refers to as "catered hate speech." From their vantage point it is a good strategy, because colleges are supposed to be places where new ideas are entertained and controversial views are aired. And if some reject that premise, there is always the First Amendment.

Most colleges and universities, especially those with residence halls (where there is ample opportunity for something to go wrong, particularly when students have been drinking), share many of the preconditions that move students toward the extreme and thus are vulnerable to hate speech. Although most students of all ethnic groups eschew the views espoused by the speaker, the ramifications for the institution are immense, since the speech pumps emotions. As Ruth Sidel (1994) concluded from her study of bias on college campuses, so many people with very different backgrounds and orientations spend so much time together within a rather contained environment, that issues and incidents based on difference can readily become highly charged, intensify quickly, and explode.

Several questions arise. First, what are the prospects that the conditions giving rise to hateful speech will remain? Second, what can be done to minimize the likelihood of its occurrence on a college campus? Third, what should be done if it does occur?

HATE SPEECH'S FUTURE PROSPECTS

Today's students are not the first to have felt and acted on anger, nor is bigotry a new phenomenon on college campuses. In the past, controversial speakers invited by students were more likely to be focused on policy or philosophical issues—pro- or anti–civil rights, pro-or anti-war, pro- or anti-religion, pro– or anti-abortion, pro- or anti-communism, etc.—not on denigrating groups of people based on their race, ethnicity, religion, sexual orientation, etc. If students did invite a bigoted speaker, their goal in doing so would be to expose the fallacies of that person's ideas, not to celebrate them. Furthermore, over the first three decades of the post–World War II era, public expressions of bigotry became increasingly less acceptable, as more Americans—often led by college students—saw value in tearing down barriers between people.

However, significant evaporation of this consensus had occurred by the mid 1970s. As has been previously discussed, some pin the change on the transition from fighting for civil rights to fighting to eradicate prejudice. Even if that opinion is accurate, was there any moral alternative to seeking to put prejudice into our past? Moreover, the assessment seems to ignore the general American transformation into the "me generation," when it became acceptable (even psychologically healthy) for people to focus on themselves—or to put it differently, when the balance was lost between the American value of individualism and the American value of communitarianism. Thus, we find ourselves a society increasingly fragmented in numerous dimensions, race and ethnicity being only two.

This fragmentation, heightened by uncertainty regarding the economic future, pushed Americans to search for something that can produce more surety. Many did not have to look far; they renewed the old feeling that self-interest is best promoted through identity politics, this time based more on race than on national origin. Thus, the great American center—fiscally conservative, socially more progressive, and mostly white—began to lean in a more conservative direction, leaving economically disadvantaged minorities and liberal whites without the majority that they once enjoyed. Public policy began to shift away from a governmental commitment to improve the lot of the poor and the disenfranchised, so much so, Elizabeth Kim (1993: 54) contends, that minority groups were left "scrambl[ing] to pick up the pieces in the aftermath of the eighties, many with revenge on their agendas." This has not gone unnoticed by those whites who are fearful of their own loss of position; and so the identity politics intensify. Thus, unless something is done to minimize the group-identity focus that characterizes our polity, ethnic rivalries may well continue to escalate in our society (and at our colleges and universities, as each becomes more diverse).

On the other hand, the campus situation would improve if conditions on the macro level were to improve; that is, if the economy were to grow at a rate that resulted in low unemployment and in good jobs for people with all levels of education and there were to be renewed commitment to intergroup harmony across the nation, students, too, would be less inclined toward intergroup hostility. The challenge regarding the economy has proven elusive for both liberals and conservatives, Republicans and Democrats.

But irrespective of the approach taken by the various players—whether they see the goal being achieved through big government or big business, public and private partnerships, or a laissez-faire economy—a compelling argument can be made that each truly wants our nation to enjoy a future of prosperity. However, an equally compelling case can be made that little more than lip service has been paid in recent years by most of those players to the second challenge.

America sorely needs leadership from people in influential positions, both elected and ascribed—particularly from those who are white—to topple the walls that divide Americans, an undertaking as sustained as that which toppled the Berlin Wall. This leadership needs to look beyond the alienating policies of the past: policies that government alone must do the job, as well as those that say that government has no role. Indeed, government does have a role, unless I misunderstand the passages in the Preamble to the Constitution about "promoting the general welfare" and "securing the blessings of liberty." The challenge, then, is to focus on approaches that will restore the balance between the American value of individualism and the American value of communitarianism.

Affirmative action, a policy that I have supported since its inception and that I continue to believe is necessary, provides a good example of the challenge. The policy has been divisive: opposed by those who believe that it holds back meritorious people who should have an equal chance (the American value of individualism); and supported by those who believe that the society benefits by providing a collective effort to overcome historical group exclusion (the American value of communitarianism). One side says that rights are being secured by the policy; the other says that rights are being violated. Everybody is correct—at least in theory. In practice, however, our earlier review of the effects of affirmative action indicates that the economic status of minorities, particularly African Americans, has not jumped in quantum proportions relative to whites. In fact, on average, there has been little change. Yes, some have advanced, but the disparities have increased significantly for those at the lower end of the economic scale. While the anger of white males regarding affirmative action is usually directed toward minorities, it would be more appropriately aimed at an economy that failed to grow as fast as women were entering the labor force.

Some messages, however, seem destined not to be heard. Thus, the arguments regarding affirmative action remain in the theoretical or philosophical realm, rather than in the practical.

If affirmative action is abandoned, race-based disparities will probably increase, as a result of the existing difference in socioeconomic condition between most whites and most blacks; that condition affects school achievement and thus career opportunity, as does the prejudicial decision making, which would be more difficult to contest than at present. On the other hand, if the policy is maintained as it stands, absent a rapidly growing economy and without the strong backing of the judiciary it will continue to serve as a lightning rod for those who need a rationale for their own economic insecurity (an increasing number), and it is likely to fall, through the political process. An attempt should be made to find an approach that is viewed as upholding the principle of equal opportunity but that does not re-segregate our society for the sake of "color-blind" decision making. Bridging that gap is not going to be easy but is not without possibility. Bobo and Kluegel (1993: 460) concluded from their attitudinal study that policies that are framed as "opportunity enhancing" are politically viable even if they are race-targeted, as long as they are accompanied by efforts "to address the denial of contemporary racial discrimination and sense of group self-interest prevalent among whites."

If we can, as a nation, achieve a new consensus about fairness, what to do when people act unfairly, and what to do if the system appears to be fair but produces an unfair outcome, we will have removed a major contributor to hateful speech, and we will have taken down enough of the walls between Americans so that they can see each other as they talk. At this point, however, everyone is clinging to ideological positions. Thus, I suspect, intergroup tension and its companion, hate speech, will remain part of our landscape.

MINIMIZING HATE SPEECH
ON COLLEGE CAMPUSES

Lani Guinier's (cited in Ewalt, 1994: 246) assessment regarding the status of race relations in America is also accurate for the campus specifically: "We've spent so much time pacing our respective corners that common ground between us is really empty. We have a strange fear of this unknown Other. If only we could make the Other look less strange." As difficult as it is now to establish common ground with the Other on college campuses, their future will have more Others than their present does, as our society continues its demographic evolution.

Colleges and universities cannot wait for that empty space to be replaced with common ground and for intergroup tolerance levels to rise in the broader society. For the reasons discussed earlier, they should anticipate the potential for problems. Their traditionally aged college students arrive on campus just as they are reaching a rebellious period. These young students are the most likely among the total enrollment to live in residence halls, join fraternities, participate in student government, and write for the campus newspaper—the places where controversy is most likely to arise. Further, the fact that the avenues for effective protest open to young adults in the wider society are rather limited makes colleges and universities a prime venue for conflict (Sidel, 1994). If college leaders are not moved by moral compulsion to provide leadership to improve intergroup relations, the desire to avoid conflict, along with the compelling evidence that unfavorable campus climates clearly stand in the way of student success, should provide sufficient incentive.

Building Community: A Useful Approach?

Ernest Boyer (cited in Peters, 1992: 265) believes that the growing pattern of "fragmentation and tribalism" that exists in our nation critically obligates higher education "to find ways to build community and bring us all together." Colleges and universities, he argues, must identify "the transcendent purposes that somehow can define the nature of community amidst diversity." Sheldon Hackney set out to tackle that issue, as he committed the National Endowment for the Humanities to supporting an initiative, based primarily at colleges, for a "national conversation" on common values and pluralism. The field, however, has been proven full of rocks and gullies, reflecting the divisions between us. Not only was the initiative criticized by conservatives for being "politically correct," it was also bashed by postmodernists (whom I heard attack Hackney at a scholarly conference during the question-and-answer period after his address, "American Pluralism and American Identity: Continuing a National Conversation") for failing to recognize

the legitimate differences among Americans, based on their historical circumstances, that should preclude a senseless quest for a
common set of values.

While a national crusade to define common values and the
nature of community is an immense undertaking, surely for individual colleges and universities it is a far less monumental task.
Many have been trying. However, New York University Law
professor Burt Neuborne (1992) argues that efforts to establish
"community" on college campuses, though well intentioned, are
misguided, since colleges are not true communities but common
enterprises. He suggests that we can bridge the gap between on one
hand popular sovereignty and majority rule (the values of community) and on the other natural law and individual rights (the values
of self) through an *idealized pluralism* that focuses on protecting
access to common enterprises. Idealized pluralism is driven by
three principles: (1) eliminating law as an obstacle to true community; (2) eliminating law as a device to compel community; and (3)
approving laws that assure equal opportunity to derive individual
benefits from significant common enterprises.

Applying this notion to higher education, he contends that
students come to a college not to become members of a true
community but to get an education; that is, they come to engage in
a common educational enterprise. Similarly, faculty and staff come
to do a job for which they were educated and that will provide
them with wages and benefits, both tangible and intangible. Accordingly, a college or university, as an educational enterprise,
"should think twice about establishing a shared community of
values that may force a dissenter to the difficult choice of submit-
ting or exiting, especially since power to protect participation in
the common enterprise exists without the necessity of coercing
community." He argues that the only way in which a college might
remotely be considered a community would be as "a community
of free inquiry, in which no idea or thought is off limits," a
conception that also precludes students and faculty from being
required to endorse a set of values with which they disagree
(Neuborne, 1992: 398).

Neuborne cites the banning of hate speech, broadly construed,
as an example of an official act intended to promote (or coerce) the
value of community that ought to be avoided. However, he believes
that the institution does have an obligation to make sure that

individuals are not denied the benefit of participation in the common educational enterprise that it provides. Thus if behavior, including speech, can be proven to interfere with the learning process—the basis of the common educational enterprise—the institution should act to preclude that behavior. Neuborne believes that threats and intimidation clearly cross the line and that sustained verbal harassment of a targeted individual may well do so, depending on the circumstances; however, "bruised emotions caused by ugly ideas and epithets, even hateful ones, do not" (Neuborne, 1992: 399). Any effort to constrain such behavior would have a counterproductive effect on the very sense of community that it would be intended to support. Thus, Neuborne (1992: 406) concludes, if official actions intended to force community are avoided and if the focus is placed on preserving equal access to the common enterprise, "true communities will emerge and a caring polity will evolve," since its individual members will be "imbued with empathy, altruism, toleration, and a sense of the long term common good."

Neuborne's thesis is an interesting one but seems to fall a bit short, given the weight of evidence that suggests that minority students are under more pressure than white students, in part because of the pervasiveness of hateful speech, and that this stress is an added source of academic vulnerability. Thus, in order to guarantee participation in the common educational enterprise, it would also be necessary to constrain the utterance of hateful thoughts—necessary, except that the courts have ruled that hateful speech as it routinely occurs cannot be constrained.[1] Rather than leave such an open hole in the notion of protecting access to the common enterprise, it seems to me that institutions of higher learning ought to pursue the community approach, keeping in mind that the primary consideration should be to sustain a community of learners.

Here I think that the experience of Swarthmore College is instructive. Although the institution has received some negative press in recent years for being a bastion of political correctness, for example when it permitted students to vote on whether to fly the American flag over the administration building, it has worked tirelessly to make all of its students feel comfortable in exploring complex societal issues. On the flag matter, Swarthmore's president, Alfred Bloom, initially consented to the request, which was made by a conservative student group, but then a socialist student group waged a protest. Bloom decided to let the student body decide through a referendum because it presented an "educational moment" that permitted the hashing out of issues. The students voted to fly the flag. This episode, as controversial as it was, demonstrates a defining characteristic of the Swarthmore community—the commitment to discourse. Thus, even on this very liberal, "politically correct" campus, the Conservative Union and the Christian Fellowship are among the college's most active groups, not because they have been compelled to act to keep their ideas from being pushed off campus but because there is a place in the campus dialogue for them (Jones, 1995).

It is possible, then, to foster a sense of community and not coerce a politically correct group-think. Granted, the issues get thorny when the differences are racially based, but I still maintain that Americans have more in common than in contrast. Great care must be taken both in courses and extracurricular activities to draw on the commonalities in the human experience so as to overcome the tendencies to particularize, rationalize, or blame that often accompany developing ethnic pride and ethnic identity under challenge. A campus that fosters dialogue, that is committed to its members testing their ideas in an open fashion, is more likely to become successful in its goal of becoming a community in which diversity and civility are compatible.

Reaching the Soul

While it is typically a group that invites a hate speaker, it is usually the individual that utters hateful speech or commits hateful acts. Thus, colleges and universities need, too, to focus on the development of the individual. Shelby Steele (1995) contends that racial tensions on college campuses do not fit the pattern of white racism and black protest but are, paradoxically, more the result of racial equality than inequality. Based on his interviews with students at Stanford, UCLA, and Berkeley, he argues that the integrated setting exposes individual differences between blacks and whites, and causes students to grapple with their own thoughts and feelings about themselves and the Other. For example, African American students on integrated campuses are confronted on a daily basis with the myth of black inferiority, as white students view them as affirmative action cases and as some black students act in a stereotypical way that reinforces the myth. This subjects them "to four unendurable feelings—diminishment, accountability to the preconceptions of whites, a powerlessness to change those preconceptions, and finally shame" (Steele, 1995: 179–80). Steele believes that it is difficult for black students to admit that they are made anxious about this, so they will usually conceal the feelings and rationalize that the history of white racism is repeating itself. Thus, rather than focusing on the real problem that underlies their racial anxiety—the unhealed wounds of the past relationship between blacks and whites—they see themselves as victims of a superior/inferior relationship and resort to the protest patterns of the civil rights era.

Steele (1995: 184) sees these festering lesions operating also among white students. He found that most of the white students he interviewed spoke "as if under a faint cloud of accusation," compelled "to assure [him] that they were not racist." His skin color alone accused and judged them, as if saying "that whatever and whenever blacks are concerned, they had reason to feel guilt." This guilt provides the basis for white racial anxiety and carries with it "the terror of discovering that one has reason to feel guilt. . . . The darkest fear of whites is that their better lot in life is at least partially the result of capacity for evil." Thus, he concludes, white students coming face to face with African Americans are also coming face to face with the possibility of their own inhumanity. However, they were not the ones responsible for our nation's history, and thus they react hostilely to those who (African Americans) accuse them, as a means of "defending their own racial innocence"—acting in a racist way to demonstrate that they are not racists (Steele, 1995: 184–85).

According to Steele (1995: 178), the result of the accumulation of these feelings and actions by white and African American students is a struggle for innocence, manifested in a troubling, volatile politics of difference "in which each group justifies itself, its sense of worth and its pursuit of power, through difference alone." The winner not only accrues the most power but also the most innocence.

Steele argues that the best way to end this fighting is for colleges and universities to emphasize commonality as a higher value than diversity or pluralism. Such a response, however, seems to ignore the basis that he himself cites for the problems. I agree that we will all benefit from understanding that we do have more in common than in difference, but how do we get to the problem addressed by Steele if we simply stress commonality? Without question, one of the primary goals of multicultural education should be the exploration of what we have in common, though it is also as important to explore different visions and outlooks and to understand the contributions of the world's many peoples. Further, it would be naive to assume that pressure from students for a multicultural curriculum will mitigate or that faculty who have sought to infuse their courses with multicultural and gender-related perspectives will return to teaching their old, more narrowly focused syllabi. The challenge, then, is to ensure that our curriculum continues to evolve in a fashion that truly shapes students as critical thinkers, not as reflections of a new (and equally limiting) dogma that discounts commonality in favor of difference.

However, we need to extend our thinking beyond the exploration of intellectual issues and public policy conceptions. At a minimum, we need to reorder institutional priorities to produce campuses that are highly student-centered, a condition that the HERI research (discussed earlier) found lowers perceptions of racial tensions among all student groups (Hurtado, 1992). But more important, if indeed it is the unresolved feelings arising from the past relationship between blacks and whites that lie at the heart of racial tensions, we need to get directly to the matter of helping students deal with these dysfunctional feelings. Thus, colleges and universities should take a multifaceted approach to assist their students to move to a new level. First, an affective dimension should be added to the instructional program, so that students can begin to explore the issues that haunt race and other intergroup relations, not just intellectually but also in a way that begins to touch one's soul; that is, to engage entering students in a seminar akin to a group therapeutic process that continues throughout the first year. Second, a strong student support services program can further the effort outside of class (particularly in the residence halls, since dorm students tend to be more available than commuters), by helping to prepare students for life in a diverse society. Third, institutions should work at providing opportunities for positive interaction among students from different groups, so that they get to know and appreciate each other as individuals. Fourth, the entire workforce must understand that every member, irrespective of the level and nature of assigned duties, shares in the responsibility of fostering positive intergroup relations and student development.

Human Relations Auditing

While these four ingredients would combine to produce a general prescription to overcome the malady cited by Steele, the recipe for each institution must be tailored to fit the college or university's own circumstances. Since the culture and climate of Brown, for example, are different from those of Duke or Miami-Dade Community College or the University of Colorado or Kean—given the unique history and institutional strengths of each and the nature of their student bodies, etc.—each needs a set of programs that will be most effective for it. And, the good ideas that emerge on each campus must be engineered to work synergistically to maximize the likelihood that the feelings underpinning intergroup hostility are changed.

An approach that is showing promise in the corporate setting—the human relations audit—could provide a means for an institution of higher learning to develop an effective and comprehensive basis for its activity. Such an audit yields definitive information regarding the status of intergroup relations, on an office-by-office and service-by-service basis (both relations among those who work in a given office or service and those between them and their clienteles). For a campus, specific areas needing improvement and their relative level of urgency would be identified, as would components that might serve as models for improvement in other parts of the institution. The audit would also provide similar information regarding student-to-student interaction in residence life, student activities, athletics, etc. As is the case in financial and operational auditing, human relations auditing is intended to reveal areas of weakness that can be strengthened in order to avoid future problems. Thus, the process also includes the development of a remedial plan (with benchmarks for success), which can focus human and monetary resources. Further, just as the other two types of audits are meant to alter behavior in accordance with "best practice," the human relations audit can reveal what practice can be considered best for intergroup relations, in order to affect behavior of individuals within the organization, as well as institutional behavior, irrespective of the vagaries of the annual budget.

PROVIDING LEADERSHIP

The best way to avert a crisis is to catalyze the institutional culture to become one that embraces all who are enrolled irrespective of background characteristics, that nurtures the intellectual capacity of students to explore difficult issues, that fosters their affective development, and that helps them to learn to live with diversity by appreciating the commonality that underlies the difference. There are so many obstacles to overcome that effective leadership is required at all levels of the institution, particularly at the top. College and university presidents cannot simply delegate the responsibility to the front line, i.e., the faculty and the student-affairs staff. Their position must be broadly understood, through a clearly articulated vision statement and policy decisions that set positive intergroup relations among the highest of institutional priorities. Further, they must be at least as active on the campus in pursuit of this goal as they are off the campus in pursuit of funds.

Using the Bully Pulpit

While such a strategy, effectively implemented, should diminish the likelihood of intergroup conflict, there is no perfect antidote. Thus, college and university presidents must be prepared to act in the event that hateful speech occurs, either from students or from catered hate speakers. In the first instance, while it may be extremely difficult for a campus speech code to withstand constitutional scrutiny, increased penalties for hate-based acts are clearly possible. Thus, for example, if the defacement of property includes hateful epithets or is clearly targeted at an individual because of that person's race, ethnicity, religion, gender, sexual orientation, etc., the institution can and should invoke stiffer penalties than it would for simple defacement. Just as important, the president should be quickly at the scene to support the victim. Using the defacement example again, the president should lead a communal clean-up effort so that the perpetrators understand that there is no community support for their actions. Further, they should use their "bully pulpit" every time that a hateful act comes to their attention.

If a hate speaker is invited to campus, presidents should not hesitate to use the bully pulpit, starting with the students who rendered the invitation.[2] They should be questioned by the president regarding their rationale for the invitation. This should not be a negotiation session, but the president should be willing to act if he or she learns that the invitation was prompted by specific events on campus or by an unwelcoming campus climate. In any event, the students should be engaged in a conversation regarding the effect that a hate speaker would have on the targeted individuals in particular and on the campus in general. The students should know that while the president supports their free speech rights, she or he also enjoys such a right and will speak out forcefully against the message brought by the hate speaker, beginning the moment that the hate speaker's contract is executed. The president should also make known that if another campus group organizes a demonstration that will occur simultaneously with the speech, he or she will be among the protesters.

Sound Policies, Effectively Implemented

If the presidential leadership proves to be unsuccessful in getting the students to withdraw the invitation (something that might well happen if the students have been politicized or are alienated), a preexisting crisis management plan needs to be implemented. (More mistakes are likely to be made if an institution waits until a crisis develops before it considers how to deal with it.) Since the institution has the legal right to regulate the time, place, and manner of campus speech, it should use this authority to assure that it does not lose control of the situation. Thus, for example, the institution should not permit a speaker's own security staff to dictate security arrangements, to act alongside campus security, or to insist that audience members be searched. If campus officials believe that greater than usual security precautions are necessary, they should make the necessary arrangements themselves, and well in advance of the event.[3] (Of course, the institution may not have such discretion with certain elected officials.)

The crisis management plan should also include efforts to reach out to campus groups who may be the targets of the hate speaker's offensive remarks. They should not be able to dictate the institution's actions, any more than those who invited the speaker, but neither should they be treated as institutional adversaries. Efforts should be made to explain the institution's support of the speech rights of the group that offered the invitation but also its opposition to the message which that group wishes delivered. The targeted group should be made aware of the president's plans to offer a different message and should be invited to join in that message. If they wish to demonstrate or to hold a competing or subsequent event with their own speaker, they should be held to the same standards as the group that invited the hate speaker. A target group that is inclined to respond to the hate speaker with another hate speaker should be dissuaded by the president, using the same bully pulpit approach that was attempted with the first group.

In interacting with the group that invited the hate speaker, the target groups, and the rest of the campus community, the president should work actively to decrease the level of emotion and to transform the situation into a teachable moment. Through it all, the president should both seek to debunk the myths and lies that are the foundation of hateful speech (with particular reference to those that the speaker is known to propagate) and should encourage true dialogue toward creating more common ground. The president cannot do it alone—other campus leaders should be engaged in the effort—but it cannot be done at all without the president's leadership.

A crisis management plan has to involve public relations and interaction with the media. Without question, there will be alumni, parents, corporate donors, political leaders, and interest groups upset by an institution's decision to permit a hate speaker to come on campus. They will see reasons that on this occasion freedom of speech should be superseded by some other constitutional protection or some other common good. It will not be easy to convince them that the only way to bar the hate speaker (assuming that all of the procedures have been followed by the sponsoring group) is to bar all outside speakers, a price that is too high for a college or university to pay. The institution must be convincing that it has neither lost control of the campus nor its willingness to be strong both in the defense of free speech and in condemnation of the hateful speech; that it will do its utmost to assure that the voices for good speech are louder than those for hate speech; and that when the hate speaker comes, the president will lead the community in responding loudly as one, "That message is not accepted on our campus!"

SOME FINAL THOUGHTS

While the period from 1992 through 1994 was an unforgettable one for Kean College and many other institutions across the nation, there seemed to be a sharp drop in the number of press reports of hate speakers on college campuses in the 1994–95 academic year. Higher education should not be lulled into thinking that the events of the preceding several years provided some sort of cathartic release that cured the problem. Indeed, the societal and campus conditions that prompted the invitation of Khalid Abdul Muhammad and other purveyors of hate to so many colleges and universities during those several years, continue to exist. Thus, as proves true time and again vis à vis urban unrest, it only takes a single incident to spark feelings powerful enough to involve a campus in a new episode of catered hate speech. Such fires also have a tendency to spread to other campuses.

Colleges and universities should occupy the moral high ground, doing all that they can to assist our nation's evolution as *E Pluribus Unum*, so that we may march forward as one nation, not hover as a cluster of fractionated groups with increasingly less in common. Central to their endeavors must be an active commitment to, not a reactive posture of, improving intergroup relations on campus. The challenge is rigorous, but not impossible.

Since the ivy-covered walls between institutions of higher education and the environment in which they function are extremely porous, the challenge would be more easily met if campus leaders were not alone in striving to develop commitment to a more embracing society. Leaders off-campus—those in charge of government agencies, corporations, not-for-profit organizations, community and religious groups, and other formal social systems—need to stand tall in the effort to bring our nation together. They can start in their own backyards, by heeding the lessons that can be learned from the spate of hateful speech episodes that have plagued our colleges and universities. They must recognize that the health of their own organizations or communities, as well as that of the society that they serve, requires that they be ever-vigilant about intergroup relationships, since it effects the internal life of their organizations or communities, as well as external perceptions of their effectiveness, relevance, and even viability. Leaders cannot afford to be complacent, assuming that their group is either immune to, or beyond the reasonable likelihood of, disruption by intolerance. Like pneumonia, hatred is always floating in the atmosphere, ready to consume a weak body that ignores its symptoms. While medicines can restore health to an infected organism if the disease is caught in time, a body that is strong has less chance of contracting the illness in the first place. Thus, leaders of all organizations would be well advised to initiate an ongoing diagnostic and preventative process aimed at long-term health in intergroup relations within the organization.

Further, just as many employers encourage their employees' community service activity and sponsor such group efforts as roadside beautification projects and holiday parties for the disadvantaged, leaders of all formal groups should extend their organization's "good citizen or neighbor" role to the arena of human relations. If their message is to be commonly understood, they must, in word and deed, preach the importance of tolerance and intergroup harmony on a continuing basis. Also, whenever the monstrous head of hatred reveals itself in their communities, they must be quick to speak out, and encourage their members to do the same. Just as college presidents should lead public cleanups of racially motivated defacement of college or student property, other leaders should also symbolically roll up their sleeves to help to remove hateful graffiti targeted at members of their organization or occurring in their community, or otherwise come to the aid and comfort of victims of hatred.

Finally, leaders on campus and off should take a cue from the president of Kean College's Pan African Student Union, who, despite all that happened at the college, has been able to maintain a sense of optimism that has waned in too many Americans, particularly the young. Of her divided institution, she says, "I think we can recover." Recognizing the importance of exploring the deep feelings that separate people, she is convinced that "we just have problems within ourselves that we have to change. But if nobody talks about it, then nothing happens" (John-Hall, 1995: B6). If America's leaders are to continue to be worthy of our followership, they have an obligation to engage our society in a discussion that has the goal of forging a renewed sense of national purpose and recreating the spirit of optimism that has historically fueled the American dream. Together with colleges and universities, which in their position at the top of our educational chain have a special responsibility to foster such dialogue, they can help convert fighting words into uniting words.

NOTES

1. There is, however, an intriguing possibility that an institution of higher learning might seek to assure a proper working environment for its employees by regulating certain speech by all members of the campus community, not just by employees, in order to protect the workplace rights *of* its employees. In its role as employer the college or university has a responsibility to remedy a hostile work environment anywhere on its grounds. Are protected-class employees any less harassed because a derogatory sign is in a dorm window rather than at the desk of a fellow employee? Or because defamatory comments are uttered by a student every time the employee passes the student's favorite walk-side bench, rather than if a co-worker had made the remark? While a limited approach such as this would not deal with the student-to-student speech that is so offensive, since it would need to be geared very specifically to protect employees, it would have a serendipitous effect of making the campus more hospitable to students as well.

2. The event should not come as a surprise to the president. The institution should have procedures in place that must be followed by groups seeking to use campus facilities or to spend funds (including student fees) that are collected by the institution. Such procedures should require sufficient prior notice to permit the institution to prepare for the event. It is incumbent upon the campus officials involved in the activities process to inform the president immediately upon learning that a student group intends to invite a controversial speaker, particularly a hate speaker.

3. Some institutions have sought to discourage groups from inviting hate speakers by passing the costs of additional security or damage insurance policies on to the group. If this is not done across the board, it is likely to be ruled unconstitutional. Thus, if the institution does not pass on to the sponsoring group the additional costs for any event involving outsiders—whether one police officer to oversee parking for a visiting ballet company or a major security detail for a political rally in support of a Democratic or Republican candidate or for a Rolling Stones concert—it probably cannot pass on the costs of security for a hate speaker. Similarly, its criteria for requiring a damage insurance policy must be clearly stated and equitably applied.

REFERENCES

Adams, Russell. "Hate Speech on Campus." Paper presented at the QEM Biannual Conference. Washington, DC, July 15, 1994.

Bobo, Lawrence and James R. Kluegel. "Opposition to Race-Targeting: Self-Interest, Stratification Ideology, or Racial Attitudes." *American Sociological Review* v. 58 n. 4 (December 1993), pp. 443–464.

Ewalt, Patricia. "On Not Knowing." *Social Work* v. 39 n. 3 (May 1994), pp. 245–246.

Hurtado, Sylvia. "The Campus Racial Climate, Contexts of Conflict." *Journal of Higher Education* v. 63 n. 5 (September/October 1992), pp. 539–569.

John-Hall, Annette. "N.J. College Still Feels Speech's Stigma." *Philadelphia Inquirer*. January 8, 1995, pp. B1, B6.

Jones, Maggie. "The Prince of P(erpetual) C(onversation)." *Philadelphia Magazine* v. 86 n. 8 (August 1995), pp. 67–77.

Kim, Elizabeth C. "Toward a Cord of Solidarity: Progressive Social Change in the 1990s." *Monthly Review* v. 45 n. 4 (September 1993), pp. 2–57.

Neuborne, Burt. "Ghosts in the Attic: Idealized Pluralism, Community and Hate Speech." *Harvard Civil Rights—Civil Liberties Review* v. 27 n. 2 (Summer 1992), pp. 371–406.

Peters, Ronald M., Jr. *The Next Generation, Dialogues Between Leaders and Students*. Norman, OK: University of Oklahoma Press, 1992.

Sidel, Ruth. *Battling Bias, The Struggle for Identity and Community on College Campuses*. New York: Viking, 1994.

Steele, Shelby. "The Recoloring of Campus Life: Student Racism, Academic Pluralism and the End of a Dream." *Campus Wars: Multiculturalism and the Politics of Difference*, ed. John Arthur and Amy Shapiro. Boulder, CO: Westview Press, 1995, pp. 176–187.

Bibliography

Abalos, David. "Multicultural Education in the Service of Transformation." *Celebrating Diversity: Global Approach to Literature and World Culture, Conference Proceedings*. Montclair State College, March 10, 1989.

Abernathy, Virginia. *Population Politics, The Choices That Shape Our Future*. New York: Plenum Press, 1993.

Adams, Russell. "Hate Speech on Campus." Paper presented at the QEM Biannual Conference. Washington, DC, July 15, 1994.

Alexander, Edward. "Multiculturalists and Anti-Semitism." *Society* v. 31 n. 6 (September/October 1994), pp. 58–64.

Altman, Andrew. "Liberalism and Campus Hate Speech." *Campus Wars: Multiculturalism and the Politics of Difference*, ed. John Arthur and Amy Shapiro. Boulder, CO: Westview Press, 1995, pp. 122–134.

Anderson, P. and T. Farragher. "States Spend Billions to Provide Services to Illegal Immigrants." *Philadelphia Inquirer*. September 15, 1994, p. A4.

Anti-Defamation League. "ADL Special Summary Report: 1994 Audit of Anti-Semitic Incidents, Overview." New York: Anti-Defamation League, 1995.

Ashraf, Javed. "Differences in Returns to Education: An Analysis by Race." *American Journal of Economics and Sociology* v. 53 n. 3 (July 1993), pp. 281–290.

Associated Press. "At Rutgers, Bias Incidents Follow Protests Over President's Remarks." *Philadelphia Inquirer*. February 23, 1995, p. S7.

———. "Court Overturns Stanford Code on Bigoted Speech." *The New York Times*. March 1, 1995, p. B8.

————. "Rutgers Minority Recruiting Down." *Philadelphia Inquirer*. May 29, 1995, p. S8.

Ayres, B. Drummond, Jr. "University Regents in California Battle Over Affirmative Action." *The New York Times*. July 21, 1995, pp. A1, A14.

Badgett, M. V. Lee. "Where the Jobs Went in the 1990–91 Downturn: Varying (Mis)Fortunes of Homogenous Distress?" Paper presented at the National Conference on Race Relations and Civil Rights in the Post Reagan-Bush Era. Minneapolis, MN, October 1994.

Banks, James A. "The Historical Reconstruction of Knowledge About Race: Implications for Transforming Teaching." *Educational Researcher* v. 24 n. 2 (March 1995), pp. 15–25.

Barr, Kellie E. M., Michael P. Farrell, Grace M. Barnes, and John W. Welte. "Race, Class, and Gender Differences in Substance Abuse: Evidence of Middle Class/Underclass Polarization Among Black Males." *Social Problems* v. 40 n. 3 (August 1993), pp. 314–327.

Belsky, Gary and Susan Berger. "Women Could Be Big Losers if Affirmative Action Falls." *Money* v. 24 n. 8 (August 1995), pp. 20–22.

Berman, Paul. "The Other and the Almost the Same." *The New Yorker*. February 28, 1994, pp. 61–71.

Bernstein, Richard. "Play Penn." *The New Republic* v. 209 n. 5 (August 2, 1993), pp. 16–19.

Billings, Jessica C. "Racism in the '90s: Is It Hip to Hate?" *Education Digest* v. 58 n. 2 (December, 1992), pp. 35–39.

Birnbaum, Robert. "Administrative Commitments and Minority Enrollments: College Presidents' Goals for Quality and Access." *Review of Higher Education* v. 11 n. 4 (Summer 1988), pp. 435–457.

Bobo, Lawrence and James R. Kluegel. "Opposition to Race-Targeting: Self-Interest, Stratification Ideology, or Racial Attitudes." *American Sociological Review* v. 58 n. 4 (December 1993), pp. 443–464.

Bren, Vicki L. "Memorandum to Stephen Wiley, Re: Free Speech on College Campuses—Kean College." December 28, 1993.

Browder, Lesley H., Jr. "'Can We All Get Along?' The Politics of Diversity," *Leadership and Diversity in Education*, ed. Joel L. Burdin. Lancaster, PA: Technomic Publishing, 1994, pp. 36–54.

Brown, Darryl. "Racism and Race Relations in the University." *Virginia Law Review* v. 76. (1990), pp. 295–335.

Bruning, Fred. "Black and White in America." *MacLean's* v. 105 n. 22 (June 1, 1992), p. 11.

Burd, Stephen. "Humanities Endowment Approves Grants for 'National Conversation.'" *The Chronicle of Higher Education*. April 14, 1995, p. A34.

Bush, George. "Excerpts from President's Speech to University of Michigan Graduates." *The New York Times.* May 5, 1991, p. A32.

Caputo, Richard K. "Family Poverty, Unemployment Rates, and AFDC Payments: Trends among Blacks and Whites." *Families in Society: The Journal of Contemporary Human Services* v. 74 n. 9 (November 1993), pp. 515–526.

Card, David and Thomas Lemieux. "Changing Wage Structure and Black-White Wage Differentials." *The American Economic Review* v. 84 n. 2 (May 1994), pp. 29–33.

Carvagal, Doreen. "Protest against President Halts Basketball Game at Rutgers." *The New York Times.* February 8, 1995. p. B1.

Chira, Susan. "Teaching History So That Cultures Are More Than Footnotes." *The New York Times.* July 10, 1991, p. A17.

Clinton, William J. "Excerpts from Clinton Talk on Affirmative Action." *The New York Times.* July 20, 1995, p. B10.

Cockburn, Alexander. "Bush and P.C.—A Conspiracy So Immense . . . ." *The Nation* v. 252 n. 20 (1991), pp. 685–686.

Cohen, Richard. "Nixon's the One." *Second Thoughts about Race in America,* ed. Peter Collier and David Horowitz. Lanham, MD: Madison Books, 1991, pp. 19–24.

Cohen, Robert. "Farrakhan Suspends Lecturer." *Newark Star Ledger.* February 4, 1994, pp. 1, 18.

Collison, Michelle N.-K. "Young People Found Pessimistic about Relations between the Races." *The Chronicle of Higher Education.* March 25, 1992, pp. A1, A32.

———. "Survey Finds Many Freshmen Hope to Further Racial Understanding." *The Chronicle of Higher Education.* January 13, 1993, pp. A29, A32.

Commissioner's Task Force on Minorities. *A Curriculum of Inclusion.* Albany, NY: New York State Department of Education, 1989.

Commission on Minority Participation in Education and American Life. *One-Third of a Nation.* Washington, DC: American Council on Education and Education Commission of the States, 1988.

Commission on Racism, Racial Violence and Religious Violence. *Report of the Commission on Racism, Racial Violence and Religious Violence.* Trenton, NJ: NJ Department of Law and Public Safety, 1993.

Crosson, Patricia H. "Four-Year College and University Environments for Minority Degree Achievement." *The Review of Higher Education* v. 11 n. 4 (Summer 1988), pp. 365–382.

Cudjoe, Selwyn R. "Time for Serious Scholars to Repudiate Nation of Islam's Diatribe against Jews." *The Chronicle of Higher Education.* May 11, 1994, pp. B3, B5.

Darity, William, Jr. "The Undesirables, America's Underclass in the Managerial Age: Beyond the Myrdal Theory of Racial Inequality." *Daedalus* v. 124 n. 1 (Winter 1995), pp. 145–165.

D'Aurizio, Elaine. "Campus Speech Codes, Policing Bias, Many NJ Colleges Try to Control Language of Hate." *Bergen Record.* June 2, 1993, pp. A1, A14.

Delgado, Richard. "Campus Antiracism Rules: Constitutional Narratives in Collision." *Northwestern University Law Review* v. 85 n. 2 (1991), pp. 343–387.

————. "Words That Wound: A Tort Action for Racial Insults, Epithets, and Name Calling." *Words That Wound: Critical Race Theory, Assaultive Speech and the First Amendment,* ed. Mari J. Matsuda, Charles R. Lawrence, III, Richard Delgado, and Kimberle Williams Crenshaw. Boulder, CO: Westview Press, 1993, pp. 93–111.

Drucker, Peter. "Political Correctness and American Academe." *Society* v. 32 n. 1 (November/December 1994), pp. 58–63.

D'Souza, Dinesh. "The Visigoths in Tweed." *Forbes* v. 147 (April 1,1991), pp. 81–86.

Dziech, Billie Wright. "Coping with the Alienation of White Male Students." *The Chronicle of Higher Education.* January 13, 1995, pp. B1–B2.

Editors of the *Boston Globe.* "Mass. Students Upbeat Amid Sobering Problems." *Boston Globe.* September 12, 1993.

Editors of *Perspective, the Campus Legal Monthly.* "First Amendment on Campus: Four Exceptions." *Perspective, the Campus Legal Monthly* v. 6 n. 1 (January 1991), pp. 1–2.

Editors of the *Philadelphia Inquirer.* "Confederate Flag Dispute Widens at U. of Delaware." *Philadelphia Inquirer.* May 8, 1995, p. B2.

Editors of *Society.* "Social Science and the Citizen." *Society* v. 32 n. 2 (January/February 1995), pp. 2–4.

Editors of *The Chronicle of Higher Education.* "'In' Box." *The Chronicle of Higher Education.* January 13, 1995a, p. A15.

————. "'In' Box." *The Chronicle of Higher Education.* July 7, 1995b, p. A13.

Editors of *The Economist.* "America's Blacks, A World Apart." *The Economist* v. 318 (March 30, 1991), pp. 17–21.

————. "Illegal Immigrants, To the Rescue." *The Economist* v. 332 n. 7879 (September 3, 1994), p. 35.

————. "South Carolina, A Rebel Tamed?" *The Economist* v. 331 (June 11, 1994), pp. 23–24.

Editors of *The New York Times.* "Affirmative Action Will Be Examined in Senate." *The New York Times.* February 6, 1995, p. A15.

Edmondson, Brad. "The Trend You Can't Ignore." *American Demographics* v. 16 n. 7 (July 1994), p. 2.

Edsall, T. "Christian Coalition Sounds Charge for '96." *Washington Post.* September 17, 1994, p. A4.

Eisen, Arnold. "Limits and Virtues of Dialogue." *Society* v. 31 n. 6 (September/October 1994), pp. 17–22.

Elfin, Mel and Sarah Burke. "Race on Campus." *US News and World Report.* April 19, 1993, pp. 52–56.

Ellison, Christopher G. and Daniel A. Powers. "The Contact Hypothesis and Racial Attitudes among Black Americans." *Social Science Quarterly* v. 75 n. 2 (June 1994), pp. 385–400.

Ewalt, Patricia. "On Not Knowing." *Social Work* v. 39 n. 3 (May 1994), pp. 245–246.

Exter, Thomas. "The Declining Majority." *American Demographics* v. 15 n. 1 (January 1993), p. 59.

Ferguson, Ronald F. "Shifting Challenges: Fifty Years of Economic Change Toward Black-White Earnings Equality." *Daedalus* v. 124 n. 1 (Winter 1995), pp. 37–76.

Florio, Gwen. "Campus Polarized after Confederate-flag Flap." *Philadelphia Inquirer.* November 28, 1994. pp. S1, S9.

Fonte, John. "The Naive Romanticism of the History Standards." *The Chronicle of Higher Education.* June 9, 1995, p. A48.

Galis, Leon. "Merely Academic Diversity." *Journal of Higher Education* v. 64 n. 1 (January/February 1993), pp. 93–101.

Gates, Henry Louis, Jr. "Black Demagogues and Pseudo-Scholars." *The New York Times.* July 20, 1992, p A19.

————. "Let Them Talk: Why Civil Liberties Pose No Threat to Civil Rights." *The New Republic* v. 209 n. 12–13 (September 20 and 27, 1993), pp. 37–49.

Gibbs, Annette. *Reconciling Rights and Responsibilities of Colleges and Students: Offensive Speech, Assembly, Drug Testing and Safety; ASHE/ERIC Higher Education Research Report No. 5.* Washington, DC: The George Washington University, 1992.

Giles, Michael W. and Kaenan Hertz. "Racial Threat and Partisan Identification." *American Political Science Review* v. 88 n. 2 (June 1994), pp. 317–326.

Giroux, Henry. "Teaching in the Age of 'Political Correctness,'" *The Educational Forum* v. 59 n. 2 (Winter 1995), pp. 130–139.

Gomez, Elsa. Letter to Chancellor Edward D. Goldberg, December 20, 1993.

————. "December 9 Statement from Dr. Gomez," reprinted in *Kean Today.* January 13, 1994, p. 4.

————. "Administrative Report, Special Edition." March 4, 1994.

Goode, Stephen. "All Opinions Welcome—Except the Wrong Ones." *Insight* (April 22, 1991), pp. 8–17.

Goodman, Howard. "Blacks, Jews Strive amid New Wounds." *Philadelphia Inquirer*. January 30, 1994, pp. E1–E2.

Gose, Ben. "Penn to Replace Controversial Speech Code. Will No Longer Punish Students for Insults." *The Chronicle of Higher Education*. June 29, 1994, p. A30.

————. "Growth of Minority Enrollment Slowed to 2.6 % in 1993." *The Chronicle of Higher Education*. March 17, 1995, p. A34.

Gray, Jerry. "House Leader Refers to Colleague with Anti-Gay Slur." *The New York Times*. January 28, 1995, p. A1.

Green, John C. "The Grassroots Clout of the Religious Right." *The Chronicle of Higher Education*. October 26, 1994, pp. B1–B2.

Grey, Thomas C. "Civil Rights vs. Civil Liberties, The Case of Discriminatory Verbal Harassment." *Journal of Higher Education* v. 63 n. 5 (September/October 1992), pp. 485–516.

Gunther, Gerald. "Good Speech, Bad Speech—No." *Campus Wars: Multiculturalism and the Politics of Difference*, ed. John Arthur and Amy Shapiro. Boulder, CO: Westview Press, 1995, pp. 109–113.

Hacker, Andrew. "The Myths of Racial Division." *The New Republic* v. 206 n. 12 (March 23, 1992), pp. 21–25.

Hager, George. "Commission Moves Carefully on Entitlement Cuts." *Congressional Quarterly* v. 52 n. 32 (August 13, 1994), p. 2318.

Hamilton, Charles V. "Affirmative Action and the Clash of Experiential Realities." *The Annals of the American Academy of Political and Social Science* v. 523 (September 1992), pp. 10–18.

Harvey, William B. "Faculty Responsibility and Tolerance." *Thought and Action, the NEA Higher Education Journal* v. 7 n. 2 (Fall 1991), pp. 115–136.

Heller, Scott. "Frame-Up of Multicultural Movement Dissected by Scholars and Journalists." *The Chronicle of Higher Education*. November 27, 1991, pp. A15–A17.

Henneberger, Melinda. "D'Amato Gives a New Apology on Ito Remarks." *The New York Times*. April 7, 1995, p. A1.

Hirsch, E. D. *Cultural Literacy: What Every American Needs to Know*. Boston: Houghton Mifflin, 1987.

Hodulik, Patricia. "Racist Speech on Campus." *Wayne Law Review* v. 37 (1991), pp. 1433–1450.

Holmes, Steven A. "Farrakhan Is Warned over Aide's Invective." *The New York Times*. January 25, 1994, p. A1.

————. "White House Signals an Easing on Affirmative Action." *The New York Times*. February 25, 1995, p. 9.

Hook, Janet. "House Denounces Remarks as 'Racist' Speech." *Congressional Quarterly* v. 52 n. 8 (February 26, 1994), p. 458.

Hummer, Robert A. "Racial Differences in Infant Mortality in the U.S.: An Examination of Social and Health Determinants." *Social Forces* v. 72 n. 1 (December 1993), pp. 529–554.

Hurtado, Sylvia. "The Campus Racial Climate, Contexts of Conflict." *Journal of Higher Education* v. 63 n. 5 (September/October 1992), pp. 539–569.

Idelson, Holly. "House Hate Crimes Measure Would Increase Sentences." *Congressional Quarterly* v. 51 n. 38 (September 25, 1993), p. 2563.

Israel, Michael. "Hate Speech and the First Amendment." Unpublished manuscript shared with members of Kean College Board of Trustees, 1994.

Jaschik, Scott. "Minority Scholarships: A Chronology." *The Chronicle of Higher Education*. November 9, 1994, p. A30.

————. "Blow to Affirmative Action." *The Chronicle of Higher Education*. June 23, 1995a, pp. A21–23.

————. "'No' on Black Scholarships." *The Chronicle of Higher Education*. June 2, 1995b, pp. A25, A29.

————. "U.S. Report Questions 'Bakke' Defense of Affirmative Action." *The Chronicle of Higher Education*. July 7, 1995c, p. A20.

John-Hall, Annette. "N.J. College Still Feels Speech's Stigma." *Philadelphia Inquirer*. January 8, 1995, pp. B1, B6.

Johnson, James H., Jr. and Walter C. Farrell, Jr. "Race Still Matters." *The Chronicle of Higher Education*. July 7, 1995, p. A48.

Jones, Charles H. "Equality, Dignity and Harm: The Constitutionality of Regulating American Campus Ethnoviolence." *Wayne Law Review* v. 37 (1991), pp. 1383–1432.

Jones, Maggie. "The Prince of P(erpetual) C(onversation)." *Philadelphia Magazine* v. 86 n. 8 (August 1995), pp. 67–77.

Kahlenberg, Richard. "Class, Not Race, An Affirmative Action That Works." *The New Republic* v. 212 n. 14 (April 3, 1995), pp. 21–27.

Kaplin, William A. "A Proposed Process for Managing First Amendment Aspects of Campus Hate Speech." *Journal of Higher Education* v. 63 n. 5 (September/October 1992), pp. 517–538.

Kaus, Mickey. "TRB in Washington, Speech Defect." *The New Republic* v. 208 n. 24 (June 14, 1993), pp. 6, 49.

Kean, Thomas. "The Way to Handle Hatemongers, Confront Their Ideas Forcefully." *Bergen Record*. May 22, 1994, p. A23.

Kean College. "Controversy Follows Muhammad Speech." *Kean Today*. January 13, 1994, pp. 1, 4.

Kellough, J. Edward. "Affirmative Action in Government Employment." *The Annals of the American Academy of Political and Social Science* v. 523 (September 1992), pp. 117–130.

Kennedy, Randall. "Should Private Universities Voluntarily Bind Themselves to the First Amendment? No!" *The Chronicle of Higher Education.* September 21, 1994, pp. B1–B2.

Kilbourne, Barbara, Paula England, and Kurt Beron. "Effects of Individual, Occupational, and Industrial Characteristics of Earnings: Intersections of Race and Gender." *Social Forces* v. 72 n. 4 (June 1994), pp. 1149–1176.

Kilson, Martin and Clement Cottingham. "Thinking About Race Relations, How Far Are We Still from Integration?" *Dissent* v. 38 n. 4 (Fall 1991), pp. 520–530.

Kim, Elizabeth C. "Toward a Cord of Solidarity: Progressive Social Change in the 1990s." *Monthly Review* v. 45 n. 4 (September 1993), pp. 52–57.

Klein, Joe. "Race: The Issues." *Second Thoughts about Race in America,* ed. Peter Collier and David Horowitz. Lanham, MD: Madison Books, 1991, pp. 37–50.

Kovar, Mary Grace. "Mortality among Minority Populations in the United States." *American Journal of Public Health* v. 82 n. 8 (August 1992), pp. 1168–1170.

Kristol, Irving. "The Tragedy of Multiculturalism." *Wall Street Journal.* July 31, 1991, p. A10.

Lange, Ellen E. "Racist Speech on Campus: A Title VII Solution to a First Amendment Problem." *Southern California Law Review* v. 64 (1990), pp. 105–134.

Lawrence, Charles R., III. "If He Hollers Let Him Go: Regulating Racist Speech on Campus." *Duke Law Review* v. 1990 n. 3 (June 1990), pp. 431–483.

Leatherman, Courtney. "The Minefield of Diversity, How Debate Over Expanding a Multicultural Requirement at the U. of Oregon Got Ugly." *The Chronicle of Higher Education.* June 15, 1994, p. A15, A17–A18.

Lester, Julius. "Whatever Happened to the Civil Rights Movement?" *Second Thoughts about Race in America,* ed. Peter Collier and David Horowitz. Lanham, MD: Madison Books, 1991, pp. 3–9.

Lichter, Daniel T. and David J. Eggebeen. "Rich Kids, Poor Kids: Changing Income Inequality among American Children." *Social Forces* v. 71 n. 3 (March 1993), pp. 761–780.

Locke, Michelle. "University Eyes End to Race-based Policies." *Philadelphia Inquirer.* July 21, 1995, pp. A1, A14.

Loury, Glenn C. "Incentive Effects of Affirmative Action." *The Annals of the American Academy of Political and Social Science* v. 523 (September 1992), pp. 19–29.

Magner, Denise K. "Gathering to Assess Battle Against 'Political Correctness,' Scholars Look for New Ways to Resist 'Illiberal Radicals.'" *The Chronicle of Higher Education.* October 30, 1991, pp. A17–A19.

Marcus, Laurence R. "Federal Civil Rights Enforcement in Higher Education: Shadow or Substance." *Educational Policy* v. 2 n. 2 (1988), pp. 189–208.

————. "State-level Efforts to Improve Racial/Ethnic Harmony on Campus." Paper presented at the National Conference on Racial and Ethnic Relations in American Higher Education. Oklahoma City, June 1989.

Marcus, Laurence R. and Benjamin D. Stickney. "A Concluding Note: The Challenge Ahead." *Politics and Policy in the Age of Education,* ed. Laurence R. Marcus and Benjamin D. Stickney. Springfield, IL: Charles C Thomas Publishers, 1990.

Matsuda, Mari J. "Public Response to Racist Speech: Considering the Victim's Story." *Words That Wound: Critical Race Theory, Assaultive Speech and the First Amendment,* ed. Mari J. Matsuda, Charles R. Lawrence, III, Richard Delgado, and Kimberle Williams Crenshaw. Boulder, CO: Westview Press, 1993, pp. 17–51.

Matsuda, Mari J. and Charles R. Lawrence, III. "Epilogue: Burning Crosses and the R.A.V. Case." *Words That Wound: Critical Race Theory, Assaultive Speech and the First Amendment,* ed. Mari J. Matsuda, Charles R. Lawrence, III, Richard Delgado, and Kimberle Williams Crenshaw. Boulder, CO: Westview Press, 1993, pp. 133–136.

Matsuda, Mari J., Charles R. Lawrence, III, Richard Delgado, and Kimberle Williams Crenshaw. "Introduction." *Words That Wound: Critical Race Theory, Assaultive Speech and the First Amendment,* ed. Mari J. Matsuda, Charles R. Lawrence, III, Richard Delgado, and Kimberle Williams Crenshaw. Boulder, CO: Westview Press, 1993, pp. 1–14.

Maxwell, Nan L. "The Effect on Black-White Wage Differences of Differences in the Quantity and Quality of Education." *Industrial and Labor Relations Review* v. 47 n. 2 (January 1994), pp. 249–264.

McAneny, Leslie. "Ethnic Minorities View the Media's View of Them." *The Gallup Poll Monthly* n. 347 (August 1994), pp. 31–41.

McAneny, Leslie and Lydia Saad. "America's Public Schools: Still Separate? Still Unequal?" *The Gallup Poll Monthly* n. 344 (May 1994), pp. 23–29.

McClain, John D. "Blacks' Academic Gains No Match for Bias, Market Forces, Study Says." *Philadelphia Inquirer*. April 30, 1995, p. A9.

McClelland, Katherine E. and Carol J. Auster. "Public Platitudes and Hidden Tensions, Racial Climates at Predominantly White Liberal Arts Colleges." *Journal of Higher Education* v. 61 n. 6 (November/December 1990), pp. 607–642.

McClelland, Kent and Christopher Hunter. "The Perceived Seriousness of Racial Harassment." *Social Problems* v. 39 n. 1 (February 1992), pp. 92–107.

McConnell, Scott and Eric Breindel. "Head to Come. Is 'White Nationalism' the Problem?" *The New Republic*. January 8 and 15, 1990, pp. 18–21.

McDaniel, Antonio. "The Dynamic Racial Composition of the United States." *Daedalus* v. 124 n. 1 (Winter 1995), pp. 179–198.

Merelman, Richard M. "Racial Conflict and Cultural Politics in the United States." *Journal of Politics* v. 56 n. 1 (February 1994), pp. 1–20.

Meyers, Michael. "Black/Jewish Splits." *Society* v. 31 n. 6 (September/October 1994), pp. 23–27.

Michelman, Frank. "Universities, Racist Speech and Democracy in America: An Essay for the ACLU." *Harvard Civil Rights—Civil Liberties Review* v.27 n. 2 (Summer 1992), pp. 339–369.

Monaghan, Peter. "Charges of Bias against Whites Erupt at Evergreen State Branch." *The Chronicle of Higher Education*. February 24, 1995, p. A38.

Mooney, Carolyn J. "Amid the Continuing Debate Over 'Political Correctness,' University of Arizona Courses Seek to Explore the Middle Ground." *The Chronicle of Higher Education*. May 29, 1991, pp. A9–A10.

Morris, Eugene. "The Difference in Black and White." *American Demographics* v. 15 n. 1 (January 1993), pp. 44–49.

Murray, Charles A. and Richard Hernstein. *The Bell Curve: Intelligence and Class Structure in American Life*. New York: The Free Press, 1994.

Nagel, Joane. "Constructing Ethnicity: Creating and Recreating Ethnic Identity and Culture." *Social Problems* v. 41 n. 1 (February 1994), pp. 152–176.

National Center for Educational Statistics. *Mini-Digest of Educational Statistics 1994*. Washington, DC: US Government Printing Office 1994a.

———. *The Pocket Condition of Education 1994*. Washington, DC: US Government Printing Office, 1994b.

National Commission on Excellence in Education. *A Nation at Risk: The Imperative for Educational Reform.* Washington, DC: US Government Printing Office, 1983.

Neuborne, Burt. "Ghosts in the Attic: Idealized Pluralism, Community and Hate Speech." *Harvard Civil Rights—Civil Liberties Review* v. 27 n. 2 (Summer 1992), pp. 371–406.

New Jersey State Assembly. "An Assembly Resolution Concerning Free Speech, Tolerance, and Responsibility, and Commending Dr. Edward Goldberg, Chancellor of Higher Education." January 10, 1994.

New York State Social Studies Review and Development Committee. *One Nation, Many Peoples: A Declaration of Cultural Interdependence.* Albany: NY State Dept. of Education, 1991.

Nicklin, Julie L. "Teacher-Education Programs Face Pressure to Provide Multicultural Training." *The Chronicle of Higher Education.* November 27, 1991, pp. A1, A16–A17.

Noley, Grayson. "Fear, Higher Education and Change." *Thought and Action, the NEA Higher Education Journal* v. 7 n. 2 (Fall 1991), pp. 105–114.

Nordheimer, Jon. "Divided by Diatribe, College Speech Ignites Furor Over Race." *The New York Times.* December 29, 1993, pp. B1, B6.

———. "Farrakhan Softens Tone But Sticks to Message." *The New York Times.* March 30, 1994, p. B4.

———. "At Rally Students Seek Resignation of Rutgers President." *The New York Times.* February 2, 1995a, p. B4.

———. "Rutgers Leader Disavows Linking Race and Ability." *The New York Times.* February 1, 1995b, p. B5.

Oldaker, Lawrence L. "Coping with 'Hate Speech' in Educational Settings." *Leadership and Diversity in Education,* ed. Joel L. Burdin. Lancaster, PA: Technomic Publishing Company, 1994, pp. 76–85.

Olivas, Michael. "The Political Economy of Immigration, Intellectual Property and Racial Harassment, Case Studies on the Implementation of Legal Change on Campus." *Journal of Higher Education* v. 63 n. 5 (September/October 1992), pp. 570–598.

O'Neil, John. "A New Generation Confronts Racism." *Educational Leadership* v. 50 n. 8 (May 1993), pp. 60–63.

O'Neill, Dave M. and June O'Neill. "Affirmative Action in the Labor Market." *The Annals of the American Academy of Political and Social Science* v. 523 (September 1992), pp. 88–103.

Orlans, Harold. "Affirmative Action in Higher Education." The Annals of the American Academy of Political and Social Science v. 523 (September 1992), pp. 144–158.

Oteri, Lisa A. and Gary D. Malaney. "Racism on Campus—The Negative Impact on Enrollment." *College and University* v. 65 n. 3 (Spring 1990), pp. 213–226.

Otto, M. "Christian Coalition Looks to November." *Philadelphia Inquirer.* September 17, 1994, p. A2.

Overpeck, Mary D., Howard J. Hoffman, and Kate Prager. "The Lowest Birth-Weight Infants and the US Infant Mortality Rate: NCHS 1983 Linked Birth/Infant Death Data." *American Journal of Public Health* v. 82 n. 3 (March 1992), pp. 441–444.

Perez, Miguel. "In Search of a Scapegoat." *Bergen Record.* March 9, 1994, p. A24.

Peters, Ronald M., Jr. *The Next Generation, Dialogues Between Leaders and Students.* Norman, OK: University of Oklahoma Press, 1992.

Phillip, Mary-Christine. "Fiscal Reality Hits Higher Education's Ivory Tower . . . Hard." *Black Issues in Higher Education* v. 11 n. 26 (February 23, 1995), pp. 8–14.

Piliawsky, Monte. "The Clinton Administration and African-Americans." *Black Scholar* v. 24 n. 2 (Spring 1994), pp. 2–10.

Poritz, Deborah T. and William C. Brown. "Letter to Elsa Gomez Re: Constitutionality of Conduct-Based Restrictions on Speakers at State Colleges." D.O.L. No. 94–80057. March 16, 1994.

Purdum, Todd S. "President Shows Fervent Support for Goals of Affirmative Action." *The New York Times.* July 20, 1995, pp. A1, B10.

Ravitch, Diane. "Multiculturalism: E Pluribus Plures." *The Key Reporter* v. 56 n. 1 (1990), pp. 1–4.

Riche, Martha Farnsworth. "We're All Minorities Now." *American Demographics* v. 13 n. 10 (October 1991), pp. 4–8.

Robeson, Paul, Jr. *Paul Robeson, Jr. Speaks to America.* New Brunswick, NJ: Rutgers University Press, 1993.

Rodgers, William M., III. "Racial Differences in Employment Shares: New Evidence from EEO-1 Files." Paper presented at the National Conference on Race Relations and Civil Rights in the Post Reagan-Bush Era. Minneapolis, MN, October 1994.

Rose, Tricia, Andrew Ross, and others. "Race and Racism: A Symposium." *Social Text* v. 13 n. 1 (Spring 1995), pp. 1–52.

Rosen, Jeffrey. "Is Affirmative Action Doomed? How the Law Is Unraveling." *The New Republic* v. 211 n. 16 (October 17, 1994), pp. 25–28, 30, 34–35.

———. "Affirmative Action: A Solution, Neither Color-blindness nor Quota-mongering." *The New Republic* v. 212 n. 19 (May 8, 1995), pp. 20, 22–25.

Rubin, James H. "Blacks Lead in Mortgage Rejection." *Philadelphia Inquirer.* July 19, 1995, p. C1.

Sanoff, Alvin P. and Scott Minerbrook and Associates. "Students Talk about Race, At Chapel Hill, N.C. Racial Tension Runs High. A Special Report." *US News and World Report.* April 19, 1993, pp. 57–64.

Schlesinger, Arthur, Jr. "Report of the Social Studies Syllabus Review Committee, A Dissenting Opinion." New York State Social Studies Review and Development Committee. *One Nation, Many Peoples: A Declaration of Independence.* Albany: NY State Department of Education, 1991, pp. 45–47.

———. "The Disuniting of America: Reflections on a Multicultural Society." *Campus Wars, Multiculturalism and the Politics of Difference,* ed. John Arthur and Amy Shapiro. Boulder, CO: Westview Press, 1995, pp. 226–234.

Schrag, Peter. "Son of 187, Anti-affirmative Action Propositions." *The New Republic* v. 212 n. 5 (January 30, 1995), pp. 16–19.

Schulte, Brigid. "African American Family Income Hasn't Risen above the 1969 Level." *Philadelphia Inquirer.* February 23, 1995, p. A3.

Schwarz, Benjamin. "The Diversity Myth: America's Leading Export." *The Atlantic Monthly* v. 275 n. 5 (May 1995), pp. 57–67.

Scott, Joan Wallach. "The Campaign against Political Correctness, What's Really at Stake?" *Change* v. 23 n. 6 (1991), pp. 30–43.

Scott, Robert. "Multiculturalism." Invited Address. Organization of African Unity Lecture Series on Multiculturalism. Ramapo College, September 26, 1991.

Seigenthaler, John. "Politically Correct Speech: An Oxymoron." *Editor and Publisher* v. 126 n. 10 (March 6, 1993), pp. 48, 38.

Shapiro, John T. "The Call for Campus Conduct Policies: Censorship or Constitutionally Permissible Limitations on Speech." *Minnesota Law Review* v. 75 (1990), pp. 201–238.

Shea, Christopher. "Sore Relations Again at Penn." *The Chronicle of Higher Education.* March 24, 1995a, pp. A39–A40.

———. "Stanford Anti-harassment Policy Violates Rights of Free Speech, Cal. Judge Rules." *The Chronicle of Higher Education.* March 10, 1995b, p A32.

———. "Stanford Gives Up Legal Battle to Keep Its Hate Speech Code." *The Chronicle of Higher Education.* March 24, 1995c, p. A40.

Sidel, Ruth. *Battling Bias, The Struggle for Identity and Community on College Campuses.* New York: Viking, 1994.

Siegel, Evan G. S. "Closing the Campus Gates to Free Expression: The Regulation of Offensive Speech at Colleges and Universities." *Emory Law Journal* v. 39 (1990), pp. 1351–1400.

Sigelman, Lee and Susan Welch. "The Contact Hypothesis Revisited: Black-White Interaction and Positive Racial Attitudes." *Social Forces* v. 71 n. 3 (March 1993), pp. 781–795.

Singer, Eleanor. "The Polls—A Review, NBC's 'R.A.C.E.'" *Public Opinion Quarterly* v. 54 n. 4 (Winter 1990), pp. 605–608.

Skerry, Peter. "The Black Alienation, Why African Americans Are Increasingly Nativist." *The New Republic* v. 212 n. 5 (January 30, 1995), pp. 15–23.

Smedley, Brian D., Hector F. Myers, and Shelly P. Harrell. "Minority Status Stresses and the College Adjustment of Ethnic Minority Freshmen." *Journal of Higher Education.* v. 64 n. 4 (July/August 1993), pp. 434–452.

Smith, James P. "Affirmative Action and the Racial Wage Gap." *The American Economic Review* v. 83 n. 2 (May 1993), pp. 79–84.

Spear, Thomas. "Attacks on 'PC' Are New McCarthyism." *Christian Science Monitor.* April 24, 1991, p. 19.

Spoto, Mary Ann. "Kean President Blasts Farrakhan Aide's Talk." *Newark Star Ledger.* December 11, 1993, p. A10.

Stassen, Martha L. A. "White Faculty Members and Racial Diversity: A Theory and Its Implications." *The Review of Higher Education* v. 18 n. 4 (Summer 1995), pp. 361–391.

Steele, Shelby. "The Recoloring of Campus Life: Student Racism, Academic Pluralism and the End of a Dream." *Campus Wars: Multiculturalism and the Politics of Difference*, ed. John Arthur and Amy Shapiro. Boulder, CO: Westview Press, 1995, pp. 176–187.

Steinberg, Jacques. "Code Hate in Yearbook Evokes Anger." *The New York Times.* June 16, 1995, p. B1.

Stern, Kenneth S. *Bigotry on Campus: A Planned Response.* New York: American Jewish Committee, 1990.

Stimpson, Catharine R. "New 'Politically Correct' Metaphors Insult History and Our Campuses." *The Chronicle of Higher Education.* May 29, 1991, p. A40.

Strossen, Nadine. "Regulating Speech on Campus: A Modest Proposal." *Duke Law Journal* v. 1990 n. 3 (June 1990), pp. 484–573.

Taylor, John. "Are You Politically Correct?" *New York Magazine.* January 21, 1991, pp. 32–40.

Taylor, Marylee. "Local Racial Inequality and White Racial Attitudes." Paper presented at the National Conference on Race Relations and Civil Rights in the Post Reagan-Bush Era. Minneapolis, MN, October, 1994.

Taylor, William L. and Susan M. Liss. "Affirmative Action in the 1990s: Staying the Course." *The Annals of the American Academy of Political and Social Science* v. 523 (September 1992), pp. 30–37.

Thomas, Melvin E., Cedric Herring, and Hayward Derrick Horton. "Discrimination over the Life Course: A Synthetic Cohort Analysis of Earnings Differences between Black and White Males." *Social Problems* v. 41 n. 4 (November 1994), pp. 608–628.

Toma, J. Douglas and Joan Stark. "Pluralism in the Curriculum: Understanding Its Foundations and Evolution." *Review of Higher Education* v. 18 n. 2 (Winter 1995), pp. 217–232.

Tomaskovic-Devey, Donald. "The Gender and Race Composition of Jobs and the Male/Female, White/Black Pay Gaps." *Social Forces* v. 72 n. 1 (September 1993), pp. 45–76.

Trustee Subcommittee (Patricia Weston Rivera, Chair). *Report of the Subcommittee*. Union, NJ: Kean College Board of Trustees, June 1994.

Turner, Caroline Sotello Viernes. "Guests in Someone Else's House: Students of Color." *The Review of Higher Education* v. 17 n. 4 (Summer 1994), pp. 355–370.

Usdan, Michael, Debra Y. Delgado, and Charlotte Swift. "A Healthy Future for Our Children." *Futures Research Quarterly* v. 10 n. 2 (Summer 1994), pp. 83–95.

Wallace, John M., Jr. and Jerald G. Bachman. "Explaining Racial/Ethnic Differences in Adolescent Drug Use: The Impact of Background and Life Style." *Social Problems* v. 38 n. 3 (August 1991), pp. 333–354.

Weinstein, Laurence A. "Policing Prejudice." *AGB Reports* v. 32 n. 1 (January/February 1990), pp. 6–11.

White, Lawrence. "Hate Speech Codes That Will Pass Constitutional Muster." *The Chronicle of Higher Education*. May 25, 1994, p. A48.

Wilkinson, Doris. "Anti-Semitism and African Americans." *Society* v. 31 n. 6 (September/October 1994), pp. 47–50.

Williams, John B. "Affirmative Action at Harvard." *The Annals of the American Academy of Political and Social Science* v. 523 (September 1992), pp. 207–220.

Williams, Juan. "The Movement Continues." *Second Thoughts About Race in America*, ed. Peter Collier and David Horowitz. Lanham, MD: Madison Books, 1991, pp. 33–36.

Wilson, Reginald. "Affirmative Action: Yesterday, Today and Tomorrow." *CUPA Journal* v. 40 n. 3 (Fall 1989), pp. 1–6.

Winkler, Karen J. "Historical Group Issues Statement on Role of Jews in Slave Trade." *The Chronicle of Higher Education*. February 17, 1995, p. A15.

Young, Iris Marion. "Social Movements and the Politics of Difference." *Campus Wars, Multiculturalism and the Politics of Difference*, ed. John Arthur and Amy Shapiro. Boulder, CO: Westview Press, 1995, pp. 199–225.

Zapler, Michael. "Kentucky Lawmaker Sets Off Affirmative Action Debate by Telling White Students They 'Lost" Scholarships." *The Chronicle of Higher Education.* October 12, 1994, p. A25.

Zuckerman, Jill and David Masci. "House Panel OKs Arts Funding, Sidesteps Obscenity Issue." *Congressional Quarterly* v. 51 n. 26 (June 26, 1993), p. 1667.

Index

About the Author

LAURENCE R. MARCUS is a professor in the Educational Administration Department of Rowan College. He has previously held positions at the New Jersey Department of Higher Education, Stockton State College in New Jersey, and the University of Massachusetts at Amherst, where he received his doctorate. His book, *The Great Educational Debate: Washington and the Schools*, coauthored with Benjamin D. Stickney, was honored by *Choice* as a 1985–86 Outstanding Academic Book.